Introduction to x64 Assembly Programming

Maxwell Vector

Contents

Chapter 1

Register and Data Movement Operations

x64 Register Architecture

Within the x64 architecture, the central processing unit encompasses a collection of registers that serve as the primary components for data storage and manipulation. The aggregate of registers includes a set of general-purpose registers that are employed in a broad range of computational contexts. Registers such as RAX, RBX, RCX, and RDX are fundamental for arithmetic operations, indexing, and logical procedures. Their overlapping and hierarchical configuration provides the capability for both whole-register operations and access to sub-register segments, thereby enabling flexible data handling. In addition to these general-purpose registers, other specialized registers, including the instruction pointer (RIP) and the flag register ($RFLAGS$), play critical roles in orchestrating control flow and condition evaluation. This architectural design ensures a uniform mechanism for operand manipulation that is essential for efficient instruction execution.

Data Movement Instructions

Data movement operations form the cornerstone of computational processes by managing the transfer of binary information between various storage locations within the processor and memory subsystems. These operations are executed by instructions that transfer data without altering its inherent value, thereby preserving data integrity during transit. The process of moving data is indispensable prior to the performance of arithmetic or logical operations, and it supports the overall workflow of instruction execution within the microarchitectural framework.

1 The MOV Instruction

The MOV instruction constitutes the archetypal mechanism for transferring data within the x64 instruction set. It accomplishes the copying of data from a source operand to a destination operand, where the source may be an immediate value, a register, or a memory location, and the destination is typically a register or a designated memory location. The operational semantics of MOV ensure that the source remains unmodified while its value is faithfully duplicated at the destination. Compliance with operand size conventions is critical, as the data is consistently aligned with the processor's 64-bit data path. This instruction encapsulates a fundamental paradigm that underlies much of the data handling and processing logic inherent in x64-based systems.

2 The LEA Instruction

The LEA (Load Effective Address) instruction diverges from conventional data transfer operations by computing a memory address rather than retrieving the data stored at that address. It performs an arithmetic evaluation on a memory operand defined by a combination of a base register, an index register, a scale factor, and a displacement constant. The effective address is typically represented by the expression $base + index \times scale + displacement$, and the resulting computed address is transferred into a specified destination register. This instruction is indispensable for tasks that require dynamic address computation, such as pointer arithmetic and complex data structure access, wherein the derivation of an address is of paramount importance.

3 Ancillary Data Movement Commands

Complementing the MOV and LEA instructions, the x64 instruction set includes a range of ancillary commands that support additional modalities of data transfer. These commands often serve specialized purposes, such as performing register-to-register exchanges and accommodating various addressing modes that are not explicitly covered by the basic MOV instruction. Although these instructions may incorporate more elaborate operand configurations, their operational intent remains consistent: namely, to effectuate precise and controlled movement of data without modifying the original binary content. This expanded suite of data movement operations contributes to a coherent and versatile framework for the management of data within the processor, ensuring that both straightforward and complex transfer scenarios are addressed in a systematic manner.

x64 Assembly Code Snippet

```
; x64 Assembly Program: Register and Data Movement Operations
↪  Example
; This program demonstrates key data movement instructions,
; including MOV, LEA, and XCHG. It computes an effective address
; using the formula:
;    Effective Address = Base + (Index × Scale) + Displacement
; and then moves data between registers and memory.

; Data Section: Define an array of integers and a variable for
↪  results.
section .data
    ; Define an array of 5 32-bit integers.
    array:   dd 10, 20, 30, 40, 50
    ; Variable to store the computed result.
    result:  dd 0

; Code Section
section .text
    global _start

_start:
    ;---------------------------------------------------------------;
    ; Step 1: Load the Base Address of the Array
    ;---------------------------------------------------------------;
    ; Load the base address of 'array' into RDI.
    lea rdi, [rel array]        ; rdi now holds the starting address
    ↪  of array

    ;---------------------------------------------------------------;
    ; Step 2: Compute the Effective Address for a Specific Element
    ;---------------------------------------------------------------;
    ; We want to access the third element of the array (index 2).
    ; Since each element is 4 bytes (a dword), the formula is:
    ;    Effective Address = Base + (Index × 4) + 0
    mov rsi, 2                  ; rsi = index = 2
```

```asm
lea rax, [rdi + rsi*4]        ; rax = address of array[2]

;---------------------------------------------------------------;
; Step 3: Data Movement Using the MOV Instruction
;---------------------------------------------------------------;
; Retrieve the value from the computed effective address.
mov ebx, [rax]                ; ebx = array[2] (expected value: 30)
; Store the retrieved value into the memory variable 'result'.
mov [result], ebx             ; result now holds the value 30


;---------------------------------------------------------------;
; Step 4: Further Data Movement and Arithmetic Operations
;---------------------------------------------------------------;
; Load an immediate value into RCX.
mov rcx, 100                  ; rcx = 100
; Copy RCX to RDX.
mov rdx, rcx                  ; rdx = 100

; Add the value in RDX to EBX.
add ebx, edx                  ; ebx = 30 + 100 = 130
; Update the 'result' variable with the new sum.
mov [result], ebx             ; result updated to 130


;---------------------------------------------------------------;
; Step 5: Use an Ancillary Instruction (XCHG)
;---------------------------------------------------------------;
; Swap the values in RCX and RDX.
xchg rcx, rdx                 ; exchange rcx and rdx

; Move the final computed value from EBX to EAX.
mov eax, ebx                  ; eax = 130


;---------------------------------------------------------------;
; Step 6: Exit the Program via Linux System Call
;---------------------------------------------------------------;
; Prepare the exit system call (syscall number 60).
mov rax, 60                   ; syscall: exit
xor rdi, rdi                  ; set exit code to 0
syscall                       ; make the system call to exit
```

Chapter 2

Integer Arithmetic Operations

Addition Operations

Integer addition represents the most fundamental operation in arithmetic, wherein two discrete values are consolidated into a single cumulative result. This operation is executed by the arithmetic logic unit (ALU) through binary addition, a process that entails the bitwise summation of corresponding positions in the operands. When the summation at any bit position exceeds the binary capacity, a carry is generated and propagated to higher-order bits, thereby preserving the integrity of the overall computation. The process adheres to well-established mathematical properties such as commutativity and associativity, which not only aid in the theoretical formulation of arithmetic but also provide practical benefits for the optimization of hardware implementations. In mathematical notation, the addition of two integers a and b is expressed as $a + b$, underscoring the operator's simplicity and omnipresence in computational procedures.

Subtraction Operations

Subtraction is the operation responsible for determining the difference between two integer values. This process is fundamentally related to addition and is frequently implemented using the method of two's complement representation. In this approach, the subtrahend is first inverted and incremented to form its two's complement, which is then added to the minuend. This procedure transforms the subtraction operation into an additive process, thereby leveraging the existing hardware designed for addition. The method inherently establishes the handling of underflow conditions through the use of borrow flags that signal when a particular bitwise subtraction requires compensation. In formal terms, the subtraction of an integer b from an integer a is symbolically represented as $a - b$, and the underlying algorithm meticulously accounts for the borrow propagation that ensures an accurate result in binary form.

Multiplication Operations

Multiplication involves combining integer operands in a manner that abstracts the concept of repeated addition into a singular, efficient operation. Modern computing architectures employ advanced techniques that build partial product arrays, which are subsequently accumulated using shift-add methods. Each bit of one operand, when multiplied by the entirety of the second operand, produces a partial product that is aligned according to its positional weight in the binary number system. The aggregation of these partial products yields the final product, which is mathematically conveyed as $a \times b$ for two integers a and b. The complexity of this operation arises from the necessity to manage carry propagation across multiple layers of partial products, as well as the requirement to detect and signal arithmetic overflow when the product exceeds the representable range. The systematic design of hardware multipliers within the ALU encapsulates these challenges while maintaining high throughput and accuracy.

Division Operations

Division constitutes one of the more intricate arithmetic operations, as it entails partitioning a dividend by a divisor to extract two separate components: the quotient and the remainder. In practice, division is executed by iteratively subtracting scaled versions of the divisor from the dividend until the residual value is less than the divisor. This iterative process is refined in hardware by employing sophisticated algorithms such as non-restoring or SRT division, which accelerate convergence to the final result. The operation is formally denoted by $a \div b$, where a represents the dividend and b the divisor, and it inherently produces a quotient along with a corresponding remainder that satisfies the equation $a = (a \div b) \times b + r$. Considerations for division extend to the proper handling of signed integers, where the accurate interpretation of negative operands requires careful management of sign extension and adjustment during both the iterative subtraction and subsequent result representation.

x64 Assembly Code Snippet

```
; x64 Assembly Code snippet for Integer Arithmetic Operations
; This program demonstrates addition, subtraction, multiplication,
↪   and division
; operations based on the formulas discussed in this chapter.
;
; Equations demonstrated:
;    Addition:        result = a + b
;    Subtraction:  ~  result = a - b
;    Multiplication: result = a * b
;    Division:        dividend = (quotient * b) + remainder
;
; The code uses the System V AMD64 ABI (Linux) for demonstration
↪   purposes.
; Assemble with: nasm -f elf64 filename.asm
; Link with: ld -o output filename.o

global _start

section .data
    ; Define two 32-bit integer operands.
    a            dd 25            ; Operand: 25
    b            dd 7             ; Operand: 7

    ; Variables to store results.
    sum_res      dd 0             ; Stores result of addition (a +
    ↪   b)
    sub_res      dd 0             ; Stores result of subtraction (a
    ↪   - b)
    mul_res      dq 0             ; Stores result of multiplication
    ↪   (a * b) (64-bit)
    quo_res      dd 0             ; Stores quotient from division (a
    ↪   / b)
    rem_res      dd 0             ; Stores remainder from division
    ↪   (a % b)

section .text
_start:
    ;-----------------------------------
    ; Addition Operation: sum = a + b
```

```
;------------------------------------
mov eax, [a]            ; Load a into eax
mov ebx, [b]            ; Load b into ebx
mov ecx, eax            ; Copy a into ecx for addition
add ecx, ebx            ; ecx = a + b
mov [sum_res], ecx      ; Store the result in sum_res


;------------------------------------
; Subtraction Operation: diff = a - b
;------------------------------------
mov eax, [a]            ; Load a into eax
mov ebx, [b]            ; Load b into ebx
mov ecx, eax            ; Copy a into ecx for subtraction
sub ecx, ebx            ; ecx = a - b
mov [sub_res], ecx      ; Store the result in sub_res


;------------------------------------
; Multiplication Operation: prod = a * b
;------------------------------------
mov eax, [a]            ; Load a into eax (dividend for
↪   multiplication)
mov ebx, [b]            ; Load b into ebx (multiplier)
imul ebx                ; eax = eax * ebx, edx:eax holds 64-bit
↪   result
; Save the 64-bit product into memory (mul_res)
mov dword [mul_res], eax        ; Lower 32 bits
mov dword [mul_res+4], edx      ; Higher 32 bits


;------------------------------------
; Division Operation: quotient and remainder = a / b
; For division, the dividend must reside in rdx:rax.
; Here, we utilize cdq to sign-extend eax into edx.
;------------------------------------
mov eax, [a]            ; Load a into eax (dividend)
cdq                     ; Sign-extend eax into edx (prepare for
↪   division)
mov ebx, [b]            ; Load b into ebx (divisor)
idiv ebx                ; Divide edx:eax by ebx; quotient in eax,
↪   remainder in edx
mov [quo_res], eax      ; Store the quotient in quo_res
mov [rem_res], edx      ; Store the remainder in rem_res


;------------------------------------
; Exit: Terminate the program using a Linux syscall.
;------------------------------------
; The exit system call requires:
;    rax = 60 (sys_exit)
;    rdi = exit code (0 for success)
mov rax, 60             ; Syscall number for exit (60)
xor rdi, rdi            ; Set exit code to 0
syscall                 ; Make the syscall to exit
```

Chapter 3

Bitwise Logical Operations

Bitwise AND Operation

The bitwise AND operation, denoted by $\wedge$, performs a logical conjunction on corresponding bits of two fixed-width binary operands. Given two binary numbers $a = a_{n-1}a_{n-2}\ldots a_0$ and $b = b_{n-1}b_{n-2}\ldots b_0$, the operation $a \wedge b$ produces a result $c = c_{n-1}c_{n-2}\ldots c_0$, where each bit c_i is defined as

$$c_i = a_i \wedge b_i.$$

A bit c_i is set to 1 if and only if both a_i and b_i are 1; otherwise, it is set to 0. This operator is instrumental in bit masking, whereby selective extraction or clearance of bits is required. Its algebraic properties, such as commutativity ($a \wedge b = b \wedge a$) and associativity ($a \wedge (b \wedge c) = (a \wedge b) \wedge c$), afford a robust framework for simplifying and optimizing logical expressions in digital circuitry.

Bitwise OR Operation

The bitwise OR operation, symbolized by $\vee$, evaluates the union of bits from two binary operands. For operands a and b, the expression $a \vee b$ yields a binary result c, where each bit is determined by

$$c_i = a_i \vee b_i.$$

Here, c_i is set to 1 if at least one of the bits a_i or b_i is 1, and it is set to 0 only when both a_i and b_i are 0. This property renders the operator valuable in contexts where aggregation of bitwise flags or the setting of specific bits within a data structure is desired. The operation adheres to idempotency, as exemplified by the identity $a \lor a = a$, which further simplifies the analysis of logical combinations within digital systems.

Bitwise XOR Operation

The bitwise exclusive OR (XOR) operation, represented by $\oplus$, generates a result by comparing the corresponding bits of two operands and outputting a 1 if they differ. Mathematically, for binary numbers a and b, the operation is defined as

$$c_i = a_i \oplus b_i,$$

where c_i equals 1 precisely when $a_i \neq b_i$ and equals 0 when $a_i = b_i$. The XOR operator is uniquely characterized by its self-inverse property, formally stated as

$$(a \oplus b) \oplus b = a,$$

which makes it particularly useful in applications such as bit toggling and error detection. Its non-linear behavior also underlies many cryptographic schemes, where it contributes to both diffusion and confusion in the transformation of data.

Bitwise NOT Operation

The bitwise NOT operation, denoted by $\neg$, is a unary operator that inverts every bit of its operand. For a binary number $a = a_{n-1}a_{n-2}\ldots a_0$, the resulting number $c = c_{n-1}c_{n-2}\ldots c_0$ is computed by

$$c_i = \neg a_i,$$

such that each 0 in a becomes a 1 in c, and each 1 becomes a 0. In systems with fixed-bit widths, this operation is mathematically equivalent to computing

$$c = 2^n - 1 - a,$$

where n represents the number of bits. This bit inversion is a central feature in the two's complement representation used for encoding negative numbers, underscoring the profound interplay between arithmetic and logic at the bit level.

x64 Assembly Code Snippet

```
; Comprehensive x64 Assembly Code Snippet for Bitwise Logical
↪   Operations
; This code illustrates the following operations:
;   - Bitwise AND:    c = a & b      where each bit c_i = a_i & b_i.
;   - Bitwise OR:     c = a | b      where each bit c_i = a_i | b_i.
;   - Bitwise XOR:    c = a ^ b      where each bit c_i = a_i ^ b_i.
;   - Bitwise NOT:    c = ~a         where each bit c_i = NOT a_i,
;                             which is equivalent to c = 2^n - 1 - a for
↪   an n-bit number.
;
; Assemble with: nasm -f elf64 filename.asm
; Link with: ld -o filename filename.o

SECTION .data
    ; Define two sample 64-bit values
    value1    dq 0xAA55AA55AA55AA55    ; Example value,
    ↪   pattern:10101010...
    value2    dq 0xF0F0F0F0F0F0F0F0    ; Example value,
    ↪   pattern:11110000...

SECTION .bss
    ; Reserve space to store results of the bitwise operations
    result_and    resq 1    ; Result for Bitwise AND (value1 & value2)
    result_or     resq 1    ; Result for Bitwise OR  (value1 | value2)
    result_xor    resq 1    ; Result for Bitwise XOR (value1 ^ value2)
    result_not    resq 1    ; Result for Bitwise NOT (~value1)

SECTION .text
global _start
_start:
    ;-------------------------------------------------------
    ; Load sample values from memory into registers.
    ;-------------------------------------------------------
    mov rax, [value1]    ; rax <- value1
    mov rbx, [value2]    ; rbx <- value2

    ; Save original value1 in rcx for multiple reuse.
    mov rcx, rax         ; rcx <- value1

    ;-------------------------------------------------------
    ; Bitwise AND Operation:
    ; Compute rax = value1 AND value2, where each bit of rax:
    ;   rax_bit = 1 if (value1_bit == 1 and value2_bit == 1)
```

24

```asm
;------------------------------------------------------------
mov rax, rcx              ; restore value1 into rax
and rax, rbx              ; rax = rax & rbx
mov [result_and], rax


;------------------------------------------------------------
; Bitwise OR Operation:
; Compute rax = value1 OR value2, where each bit of rax:
;   rax_bit = 1 if (value1_bit == 1 or value2_bit == 1)
;------------------------------------------------------------
mov rax, rcx              ; reload original value1 into rax
or rax, rbx               ; rax = rax | rbx
mov [result_or], rax


;------------------------------------------------------------
; Bitwise XOR Operation:
; Compute rax = value1 XOR value2, where each bit of rax:
;   rax_bit = 1 if (value1_bit != value2_bit)
;   and the self-inverse property holds: (a ^ b) ^ b == a
;------------------------------------------------------------
mov rax, rcx              ; reload original value1 into rax
xor rax, rbx              ; rax = rax ^ rbx
mov [result_xor], rax


;------------------------------------------------------------
; Bitwise NOT Operation:
; Compute rax = NOT value1, where each bit of rax is the
;   inversion of value1.
; For an n-bit number, this is equivalent to: rax = 2^n - 1 -
;   value1.
;------------------------------------------------------------
mov rax, rcx              ; reload original value1 into rax
not rax                   ; rax = ~rax
mov [result_not], rax


;------------------------------------------------------------
; Exit the program cleanly.
;------------------------------------------------------------
mov rax, 60               ; syscall for exit (Linux x64)
xor rdi, rdi              ; exit status 0
syscall
```

Chapter 4

Shift and Rotate Operations

Bit Shifting Instructions

Bit shifting instructions perform the fundamental operation of repositioning the binary digits within a fixed-width operand. The left shift operation, denoted by SHL, moves each bit in an n-bit value to the left by a specified count k, effectively multiplying the operand by 2^k under modulo 2^n arithmetic. In formal terms, given an unsigned integer a, a left shift by k positions can be expressed as

$$a \times 2^k \pmod{2^n},$$

where the vacated least-significant positions are filled with zeros. This operation is intrinsic to rapid scaling and bit-level data masking, facilitating efficient multiplication by powers of two with minimal computational overhead. Conversely, the right shift operation, symbolized by SHR, repositions the bits of an n-bit operand to the right by k positions. For unsigned values, the mathematical equivalent is the integer division of a by 2^k, discarding any remainder. In precise terms,

$$\lfloor a/2^k \rfloor,$$

characterizes the effect of a right shift, wherein zeros are shifted into the most-significant positions, and the bits shifted out from the least-significant end are lost. The deterministic and single-cycle execution of these shift instructions underlies their ubiquity in performance-critical and resource-constrained environments, emphasizing the importance of these operations in both algorithmic refinements and low-level hardware design.

Bit Rotate Instructions

Rotate instructions extend the capabilities of shifting by cyclically permuting the bits within an operand such that no bit is discarded. The left rotate instruction, indicated by ROL, cyclically shifts the bits to the left while reinserting the bits that overflow from the most-significant positions into the least-significant positions. If an n-bit operand is rotated left by k positions, then the bit originally at position i is repositioned to position

$$(i + k) \mod n.$$

This cyclic property ensures that the complete bit pattern is preserved, yielding a bijective transformation that is invaluable in contexts such as cryptographic routines and digital signal processing where reversibility is vital.

Similarly, the right rotate instruction, denoted by ROR, performs the cyclic shift in the opposite direction. In a right rotate by k positions, the bit originally at position i is transferred to position

$$(i - k) \mod n.$$

Such a rotation reintroduces the bits displaced from the lower-order end into the higher-order positions, thereby conserving the aggregate information contained within the binary representation. The precise control and invariance offered by the rotate operations facilitate complex bit permutations and cyclic redundancy mechanisms, coupled with the constant-time execution characteristic of these instructions.

The rigorous operational semantics of both shift and rotate instructions reveal their pivotal roles in low-level bit manipulation. The ability to manipulate binary data efficiently through these elementary operations enables the construction of sophisticated algorithms and architectural optimizations, all while maintaining computational precision and operational expediency.

x64 Assembly Code Snippet

```
;------------------------------------
; This x64 Assembly program demonstrates the use of bit shifting and
↪  rotate
; instructions. It calculates the following:
;
; 1. Left Shift Operation:
;    Given an unsigned integer 'a' in RAX, a left shift by 'k' bits
↪  (SHL)
;    multiplies 'a' by 2^k modulo 2^64. For k=3, this computes:
;       a << 3    a * 2^3 (mod 2^64)
;
; 2. Right Shift Operation:
;    The SHR instruction divides the value by 2^k, discarding any
↪  fractional part.
;       (a << 3) >> 3    floor((a * 8) / 8)  = a
;
; 3. Rotate Instructions:
;    The ROL (rotate left) and ROR (rotate right) instructions
↪  cyclically shift
;    the bits of a register such that no bit is lost. For a rotation
↪  by 4 bits,
;    the bit originally at position i moves to:
;       ROL: (i + 4) mod 64
;       ROR: (i - 4) mod 64
;
; 4. Final Computation:
;    The program combines the results by performing a bitwise OR on
↪  the two
;    shift results and then an XOR with the rotated value.
;
; The final result is printed using the C library's printf function.
;------------------------------------

global main
extern printf

section .data
    ; Format string for printing the final 64-bit result (newline
    ↪  terminated)
    format db "Final Result: %ld", 10, 0

section .text
main:
    ;-------------------------------------------------------------
    ; 1. Bit Shifting Operations
    ;-------------------------------------------------------------
    ; Load an initial unsigned integer value into RAX
    mov rax, 12345          ; Original value, a

    ; Left Shift: Multiply a by 2^3 (i.e., 8) modulo 2^64
```

```
mov rcx, 3                    ; Shift count k = 3
shl rax, cl                   ; RAX = a << 3, equivalent to a * 8
↪  mod 2^64

; Save the left-shifted result into RBX for demonstration
↪  purposes
mov rbx, rax

; Right Shift: Divide the left-shifted value by 2^3, discarding
↪  remainder
shr rbx, cl                   ; RBX = (a * 8) >> 3, which recovers
↪  the original a


;-----------------------------------------------------------------
; 2. Bit Rotate Operations
;-----------------------------------------------------------------
; Load a 64-bit test pattern into RDX to demonstrate the rotate
↪  instructions
mov rdx, 0xA5A5A5A5A5A5A5A5    ; Test pattern in hexadecimal

; Rotate Left: Cyclically shift RDX left by 4 bits.
mov rcx, 4                     ; Rotate count = 4 bits
rol rdx, cl                    ; RDX = RDX rotated left by 4 bits

; Rotate Right: Rotate RDX right by 4 bits to recover the
↪  original pattern
ror rdx, cl                    ; RDX = RDX rotated right by 4 bits


;-----------------------------------------------------------------
; 3. Combining the Results
;-----------------------------------------------------------------
; Combine the outcomes of the shift operations:
;    Final_Result = (Left_Shift_Result OR Right_Shift_Result) XOR
↪  Rotated_Value
or rax, rbx                    ; RAX now holds the bitwise OR of the
↪  left and right shifts
xor rax, rdx                   ; Final result is obtained in RAX
↪  after XOR with rotated value


;-----------------------------------------------------------------
; 4. Printing the Final Result
;-----------------------------------------------------------------
; Setup parameters for the printf function (System V AMD64
↪  calling convention):
;    RDI: Format string pointer
;    RSI: Value to be printed (final result)
mov rdi, format               ; Load address of the format string
↪  into RDI
mov rsi, rax                  ; Load the final result into RSI
xor rax, rax                  ; Clear RAX (required for variadic
↪  functions like printf)
call printf                   ; Call printf to output the result
```

```
;-----------------------------------------------------------------
; 5. Exiting the Program
;-----------------------------------------------------------------
; Exit using the Linux syscall interface:
mov rax, 60                 ; Syscall number for exit is 60 on
↪  Linux x64
xor rdi, rdi                ; Exit code 0
syscall                     ; Make the syscall to exit the program
```

Chapter 5

Loop Implementation: Simple Loop

Fundamentals of Iterative Constructs in Assembly

Assembly language programming requires explicit construction of control flow mechanisms to enable iterative operations. At this low level, the responsibility for maintaining and directing the sequence of instructions falls entirely on the programmer. In contrast to high-level language constructs that implicitly manage loop structures, iteration in assembly is orchestrated through the deliberate use of jump instructions and counter registers. A loop in this context is defined by a designated entry point in the code, a block of instructions to be repeated, and well-specified termination criteria. The underlying mechanism leverages the deterministic behavior of the central processing unit to guarantee that each cycle of iteration satisfies the conditions established by the programmer.

This chapter examines the theoretical basis and practical implications of implementing a simple loop. The iterative construct is achieved by combining explicit counter manipulations with conditional and unconditional jump operations. The resulting structure not only enables repeated execution of a sequence of operations but also ensures that control over the loop's duration and termination is maintained with precise granularity. Such control is indispensable when iterating over data in a fixed or variable-sized collection, where the accuracy of the loop counter and the veracity of the conditional check directly impact the correctness of the computation.

Control Flow via Jump Instructions

At the assembly level, the concept of a loop is fundamentally inter-twined with the mechanism of jump instructions. These instructions alter the normal sequential flow of execution by transferring control from one location in the code to another. Two primary classes of jump instructions are employed in the construction of loops: unconditional jumps and conditional jumps. An unconditional jump transfers execution to a specified label without any regard for the state of the processor's flags, thereby serving as the backbone for reentering the loop body.

Conditional jumps, on the other hand, rely on the state of one or more status flags that have been altered by preceding arithmetic or logical operations. For instance, following an operation that decrements a counter register, a conditional jump may be executed to test whether the updated value satisfies a predetermined condition, such as non-zero. In this manner, conditional jump instructions provide a means of dynamically determining whether the loop should continue to iterate or terminate. The precision with which these instructions evaluate conditions is critical, as even minor deviations in the management of status flags may lead to loop misbehavior or inadvertent infinite repetition.

The mathematical underpinnings of these operations emerge from the discrete nature of the loop counter and the binary conditions that govern jump execution. The relationship between a loop counter, say stored in register RCX, and the corresponding condition test is expressed in a form akin to testing whether $RCX > 0$. The systematic decrement or increment of RCX and the subsequent evaluation through a conditional jump instruction enable the implementation of iteration that is both efficient and amenable to formal analysis.

Counter Mechanisms in Loop Structures

The role of counter registers in the context of a simple loop is central to the execution of iterative logic. A counter register is typically initialized with a value that represents the total number of iterations required. Its value is then modified, commonly decremented by one after each complete traversal of the loop body. The progression of the loop is governed by periodic evaluations of the counter's value; the loop continues to execute if the counter has not reached a terminal value and ceases otherwise.

This explicit control of the iteration count provides an exact correspondence between the number of loop iterations and the initial value loaded into the counter register. In many architectures, operations that both decrement the counter and conditionally branch based on its value are available. These compound operations embody the dual utility of the counter: to function simultaneously as an iterator and as a condition flag indicator. Such mechanisms underscore the efficiency in implementing loops by minimizing the number of discrete instructions required to manage control flow, thereby reducing both the code footprint and the cycle count per iteration.

A critical aspect of this approach is the maintenance of consistent state between the counter and the conditional checks that underpin the jump instructions. The deterministic decrementing of the counter, combined with a corresponding branch instruction that evaluates whether the value has attained a specified boundary (commonly zero), forms the essence of a well-structured loop. This close coupling between arithmetic operations and branch evaluations is a hallmark of assembly-level loop constructs, ensuring that every iteration is rigorously accounted for in the execution of the program.

Synthesis of Jump and Counter-Based Techniques

The integration of jump instructions and counter manipulations culminates in an iterative structure that is both robust and efficient. The journey through the loop begins with the initialization of a counter register to a predetermined value, followed by the placement of a loop label that marks the beginning of the iterative block. Within the loop body, necessary data processing and arithmetic computations are carried out. Upon completion of these operations, the counter register is updated—typically decremented—and a conditional check is performed.

If the counter still indicates that further iterations are required (for example, if the counter does not equal zero), a conditional jump instruction directs the control flow back to the loop label. This cyclical pattern of execution continues until the counter reaches its terminal condition, at which point the loop is exited and the subsequent sequence of instructions is executed. This synthesis not only highlights the interplay between control flow and iterative counting but also exemplifies the level of explicit management required in assembly programming.

The effectiveness of this approach is rooted in the processor's ability to perform rapid updates of registers and status flags, thereby allowing a seamless transition between iterations with minimal overhead. The explicit nature of jump and counter-based loop implementations lends itself to rigorous analysis, ensuring that the iterative behavior is both predictable and verifiable. As a fundamental mechanism for data iteration, the techniques discussed herein serve as a basis for more complex control structures and lay the groundwork for a deeper understanding of low-level system operations.

x64 Assembly Code Snippet

```
; This x64 Assembly code demonstrates a simple loop using explicit
↪   counter manipulation
; and jump instructions to sum the elements of an array. The
↪   algorithm initializes a counter,
; iterates over each element, adds the element to an accumulator,
↪   and then decrements the counter.
; When the counter reaches zero, the loop exits and the program
↪   terminates.

section .data
    ; Define an array of 64-bit integers.
    numbers dq 10, 20, 30, 40, 50    ; Array: 5 elements
    n       dq 5                      ; Number of elements in the array

section .text
    global _start

_start:
    ; Initialize the registers:
    ; rbx points to the start of the array.
    ; rcx holds the loop counter (number of elements to process).
    ; rax is cleared to 0 and used as an accumulator for the sum.
    mov rbx, numbers     ; rbx = address of the array "numbers"
    mov rcx, [n]         ; rcx = number of elements (5)
    xor rax, rax         ; Clear rax to 0 (accumulator for the sum)

loop_start:
    ; Check termination condition: if counter (rcx) is zero, exit
    ↪   the loop.
```

```
        cmp rcx, 0
        je loop_exit

        ; Load the current array element and add it to the accumulator.
        add rax, [rbx]

        ; Advance the pointer to the next 64-bit integer in the array.
        add rbx, 8

        ; Decrement the loop counter.
        dec rcx

        ; Unconditionally jump back to the start of the loop.
        jmp loop_start

loop_exit:
        ; After the loop, rax contains the sum of the array elements.
        ; For demonstration, we exit the program using the sum as the
        ↪ exit status.
        mov rdi, rax            ; rdi = exit code (sum)
        mov rax, 60             ; syscall number for exit in Linux x64
        syscall
```

Chapter 6

Conditional Branching: If–Else Constructs

Foundations of Decision-Making Constructs

Conditional branching in assembly language embodies the explicit formulation of decision-making structures. The mechanism operates by evaluating Boolean conditions derived from comparisons and arithmetic calculations, with the outcome manifesting in the status flags of the processor. When an arithmetic or logical instruction is executed, specific flags such as the Zero Flag (ZF), the Sign Flag (SF), or the Carry Flag (CF) are set or cleared in accordance with the result. These flags subsequently serve as the basis for evaluating predicates of the form

$$P : \mathbb{S} \to \{0, 1\},$$

where $\mathbb{S}$ represents the state space of the processor. In the context of an if–else construct, decision making is accomplished by transferring control to one of two distinct execution paths based on the Boolean evaluation of the condition.

Mechanics of Flag Evaluation and Conditional Jumps

The architecture of conditional branching is predicated on the precise manipulation of flag registers and the judicious use of jump instructions. Following the execution of a comparison or arithmetic operation, the processor's internal state reflects the outcome via its flag bits. For instance, if a comparison determines that two operands are equal, the condition $operand_1 = operand_2$ results in the activation of the Zero Flag (ZF). The role of the flag is then to serve as a criterion with which a conditional jump instruction determines the subsequent control flow. In this manner, a jump instruction may be rendered contingent upon the outcome of the prior operation, thereby redirecting program execution in a manner that mirrors the high-level if–else decision-making structure. The transition is mathematically analogous to a mapping

$$T : \{0, 1\} \rightarrow \mathcal{L},$$

where $\{0, 1\}$ represents the Boolean outcome and $\mathcal{L}$ denotes the set of possible instruction addresses.

Structural Composition of If–Else Constructs

The synthesis of an if–else structure in assembly is achieved through the integration of conditional and unconditional jump instructions. Initially, a predicate is evaluated via a comparison instruction, which updates the status flags in the processor. A subsequent conditional jump instruction then inspects the appropriate flag to decide whether to divert control flow to a designated code block associated with the true branch. Should the condition evaluate as false, execution logically proceeds to the instructions assigned to the alternative (or else) branch. This explicit control of the flow is conceptually analogous to partitioning the execution space into two disjoint segments, each corresponding to one outcome of the Boolean predicate. The divergence in execution is represented as a bifurcation in the control flow graph, with one branch activated when the predicate is true and the other when it is false.

Synthesis and Interdependence of Control Flow and Conditional Evaluation

The interdependence between conditional evaluation and control flow represents a critical element in the construction of decision-making structures. Given a condition expressed as

$$C : \text{State} \to \{0, 1\},$$

the operation of a conditional branch can be rigorously formulated. Should C evaluate to 1, the control flow is diverted to an alternate block of instructions; otherwise, the execution continues linearly. This binary decision framework is central to algorithmic branching, where the explicit redirection of program counters is contingent upon the mathematical evaluation of a predicate. The deterministic execution of assembly instructions ensures that each evaluation of the condition leads to a predictable modification in program behavior, thereby establishing a robust foundation upon which more intricate control flow mechanisms may be constructed.

x64 Assembly Code Snippet

```
;-------------------------------------------------------------
; x64 Assembly Code Demonstrating Conditional Branching (If-Else)
; This example illustrates the evaluation of processor flags (ZF,
↪  SF, CF)
; and the subsequent redirection of control flow using conditional
↪  jumps.
; It concretely models the mapping:
;    T: {0,1} ->
; whereby a Boolean evaluation (0 for false, 1 for true) selects the
↪  jump
; destination (instruction label) analogous to an if-else construct.
;-------------------------------------------------------------

section .data
    ; Define two 64-bit numbers for comparison
    num1    dq 10                   ; First operand (10)
    num2    dq 20                   ; Second operand (20)

    ; Define messages for the true (equal) and false (not equal)
    ↪  branches.
    trueMsg  db "Condition True: num1 equals num2", 10, 0
    falseMsg db "Condition False: num1 not equal to num2", 10, 0

section .bss
    ; No uninitialized data required for this example.

section .text
    global _start

_start:
    ;-------------------------------------------------------------
```

```asm
        ; Load operands into registers.
        ; The essential comparison updates the status flags based on:
        ;      P: State -> {0, 1}
        ; where P evaluates the truth of (num1 == num2).
        ;--------------------------------------------------------------
        mov rax, [num1]            ; RAX := num1
        mov rbx, [num2]            ; RBX := num2

        cmp rax, rbx               ; Compare num1 and num2.
        je branch_true             ; If equal (ZF = 1), jump to
        ↪  branch_true.

                                   ; Otherwise, flow continues to
                                   ↪  branch_false.


        ;--------------------------------------------------------------
        ; False Branch: num1 != num2
        ;--------------------------------------------------------------
branch_false:
        mov rdi, falseMsg          ; RDI points to the false message.
        call print_string         ; Call subroutine to print the
        ↪  message.
        jmp end_program            ; Jump unconditionally to
        ↪  end_program.


        ;--------------------------------------------------------------
        ; True Branch: num1 == num2
        ;--------------------------------------------------------------
branch_true:
        mov rdi, trueMsg           ; RDI points to the true message.
        call print_string         ; Call subroutine to print the
        ↪  message.

end_program:
        ;--------------------------------------------------------------
        ; Exit the program gracefully.
        ;--------------------------------------------------------------
        mov rax, 60                ; Syscall number for exit.
        xor rdi, rdi               ; Exit code: 0.
        syscall                    ; Make the syscall.


;--------------------------------------------------------------
; print_string: Subroutine to Output a Null-Terminated String
; This routine calculates the string length by scanning for the null
↪  byte.
; It then performs a write syscall to output the string to stdout.
;--------------------------------------------------------------
print_string:
        push rax                   ; Save registers that will be
        ↪  modified.
        push rbx
        push rcx
        push rdx
        push r8
```

```asm
        ; Preserve the original string pointer.
        mov r8, rdi                 ; Store pointer in R8.
        mov rcx, rdi                ; Use RCX as iterator for length
        ↪ calculation.
        xor rdx, rdx                ; Clear RDX which will count string
        ↪ length.

calc_len:
        cmp byte [rcx], 0           ; Check if current byte is null.
        je  len_found               ; If null terminator found, exit
        ↪ loop.
        inc rcx                     ; Move to next character.
        inc rdx                     ; Increment length counter.
        jmp calc_len

len_found:
        ; Write the string to stdout using write syscall.
        mov rax, 1                  ; Syscall number for sys_write.
        mov rdi, 1                  ; File descriptor 1 (stdout).
        mov rsi, r8                 ; Restore string pointer from R8.
        syscall                     ; Execute the write syscall.

        pop r8                      ; Restore registers.
        pop rdx
        pop rcx
        pop rbx
        pop rax
        ret
```

Chapter 7

Using the Stack: Push and Pop

Fundamental Role of the Stack in Temporary Storage

The stack constitutes a discrete area of memory dedicated to transient data storage, where data is organized according to a last-in, first-out (LIFO) discipline. This mechanism is pivotal in processor architectures, particularly during the execution of subroutine calls and in the preservation of registers. The stack permits the temporary retention of values that are ephemeral in nature, thereby enabling efficient procedural abstraction and the seamless management of intermediate computational results. Within this framework, the stack pointer, denoted by rsp, serves as a dynamic indicator of the current top of the stack, adjusting in response to operations that deposit or retrieve data.

Push Operation: Mechanism and Semantics

The push operation is instrumental in augmenting the stack with new data elements. Formally, when a push instruction is executed, the processor decrements the stack pointer by the size of the data element, typically expressed as δ, and subsequently writes the operand into the memory location indicated by the updated pointer. In architectures where the data size corresponds to a machine word, the updated stack pointer may be represented by the transformation

$$rsp' = rsp - \delta.$$

This arithmetic adjustment reflects the downward growth of the stack and ensures that the most recently pushed value occupies the lowest address among stored elements. The action not only provides temporary storage but also systematically preserves the state required for the later restoration of the computational context.

Pop Operation: Mechanism and Semantics

In contrast to the push operation, the pop instruction is responsible for retrieving and removing the most recently stored value from the stack. The process involves reading the data from the memory location currently referenced by the stack pointer and then incrementing the pointer by δ, thus re-establishing the previous state of the stack. This increment can be succinctly denoted as

$$rsp' = rsp + \delta,$$

which mathematically mirrors the logical reversal of the push operation. The disciplined use of the pop operation ensures adherence to the LIFO structure, permitting the reliable recovery of temporary values and facilitating the restoration of a prior execution context.

Stack Frame Construction and Management

Beyond the primitive push and pop operations, the concept of a stack frame is central to the encapsulation of a subroutine's execution environment. A stack frame typically encompasses local variables, saved registers, and other context-specific data that are essential for the proper handling of procedural calls and returns. The establishment of a stack frame is generally initiated by a series of push operations that secure the caller's contextual values, followed by an allocation of additional space for local variables, thereby demarcating a boundary for the current procedure's operational scope. The maintenance of this boundary is critical, as it affords an invariant structure whereby the return address and the previous base pointer are preserved. In many processor conventions, a separate base pointer, often denoted by *rbp*, is used to provide a stable frame of reference, such that the relative addressing of variables becomes feasible and systematic. The precise management of the stack frame, orchestrated through the judicious use of push and pop instructions, underpins the robustness of function invocation and the recursive integrity inherent in modern computing architectures.

x64 Assembly Code Snippet

```
; x64 Assembly Code Example: Demonstration of Push/Pop and Stack
↪   Frame Management
; This program illustrates the following key concepts:
;   - The push instruction: decrementing the stack pointer (rsp) and
↪   storing data.
;   - The pop instruction: reading data from memory and incrementing
↪   rsp.
;   - Stack frame construction: saving the caller's base pointer
↪   (rbp) and callee-saved registers.
;   - A sample computation involving arithmetic operations and a
↪   loop.
; The code is written for Linux x86_64 using the System V AMD64
↪   calling convention.

section .text
    global _start

;
↪   -----------------------------------------------------------------
; Function: compute
; Purpose: Receives an integer in rdi, performs arithmetic
↪   operations
;          using stack manipulation, and returns the computed result
↪   in rax.
;
↪   -----------------------------------------------------------------
compute:
    ; Function Prologue: Establish a new stack frame.
    push rbp              ; Save caller's base pointer; rsp = rsp -
    ↪   8.
    mov rbp, rsp          ; Set rbp to current rsp (new base
    ↪   pointer).

    ; Save callee-saved registers.
```

```asm
    push rbx                ; Save rbx onto the stack.
    push rsi                ; Save rsi onto the stack.

    ;
    → -------------------------------------------------------------------
    ; Begin computation:
    ; 1. Move input (in rdi) to rax.
    ; 2. Multiply the input by 2 (using left shift, akin to rsp =
    →    rsp - behavior).
    ; 3. Add a constant value and further modify the result in a
    →    loop.
    ;
    → -------------------------------------------------------------------
    mov rax, rdi            ; rax = input value.
    shl rax, 1              ; Multiply by 2.

    add rax, 10             ; Add constant 10 to the result.

    ; Use rsi to perform additional arithmetic in a loop.
    mov rsi, rax            ; Copy current result to rsi.
    mov rcx, 3              ; Set loop counter to 3.
.loop_start:
    add rsi, 5              ; In each iteration, add 5.
    loop .loop_start        ; Decrement rcx; repeat if rcx != 0.

    ; Final Computation: Move computed result from rsi back into
    →    rax.
    mov rax, rsi

    ;
    → -------------------------------------------------------------------
    ; Function Epilogue: Restore callee-saved registers and the
    →    original stack frame.
    ;
    → -------------------------------------------------------------------
    pop rsi                 ; Restore rsi.
    pop rbx                 ; Restore rbx.
    pop rbp                 ; Restore the caller's base pointer.
    ret                     ; Return; pops the return address from the
    →    stack.

;
→ -------------------------------------------------------------------
; Entry Point: _start
; Purpose: Demonstrates calling the compute function and exiting the
→    program.
;
→ -------------------------------------------------------------------
_start:
    ; Initialize input parameter.
    mov rdi, 7              ; Example input value (7) placed in rdi.
    call compute            ; Call the compute function; result
    →    returned in rax.
```

```asm
; Exit System Call: Return the computed result as the program's
↪  exit code.
mov rdi, rax            ; Move computed result into rdi (exit
↪  code).
mov rax, 60             ; Syscall number for exit on Linux
↪  (x86_64).
syscall                 ; Invoke system call to terminate the
↪  program.
```

Chapter 8

Function Calls and Returns

Mechanics of the CALL Instruction

The CALL instruction constitutes a fundamental mechanism in the x64 architecture for transferring control from one procedural context to another. At the moment of invocation, the instruction performs a dual operation. First, it automatically saves the address of the subsequent instruction onto the stack, thereby ensuring that the return point is preserved for subsequent control flow restoration. This act of saving the return address is implemented by decrementing the stack pointer, denoted by rsp, and writing the return address to that newly allocated memory location. Second, the CALL instruction computes and transfers control unconditionally to the target subroutine. The precision of this operation lies in the fact that the shift in the instruction pointer occurs atomically with the push to the stack. Such atomicity is critical in preserving the integrity of the control sequence in the presence of complex interactions between concurrent instructions and underlying processor pipelines.

Parameter Passing Conventions and Mechanism

The process of parameter passing in function calls is inextricably linked to the calling convention adopted by the system, with the x64 System V Application Binary Interface providing one of the most prevalent models. In this paradigm, several of the initial function arguments are conveyed via designated general-purpose registers such as rdi, rsi, rdx, and rcx, among others. When the number of parameters exceeds the limit imposed by the available registers, the additional parameters are transmitted through the stack. Such a scheme demands that, prior to the invocation of the CALL instruction, the calling function arrange for the proper positioning of the arguments in both the registers and, if necessary, on the stack. The semantics of parameter passing are thereby defined both by hardware mechanisms and by the prearranged protocol between caller and callee, which ensures that the requisite data is accessible in a predefined layout upon entering the subroutine.

Stack Frame Setup and Cleanup

The establishment and eventual dissolution of a stack frame are central to the proper execution of function calls. Upon entering a subroutine, the called function typically creates a new stack frame through a sequence of operations that encapsulate local variables, saved registers, and other pertinent contextual information. This process is initiated by saving the previous base pointer followed by establishing a new frame pointer, commonly designated as rbp, which provides a stable reference for accessing function arguments and local data. In addition, the callee is responsible for preserving critical register values that must be restored prior to the subroutine's exit. The cleanup of the stack frame, executed prior to the return, entails reversing the aforementioned actions: local variables are deallocated, the original frame pointer is reinstated, and any registers that were preserved are restored to their previous state. This disciplined manipulation of the stack ensures that each subroutine call operates within a self-contained context, preserving the integrity of the overall program state.

RET Instruction and the Transfer of Control

The RET instruction finalizes the function call by reverting the control flow to the location stored during the initial invocation. By reading the return address from the top of the stack, the RET instruction implicitly increments the stack pointer, restoring it to its state prior to the execution of the CALL instruction. This mechanism guarantees that the memory allocated for the return address is properly reclaimed, thereby preventing corruption of the stack. In complex procedural environments, the seamless operation of the RET instruction is crucial; it forms the nexus between the preservation of computational context and the orderly resumption of execution in the calling function. The reliability of this mechanism is a testament to the efficacy of the stack-based control flow model, as it underpins both the transfer of dynamic control and the robust management of execution state throughout nested function calls.

x64 Assembly Code Snippet

```
; x64 Assembly Code Snippet demonstrating function calls, parameter
↪   passing,
; stack frame setup/cleanup, and recursion to compute the factorial
; of a number. This code adheres to the System V AMD64 calling
↪   convention.

extern printf          ; External C library function for formatted
↪   output

section .data
    fmt_str db "Factorial of %d is %d", 10, 0    ; Format string with
    ↪   newline

section .text
    global main

;-----------------------------------------------------------------------
; main function: Entry point of the program.
; It calls the factorial function with an input value and prints the
↪   result.
;-----------------------------------------------------------------------
main:
    ; Prologue for main: establish a stack frame.
    push rbp
```

```
        mov rbp, rsp

        ; Set up the argument for factorial(n): n = 5.
        mov rdi, 5          ; First argument in rdi (n = 5)
        call factorial     ; Call factorial; result will be in rax.

        ; Prepare arguments for the printf call.
        ; According to the System V ABI:
        ;    1st argument (rdi): pointer to the format string.
        ;    2nd argument (rsi): the original input number (5).
        ;    3rd argument (rdx): the computed factorial result.
        lea rdi, [rel fmt_str]   ; Load effective address of fmt_str
        ↪  into rdi.
        mov rsi, 5               ; Second argument: the input value.
        mov rdx, rax             ; Third argument: the factorial result.
        xor rax, rax            ; Clear rax for variadic functions.
        call printf              ; Call printf to output the result.

        ; Epilogue for main: clean up the stack frame and return.
        mov rax, 0               ; Return 0 status.
        pop rbp
        ret

;-------------------------------------------------------------------------
; factorial function: Computes factorial(n) recursively.
; Parameter:
;    - n is provided in rdi.
; Returns:
;    - factorial(n) in rax.
; Uses:
;    - Callee-saved register rbx is preserved.
;-------------------------------------------------------------------------
factorial:
        ; Function prologue: establish a new stack frame and save rbx.
        push rbp
        mov rbp, rsp
        push rbx

        ; Check for the base case: if n <= 1, then factorial(n) = 1.
        cmp rdi, 1
        jle .base_case

        ; Recursive case:
        ; Save the original value of n in rbx because we will modify
        ↪  rdi.
        mov rbx, rdi
        dec rdi                  ; Prepare argument: n - 1
        call factorial           ; Recursive call to factorial(n-1); result
        ↪  in rax.
        imul rax, rbx            ; Multiply the saved n (in rbx) with the
        ↪  result.
        jmp .end_factorial
```

49

```
.base_case:
    mov rax, 1              ; For n = 0 or n = 1, return 1.

.end_factorial:
    ; Function epilogue: restore rbx and the previous stack frame.
    pop rbx
    pop rbp
    ret
```

Chapter 9

Implementing Recursion

The Recursive Paradigm in Assembly

Recursion in assembly language constitutes a paradigm wherein a routine invokes itself to decompose a computational problem into progressively simpler subproblems. At the machine level, the process is orchestrated through a disciplined sequence of control transfers, primarily mediated by the CALL and RET instructions. Each invocation triggers an automatic saving of the return address by decrementing the stack pointer rsp and writing the subsequent instruction address onto the stack. This mechanism ensures that each recursive call encapsulates its own computational context, thereby enabling a systematic return to the preceding state upon completion of the recursive operation. The recursive paradigm leverages these low-level instructions to implement algorithms that naturally embody self-similarity and iterative decomposition.

Stack Frame Organization for Recursive Calls

A critical aspect of implementing recursion in assembly is the meticulous organization of stack frames. Each recursive call necessitates the allocation of a new stack frame that captures the essential state information, including local variables, function parameters, and preserved register values. Typically, the base pointer rbp is employed to anchor these frames, providing a stable reference point for accessing function arguments and local data. The establishment of a new frame involves saving the existing rbp and updating it to point to the current top of the stack, thereby delineating the boundary for the new context. In recursive routines, the nesting of these frames creates a well-defined chain of contexts that ensures each recursive invocation maintains its integrity until control is eventually restored via the RET instruction.

Return Address Preservation in Recursive Routines

The reliable preservation of return addresses is paramount in recursive routines to maintain consistent control flow. Each invocation via the CALL instruction pushes the address of the instruction following the call onto the stack, thereby creating a unique return point for every level of recursion. Upon reaching the conclusion of a recursive invocation, the RET instruction retrieves the stored address from the stack, restores the stack pointer rsp to its prior state, and resumes execution at the correct location. This coordinated interplay between the CALL and RET instructions safeguards against erroneous control transfers and ensures that even deeply-nested recursive calls unwound in the reverse order of their establishment. The integrity of this mechanism is essential, as any deviation may lead to stack corruption or unpredictable behavior in the execution sequence.

Resource Utilization and Operational Considerations

The inherent nature of recursion in assembly introduces a set of operational considerations that relate directly to resource utilization and performance. Recursive routines intrinsically involve the repeated allocation and deallocation of stack frames, resulting in cumulative stack consumption. The careful management of the stack pointer rsp and adherence to prescribed calling conventions are critical to avoiding stack overflow or inadvertent memory corruption. Furthermore, each recursive invocation contributes to the overall execution overhead, not only through the maintenance of additional frames but also via the implicit register preservation that accompanies every call and return sequence. An understanding of these resource implications is essential for designing recursive algorithms that are both efficient and robust within the constraints imposed by the underlying hardware architecture.

x64 Assembly Code Snippet

```
; ------------------------------------------------------------------
; Recursive Factorial Function Example in x64 Assembly
; This code snippet demonstrates:
;    - The recursive paradigm using the CALL and RET instructions.
;    - Stack frame organization via RBP and RSP.
;    - Preservation of registers (e.g., RBX) across recursive calls.
;    - Resource considerations by proper allocation and deallocation
;      of stack frames in a recursive routine.
;
; The factorial function computes:
;    factorial(n) = n * factorial(n-1)    for n > 1
;    factorial(n) = 1                     for n <= 1
;
; Assemble using NASM and link on a Linux system.
; ------------------------------------------------------------------

section .data
    ; (Optional) Message format string for output (not used in this
    ↪ minimal example)
    msg db "Factorial of %d is %d", 10, 0

section .bss
    ; Uninitialized data (None needed for this code)

section .text
    global main        ; Entry point for the linker

; ------------------------------------------------------------------
; Function: fact
; Description:
;    Recursively computes the factorial of a non-negative integer n.
; Input:
;    n is passed in the RDI register.
; Output:
;    Result is returned in the RAX register.
; Clobbered:
;    RDI and RAX, while RBX is preserved.
; ------------------------------------------------------------------
fact:
    push rbp                ; Save caller's base pointer.
    mov rbp, rsp            ; Establish new stack frame.
```

53

```asm
        push rbx                ; Preserve RBX (callee-saved register).

        mov rbx, rdi            ; Save original n in RBX for later
        ↳ multiplication.
        cmp rdi, 1              ; Check if n <= 1 (base case).
        jle .Lbase_case

        dec rdi                 ; Compute n - 1.
        call fact               ; Recursive call: fact(n - 1).
        ; Upon return, factorial(n-1) is in RAX.
        imul rax, rbx           ; Multiply result by original n (stored
        ↳ in RBX).

        jmp .Lend

.Lbase_case:
        mov rax, 1              ; Base case: factorial(0) or factorial(1)
        ↳ equals 1.

.Lend:
        pop rbx                 ; Restore RBX.
        pop rbp                 ; Restore the caller's base pointer.
        ret                     ; Return to caller with result in RAX.


; ------------------------------------------------------------------
; Function: main
; Description:
;   Entry point of the program. Sets up parameters to compute
;   factorial(5) and exits with the result.
; ------------------------------------------------------------------
main:
        push rbp                ; Set up the stack frame for main.
        mov rbp, rsp

        mov rdi, 5              ; Prepare argument: n = 5.
        call fact              ; Compute factorial(5); result in RAX.

        ; Exit the program using the Linux syscall interface.
        ; The exit code is set to the computed factorial.
        mov rdi, rax           ; Move result to RDI for exit status.
        mov rax, 60            ; Syscall number for exit (Linux x64).
        syscall                ; Invoke the system call to exit.


; ------------------------------------------------------------------
; End of x64 Assembly Code Snippet
```

Chapter 10

Array Iteration and Processing

Memory Layout and Structural Organization

Arrays are defined in memory as contiguous sequences of elements, each occupying an equal number of bytes. Such a layout ensures that every element is located at a fixed offset relative to the base address of the array. For a given data type T, if an array is allocated beginning at a base address A_0, then the element at index i is stored at the memory location

$$A_i = A_0 + i \times \text{sizeof}(T),$$

where $\text{sizeof}(T)$ represents the byte-size of the data type T. This contiguous allocation is fundamental to efficient memory access, as it permits the computation of an element's address using a simple arithmetic formula. The sequential arrangement guarantees that traversals of the array can be implemented with minimal overhead by leveraging predictable address increments.

Address Calculation Mechanisms

The task of computing the address of any given element in an array is accomplished by a linear combination of the base address and an index-based offset. The offset is derived from the product of the current index and the size of each element. More formally, for the ith element, the address calculation is expressed as

$$A_i = A_0 + i \cdot e,$$

where $e = \text{sizeof}(T)$. This formula embodies the key principle that underlies pointer arithmetic in low-level programming. The arithmetic operations involved, particularly multiplication and addition, are typically optimized at the hardware level. Modern processors incorporate address-generation units that can scale indices by fixed sizes efficiently. This mechanism offloads a significant portion of the computational effort from the central processing unit, thereby streamlining the iteration over arrays. The precise management of these arithmetic operations is critical, as any miscalculation may lead to improper memory access or even violations of security policies within a system.

Iteration Strategies in Array Processing

Iterating over an array involves a systematic progression through each element by sequentially updating an index or pointer. One common strategy consists of initializing an index variable to zero and then incrementing it by one at each iteration, such that the current element is accessed by computing the address

$$A_i = A_0 + i \times e.$$

This process is repeated until the index reaches the predetermined array length. The regular spacing between array elements implies that each consecutive address is incremented by e, a property that is often termed the stride. In many processing routines, the stride directly corresponds to the size of the element, although it may be varied in cases where sub-sampling or segmented processing is required. The computation of these successive addresses is performed using arithmetic units that are optimized for such linear operations, ensuring that the overhead in each iteration is minimized.

Processing Paradigms and Data Manipulation

Beyond the mere traversal of an array, the iterative approach facilitates a wide array of data processing operations. By calculating each element's address explicitly, operations such as accumulation, search, or transformation can be applied individually to each element. The deterministic relationship

$$A_i = A_0 + i \times e$$

provides a robust framework for performing operations that require dependency on the position of elements within the array. This precise control over memory addresses allows for both uniform processing and selective manipulation based on computed conditions. Additionally, the capability to derive an element's address through multiplication and addition supports the use of various algorithmic strategies that can exploit parallelism, pipelining, and other advanced features of modern microarchitectures. The discipline in managing offsets and strides underscores the relevance of understanding hardware-level optimizations and the intricacies of memory architecture in system-level design.

x64 Assembly Code Snippet

```
; Comprehensive x64 Assembly Example for Array Iteration and
↪   Processing
;
↪   ----------------------------------------------------------------
; This example demonstrates:
;   - The memory layout of arrays (contiguous allocation).
;   - Address calculation using the formula:
;       A_i = A_0 + i * sizeof(T)
;     where T is the data type (here, a 32-bit integer, so sizeof(T)
↪   = 4).
;   - Iteration over an array by computing each element's address.
;   - Processing each element (summing the contents of the array).
;
; Assemble and link on a Linux x64 system with:
;     nasm -f elf64 array_processing.asm && ld -o array_processing
↪   array_processing.o
;
; Data Segment: Define an array of 5 integers.
SECTION .data
    array:        dd 10, 20, 30, 40, 50    ; Array elements
    array_len:    dd 5                      ; Number of elements

; BSS Segment: Reserve space for the sum result (64-bit).
SECTION .bss
    sum_result:   resq 1                    ; 8 bytes for the
    ↪   computed sum
```

```asm
; Text Segment: Beginning of the executable code.
SECTION .text
    global _start

_start:
    ; Initialize registers:
    ; rsi holds the base address (A_0) of the array.
    mov rsi, array

    ; ecx will hold the number of elements.
    mov ecx, [array_len]

    ; Clear rdx: used as the index i.
    xor rdx, rdx

    ; Clear rax: used as the accumulator for the sum.
    xor rax, rax

iterate_loop:
    ; Check if index i (in rdx) has reached the array length (in
    ↪ ecx).
    cmp rdx, rcx
    jge finish_loop          ; Exit loop if i >= length

    ; Calculate the address of array[i]:
    ; Using the equation: A_i = A_0 + i * sizeof(int)
    ; Since sizeof(int) is 4 bytes, we multiply the index i by 4.
    mov r8, rdx              ; r8 = i (copy index)
    shl r8, 2                ; r8 = i * 4 (i.e., offset in bytes)
    add r8, rsi              ; r8 now holds: A_0 + i * 4

    ; Load the 32-bit integer from the computed address and
    ↪ sign-extend to 64-bit.
    movsx r9, dword [r8]     ; r9 = array[i]

    ; Accumulate the loaded value into rax (sum).
    add rax, r9

    ; Increment the index (i = i + 1) and repeat the loop.
    inc rdx
    jmp iterate_loop

finish_loop:
    ; Store the final computed sum into memory (for verification
    ↪ purposes).
    mov [sum_result], rax

    ; Terminate the program using the Linux system call interface.
    ; System call: exit (number 60), with exit code 0.
    mov rdi, 0
    mov rax, 60
    syscall
```

Chapter 11

String Copying Routine

Properties of C-Style Null-Terminated Strings

C-style strings are defined as contiguous sequences of characters stored in memory, where the terminal element is a null byte represented by the value 0. This representation eschews the need for an explicit length field by employing a sentinel value to mark the end of the character sequence. The contiguous layout ensures that each character can be accessed via simple pointer arithmetic based on a fixed stride of one byte. Furthermore, the invariant that the terminating null character is unique in its value endows the structure with the ability to be processed in a straightforward manner by routines concerned solely with byte-wise manipulation.

Memory Addressing and Assembly-Level Considerations

At the x64 assembly level, the realization of a string copying routine necessitates a profound comprehension of memory addressing and register management. Two pointers, typically denoted as the source pointer *src* and the destination pointer *dst*, are employed to reference the original and target memory locations, respectively. Basic arithmetic operations facilitate the simultaneous incrementation of these pointers such that the transfer of each byte occurs in lock-step. The conditional evaluation of the byte just copied—through a comparison with the value 0—governs the control flow of the routine. The capability to execute load and store operations in a tight loop, combined with efficient branch instructions for conditional termination, embodies the essence of low-level data manipulation.

Algorithmic Analysis of the Copying Process

The core of the string copying routine is an iterative process that transfers individual bytes from the source to the destination until the null terminator is encountered. At each iteration, a byte is retrieved from the memory location addressed by src, and subsequently stored at the memory location indicated by dst. After the transfer, both pointers are incremented to target the next sequential memory addresses. The loop is predicated on the condition that the fetched byte differs from 0, ensuring that the sequence of characters is faithfully preserved. The theoretical underpinning of this procedure is captured by the conceptual formula:

$$dst[i] \longleftarrow src[i], \quad \text{for } i = 0, 1, 2, \ldots, \text{until } src[i] = 0.$$

This formulation both elucidates the operational mechanics and highlights the dependency on correctly managed pointer arithmetic. The absence of auxiliary counters or length indicators amplifies the critical nature of the branch condition, thereby underscoring the intricate balance between simplicity and precision inherent in assembly-level implementations.

Control Flow and Conditional Evaluation

The control structure of the string copying routine is characterized by a loop that continuously evaluates the condition of the current byte's value. Each iteration commences with the retrieval of a byte from the source address, followed by its storage at the corresponding destination location. A comparison operation immediately follows, verifying whether the transferred byte is equal to 0. This comparative evaluation acts as a gatekeeper for the iteration; should the byte be non-zero, the pointers are incremented and the copying process continues unabated. Conversely, upon detection of the null terminator, the loop terminates, signifying the completion of the copying process. Such a construct exemplifies the tight interleaving of arithmetic and logical operations within assembly code, where branch instructions are employed to enforce loop termination with minimal overhead. The deterministic progression from one memory address to the next, combined with the precise evaluation of the termination condition, forms the crux of a reliable and efficient string copying mechanism.

x64 Assembly Code Snippet

```
; =========================================
; x64 Assembly Code for a String Copying Routine (strcpy)
; Implements the conceptual formula:
;   dst[i] ← src[i], for i = 0, 1, 2, ... until src[i] == 0
; The routine uses two pointers: RSI for the source (src) and RDI
↪   for the destination (dst)
; and copies byte-by-byte until a null terminator (0) is
↪   encountered.
;
; This complete example also provides a _start entry point to
↪   demonstrate usage,
; along with a data section (source string) and a BSS section
↪   (destination buffer).
; =========================================

global _start           ; Entry point for the program (Linux x64)
global strcpy           ; Exported string copy function

section .text

; ----------------------------------
; strcpy: Copy a null-terminated string from source (RSI) to
↪   destination (RDI)
;
; Input:
;   RDI - pointer to the destination buffer (dst)
;   RSI - pointer to the source string (src)
;
; Output:
;   RAX - returns the original destination pointer (dst)
;
; Algorithm:
;   1. Save the original destination pointer in RAX (for returning
↪   later)
;   2. Load a byte from the address pointed by RSI into register AL
;   3. Store the byte from AL into the memory location pointed by
↪   RDI
```

61

```
;    4. Increment both RSI and RDI to point to the next byte
;    5. Compare the copied byte (in AL) with 0 (null terminator)
;    6. Loop if the byte is non-zero, else return
; --------------------------------
strcpy:
        mov rax, rdi            ; Save the destination pointer to return
        ↪ later

.copy_loop:
        mov al, byte [rsi]      ; Load the current byte from the source
        ↪ string
        mov byte [rdi], al      ; Store the byte into the destination
        ↪ buffer
        inc rsi                 ; Increment the source pointer
        inc rdi                 ; Increment the destination pointer
        cmp al, 0               ; Compare the byte with 0 (null
        ↪ terminator)
        jne .copy_loop          ; If not zero, continue the copy loop

        ret                     ; Return, RAX still holds the original
        ↪ destination pointer

; --------------------------------
; _start: Program's entry point to demonstrate the strcpy routine
;
; This routine sets up pointers to the source and destination,
; calls the strcpy function to perform the copying, and then exits.
; --------------------------------
_start:
        ; Load the addresses of the source string and destination buffer
        lea rsi, [rel source_str]  ; Source pointer (RSI) points to the
        ↪ source string
        lea rdi, [rel dest_str]    ; Destination pointer (RDI) points to
        ↪ the destination buffer

        call strcpy                ; Call our string copying routine

        ; Exit the program using the Linux x64 system call interface
        mov rax, 60                ; syscall number for exit is 60
        xor rdi, rdi               ; exit status 0
        syscall

; --------------------------------
; Data Section: Defines the source string (null-terminated)
; --------------------------------
section .data
        source_str db "Hello, x64 Assembly!", 0

; --------------------------------
; BSS Section: Reserves space for the destination buffer
; --------------------------------
section .bss
```

```
dest_str resb 32              ; Reserve 32 bytes for the
   ↪   destination string
```

Chapter 12

String Length Calculation

Fundamental Properties of Null-Terminated Strings

A C-style string is represented in memory as a contiguous sequence of characters terminated by a null byte, denoted by 0. The absence of an explicit length field is compensated by the presence of this sentinel value, which marks the termination of the sequence. Formally, a string can be represented as

$$S = \{s_0, s_1, \ldots, s_{n-1}, 0\},$$

where each element s_i for $0 \leq i < n$ belongs to the set of representable characters and the final element is the unique null terminator. This representation allows for a straightforward mechanism of determining the string length by testing each subsequent byte until the null value is encountered.

Algorithmic Framework for Length Computation

The routine under consideration computes the length of a string by performing a sequential scan from the beginning of the string until the null terminator is found. More precisely, if the string is defined as

$$S = \{s_0, s_1, \ldots, s_{n-1}, 0\},$$

then the length L of the string is given by

$$L = \min\{i \geq 0 \mid s_i = 0\}.$$

The algorithm initializes an index and iteratively examines each byte in memory, incrementing the index for every non-zero character. The process terminates as soon as a byte equal to 0 is detected, at which point the index reflects the number of valid characters contained in the string. This method is inherently linear, yielding a worst-case performance proportional to the number of characters preceding the null terminator.

Memory Access and Pointer Arithmetic Considerations

At the assembly language level, the routine operates on memory addresses stored in registers, which point to the beginning of the string data. The calculation of the string length is achieved through sequential memory accesses wherein a pointer is incremented by a fixed stride—typically one byte—after each read. This pointer arithmetic allows for direct and efficient traversal of memory. In each iteration, the byte located at the address pointed to by the current pointer is fetched and compared to the null terminator. The arithmetic operation that increments the pointer is conceptually equivalent to moving to the next memory cell, facilitating the linear scan required to discern the length of the string. The optimized addressing modes provided by modern architectures assist in reducing overhead and ensure that each memory access is performed with minimal latency.

Theoretical Analysis and Loop Invariants

The correctness of the string length calculation routine is underpinned by a loop invariant that maintains a consistent relationship between the number of examined characters and the state of the computation. Suppose that after i iterations, the invariant

$$\forall j \in \{0, 1, \ldots, i-1\}, \quad s_j \neq 0$$

holds true. This invariant asserts that all bytes inspected so far are non-null, ensuring that the termination condition has not been prematurely triggered. When the condition $s_i = 0$ is encountered, the invariant guarantees that the length of the string is exactly i. Furthermore, the existence of a null terminator in every properly formed C-style string ensures that the scanning process is finite and that the algorithm terminates. The linear progression of the pointer, combined with the direct comparison against the sentinel value, not only confirms the correctness of the method but also substantiates its linear time complexity, making it optimal for this class of problems.

x64 Assembly Code Snippet

```
; x64 Assembly code for computing the length of a null-terminated
↪   string.
; This implementation demonstrates pointer arithmetic, memory
↪   access, and
; loop invariants as discussed in the chapter.

section .data
    ; Define a sample C-style string (null-terminated).
    sampleString db "Hello, x64 Assembly!", 0

section .text
    global _start

;-------------------------------
; Entry Point: _start
;-------------------------------
_start:
    ; Load the address of sampleString into RDI (first argument for
    ↪   strlen)
    lea rdi, [rel sampleString]

    ; Call the strlen routine which returns the length in RAX.
    call strlen

    ; For demonstration purposes, use the computed length (in RAX)
    ↪   as the
    ; exit status when terminating the program.
    mov rdi, rax       ; Set exit code = string length.
    mov rax, 60        ; Linux system call number for exit.
    syscall

;-------------------------------
; Function: strlen
; Description:
```

```
;   Computes the length of a null-terminated string.
;   Input:  RDI = pointer to the beginning of the string.
;   Output: RAX = length of the string (number of characters until
↪   the null byte).
;
; Algorithm:
;   1. Initialize the counter (RAX) to zero.
;   2. Loop:
;       - Compare the byte at [RDI + RAX] with 0.
;       - If it's zero, the null terminator is reached; exit the
↪   loop.
;       - Otherwise, increment RAX and continue.
;
; Loop Invariant:
;   At the start of each iteration, for all indices j such that 0 <=
↪   j < RAX,
;   the content of [RDI + j] is non-zero.
;--------------------------------
strlen:
    xor rax, rax            ; Clear RAX, setting the counter to 0.

strlen_loop:
    cmp byte [rdi + rax], 0.  ; Compare current byte with null
↪   terminator.
    je .done                ; If current byte is 0, string end
↪   reached.

    inc rax                 ; Increment counter (simulate pointer
↪   arithmetic).
    jmp strlen_loop         ; Continue looping.

.done:
    ret                     ; Return with string length in RAX.
```

Chapter 13

String Comparison Routine

Formal Definition of String Equality

A null-terminated string, herein denoted by S, is defined as an ordered sequence

$$S = \{s_0, s_1, \ldots, s_{n-1}, 0\},$$

in which each element s_i for $0 \leq i < n$ is a member of the representable character set and the terminal element is the null byte, symbolized by 0. Two strings, S_1 and S_2, are considered equal if and only if they satisfy the condition

$$\forall i \geq 0, \quad s_i^{(1)} = s_i^{(2)},$$

where the equality comparison is performed sequentially up to and including the occurrence of the null terminator. In this formulation, the equality relation implies that both strings share an identical sequence of characters and terminate simultaneously.

Algorithmic Strategy for Character-by-Character Comparison

The fundamental approach to determining the equality of two strings is to conduct a sequential comparison of corresponding characters.

The algorithm initiates by setting an index $i = 0$ and proceeds as follows:

1. Evaluate whether $s_i^{(1)}$ is equal to $s_i^{(2)}$.

2. If a disparity is identified, the strings are immediately classified as unequal.

3. If both characters are identical, and neither is the null terminator, then the index i is incremented to continue the comparison.

4. The comparison terminates as soon as a null byte is encountered in either string. Consistent results across all indices up to this point imply equality.

This method encompasses two critical operational aspects. First, it relies on the early termination property which allows the procedure to halt upon detection of a mismatch, thereby yielding a performance benefit in the average case. Second, the necessity to check for the null terminator at each iteration serves as an inherent safeguard against out-of-bound memory access.

1 Sequential Comparison and Early Termination

In the sequential traversal of the strings, the algorithm maintains the operational invariant that at the beginning of each iteration the condition
$$\forall 0 \leq j < i, \quad s_j^{(1)} = s_j^{(2)}$$
holds true. The moment this invariant is violated by any index i where $s_i^{(1)} \neq s_i^{(2)}$, the procedure halts as the strings are definitively unequal. Should the algorithm reach an index where one or both characters are equal to 0, the consistent detection of the null terminator in both strings corroborates their mutual termination and, by extension, their equality.

2 Handling Divergent String Lengths

A variation in length between the two strings presents a subtle challenge in the comparison routine. By the definition of a well-formed C-style string, the null terminator functions as the sole determinant of string termination. Therefore, if one string is a proper prefix of the other, the absence of a matching null byte at the corresponding index in the longer string immediately results in a mismatch. The algorithm ensures that the ensuing traversal ceases when the first null character is encountered in either string, thereby accounting for potential discrepancies in length without necessitating an explicit pre-comparison of string lengths.

Loop Invariants and Correctness Analysis

The correctness of the string comparison procedure is substantiated by the maintenance of a loop invariant throughout its execution. At the commencement of each iteration corresponding to index i, it is assumed that for all indices j such that $0 \leq j < i$, the equality $s_j^{(1)} = s_j^{(2)}$ holds. This condition guarantees that any deviation observed at index i immediately invalidates the possibility of overall string equality. Formally, let $P(i)$ be the proposition:

$$P(i): \quad \forall j \in \{0, 1, \ldots, i-1\}, \; s_j^{(1)} = s_j^{(2)}.$$

The algorithm begins with $P(0)$, which is trivially satisfied. Upon each iteration, the veracity of $P(i+1)$ is dependent on the verification of $s_i^{(1)} = s_i^{(2)}$. The moment the invariant is broken, the algorithm terminates with a verdict of inequality. Conversely, if the invariant continues until the detection of the null terminator in both strings simultaneously, then the strings are conclusively equal. This logical structure rigorously affirms the validity and termination of the comparison routine.

Computational Complexity and Memory Considerations

Given the algorithmic design, the procedure for string comparison exhibits a worst-case time complexity of $O(n)$, where n represents the length of the string being examined. This linear complexity stems from the requirement to inspect each corresponding pair of characters until a discrepancy is encountered or the null terminator is reached. In scenarios where the strings are identical or nearly so, the performance may approach the worst-case limit.

From the perspective of memory utilization, the procedure leverages pointer arithmetic to traverse contiguous memory locations efficiently. The algorithm incrementally accesses and compares bytes stored in sequential memory cells, thus capitalizing on the spatial locality principle inherent in modern computer architectures. It is presumed that each memory access and equality comparison operates in constant time, a reasonable assumption in the context of contemporary hardware. This assessment consolidates the practical feasibility of the character-by-character comparison routine within assembly language implementations, wherein minimal overhead is incurred for each executed step.

x64 Assembly Code Snippet

```
;----------------------------------
; Function: string_compare
; Description: Compares two null-terminated strings for equality.
;              Implements a character-by-character comparison as
↪   described in
;              the chapter. It maintains the loop invariant that for
↪   all indices
;              j such that 0  j < i, s1[j] equals s2[j]. The routine
↪   exits
;              early if a mismatch is found.
;
; Parameters:
;   RDI - pointer to the first null-terminated string (s1)
;   RSI - pointer to the second null-terminated string (s2)
;
; Return Value:
;   RAX = 0   if the strings are equal
;   RAX = 1   if the strings are not equal
;
; Algorithm:
;   1. Load the current byte from each string.
;   2. Compare the bytes. If they are different, branch to
↪   .not_equal.
;   3. Check if the current byte is the null terminator. If yes, the
↪   strings are
;      equal; branch to .equal.
;   4. Otherwise, increment both pointers and repeat the process.
;----------------------------------

global string_compare

section .text
string_compare:
    ; Begin loop: compare corresponding characters.
.loop:
    ; Load one byte from each string and zero-extend it into r8 and
    ↪   r9.
    movzx r8, byte [rdi]    ; r8 <- s1[i]
    movzx r9, byte [rsi]    ; r9 <- s2[i]
```

71

```asm
    ; Compare the two loaded bytes.
    cmp r8, r9
    jne .not_equal         ; If s1[i]  s2[i], terminate early.

    ; Check for the null terminator.
    test r8, r8            ; s1[i] == 0 implies s2[i] is also 0
    ↪ (since they are equal).
    je .equal              ; Both strings have terminated, so they
    ↪ are equal.

    ; Advance both string pointers.
    inc rdi                ; Move pointer to next character in s1.
    inc rsi                ; Move pointer to next character in s2.
    jmp .loop              ; Continue with the next iteration.

.not_equal:
    ; If a mismatch is detected, return 1 (indicating inequality).
    mov eax, 1
    ret

.equal:
    ; If both strings end simultaneously and all previous characters
    ↪ are equal,
    ; return 0 (indicating equality).
    xor eax, eax
    ret
```

Chapter 14

String Concatenation Routine

Problem Definition

Let S_1 and S_2 denote two null-terminated strings, where

$$S_1 = \{s_0^{(1)}, s_1^{(1)}, \ldots, s_{n-1}^{(1)}, 0\}$$

and

$$S_2 = \{s_0^{(2)}, s_1^{(2)}, \ldots, s_{m-1}^{(2)}, 0\}.$$

The objective is to construct a single contiguous string in memory by appending the contents of S_2 to the end of S_1. In effect, the concatenated string S_C is defined by

$$S_C = \{s_0^{(1)}, s_1^{(1)}, \ldots, s_{n-1}^{(1)}, s_0^{(2)}, s_1^{(2)}, \ldots, s_{m-1}^{(2)}, 0\}.$$

This operation necessitates the precise traversal and manipulation of byte sequences in memory, and in the context of assembly language, it is typically accomplished via iterative loops that operate on individual bytes.

Algorithmic Approach

The implementation of string concatenation in an assembly loop environment involves two primary stages. The first stage identifies the end of the first string, while the second stage appends the characters from the second string.

1 Locating the Null Terminator of the First String

The algorithm commences by scanning the memory region occupied by S_1, character by character, in order to locate the null byte which signifies the termination of the string. This is achieved using a loop that incrementally advances a pointer through successive memory cells until a zero value is encountered. The traversal can be formalized by stating that, for an index i,

$$\forall j,\ 0 \leq j < i,\quad s_j^{(1)} \neq 0,$$

and the loop concludes upon finding the least index i such that $s_i^{(1)} = 0$. At this point, the pointer is positioned to receive subsequent data corresponding to the characters of S_2.

2 Sequential Appending of the Second String

Once the terminating null character in S_1 is found, the next phase of the algorithm proceeds by copying each byte from S_2 into the positions immediately following the original characters of S_1. Let p denote the pointer to the position of the null terminator in S_1, and let q represent the pointer to the beginning of S_2. An iterative loop is executed, such that during each iteration the byte at q, labeled $s_i^{(2)}$, is transferred to the memory location pointed to by p. The process is governed by the condition that the transfer continues until $s_i^{(2)} = 0$, ensuring that the null terminator of S_2 is also duly copied. Formally, if k is the index corresponding to the concatenation position in S_C, then for every i satisfying $0 \leq i \leq m$, the following relation holds:

$$s_{n+i}^{(C)} = s_i^{(2)}.$$

In this manner, the loop effectuates the direct concatenation of the character sequences.

Loop Invariants and Correctness

The correctness of the string concatenation routine is underpinned by the maintenance of key loop invariants during both stages. During the search for the null terminator in S_1, the invariant asserts that

$$\forall j,\ 0 \leq j < i,\quad s_j^{(1)} \neq 0.$$

74

This guarantees that the pointer has not prematurely encountered a termination point. Similarly, during the appending phase, the invariant is that for every index i processed, the memory region starting at the original position of S_1 and extending to the current position of the pointer accurately reflects the concatenated result. That is, for all indices $0 \leq i < k$,

$$s_i^{(C)} = \begin{cases} s_i^{(1)}, & \text{if } i < n, \\ s_{i-n}^{(2)}, & \text{if } n \leq i < n + m. \end{cases}$$

This invariant remains true until the copying process completes with the insertion of the terminating null byte from S_2 into the new combined string, thus ensuring that the resultant S_C is correctly null-terminated.

Computational and Memory Considerations

The operational complexity of the string concatenation routine is closely tied to the cumulative lengths of S_1 and S_2. The initial stage, which involves locating the end of S_1, requires a traversal of n elements in the worst case, and the subsequent copying phase involves $m + 1$ memory accesses, where the extra operation pertains to the final copying of the null terminator. Overall, the time complexity adheres to $O(n + m)$.

From a memory management perspective, the algorithm assumes that sufficient space exists beyond the termination of S_1 to accommodate the entire contents of S_2. This assumption is critical, as the routine operates under the constraint of in-place modification or within an allocated buffer defined for the resultant concatenated string. Register usage, combined with pointer arithmetic, is leveraged to minimize overhead while maintaining a tight control over memory references, thus optimizing both performance and resource utilization in a low-level assembly environment.

x64 Assembly Code Snippet

```
; x64 Assembly Routine: String Concatenation
;
; This routine concatenates two null-terminated strings S1 and S2
↪    into a single
```

```asm
; contiguous string S_C. It implements the algorithm described in
↪   the chapter:
;
;   S1 = { s^(1)_0, s^(1)_1, ..., s^(1)_(n-1), 0 }
;   S2 = { s^(2)_0, s^(2)_1, ..., s^(2)_(m-1), 0 }
;
; and produces:
;
;   S_C = { s^(1)_0, s^(1)_1, ..., s^(1)_(n-1), s^(2)_0, s^(2)_1,
↪   ..., s^(2)_(m-1), 0 }
;
; Assumptions & Calling Convention (System V AMD64):
;   - RDI: Pointer to the first string S1 (with enough allocated
↪   space for S2).
;   - RSI: Pointer to the second string S2.
;   - RAX: Will return the original pointer to S1 (i.e., S_C's
↪   start).
;
; The routine operates in two stages:
;   1. Locate the null terminator in S1 (ensuring the loop invariant
↪   that for
;      all 0 <= j < i, s^(1)_j != 0).
;   2. Sequentially copy each byte from S2 (including its null
↪   terminator) into
;      the position immediately following the end of S1. This
↪   satisfies the relation:
;         For each i in 0..m, s^(C)_(n+i) = s^(2)_i.
;
global strcat_asm
section .text

strcat_asm:
    ; Save the starting address of S1 in RAX for eventual return.
    mov     rax, rdi


    ; -----------------------------------------
    ; Stage 1: Locate the null terminator of S1.
    ; -----------------------------------------
find_null:
    cmp     byte [rdi], 0    ; Compare the current byte with zero.
    je      copy_s2          ; If found, jump to the copying stage.
    inc     rdi              ; Otherwise, move to the next
    ↪   character.
    jmp     find_null        ; Repeat the loop until a null is
    ↪   found.


    ; ---------------------------------------------------
    ; Stage 2: Append S2 to the end of S1 (copy S2).
    ; ---------------------------------------------------
copy_s2:
    mov     bl, byte [rsi]   ; Load a byte from S2 (s^(2)_i) into
    ↪   BL.
```

76

```
mov     byte [rdi], bl      ; Store the byte at the current
↪  position in S_C.
cmp     bl, 0               ; Check if the byte is the null
↪  terminator.
je      done                ; If yes, S2 copying is complete.
inc     rsi                 ; Increment S2 pointer to the next
↪  byte.
inc     rdi                 ; Increment S1 pointer (for S_C) to
↪  the next position.
jmp     copy_s2             ; Continue copying the remaining
↪  bytes.

done:
ret                         ; Return with RAX still pointing to
↪  the start of S1 (now S_C).
```

Chapter 15

Memory Copy Routine

Problem Specification

The objective is to create a routine analogous to the standard library function *memcpy*, which performs a bytewise duplication of a memory block from a source address to a destination address. Formally, given two pointers *src* and *dst* and a positive integer n, the routine must ensure that for every index i, where $0 \leq i < n$, the relation

$$dst[i] = src[i]$$

holds after execution. The design of the routine presupposes that both memory regions are valid, non-overlapping areas in a byte-addressable memory space. In addition, the copying process must be conducted efficiently, minimizing the overhead per byte transferred while rigorously maintaining data integrity.

Algorithmic Strategy and Pointer Arithmetic

The fundamental strategy relies on sequential traversal of the memory region pointed to by *src*, incrementing a counter i from 0 to $n - 1$. At each iteration, the byte located at the memory address $(src + i)$ is transferred to the corresponding location $(dst + i)$. This procedure can be encapsulated by the invariant

$$\forall i \in [0, k), \quad dst[i] = src[i],$$

where k is the current iteration index. The invariant is established at initialization with $k = 0$ and is maintained through each subsequent iteration until $k = n$, at which point the complete memory block has been accurately replicated. The use of pointer arithmetic permits the routine to operate at a low level, ensuring that the operations are conducted with minimal abstraction overhead, thereby achieving an overall time complexity of $O(n)$.

Memory Model Considerations and Data Alignment

The routine is deeply rooted in the assumptions provided by the underlying memory model. Memory is treated as a contiguous sequence of bytes, with each byte having a unique address. The efficiency of the copying process is substantially enhanced when both the source and destination addresses are aligned according to the natural word boundaries of the processor architecture. In such cases, wider data transfer techniques can be theoretically employed to increase throughput. However, in the most general formulation of the routine, the per-byte transfer paradigm is adopted to preserve generality, ensuring that the algorithm remains valid regardless of the alignment of the memory blocks. The expectation is that the hardware guarantees memory coherency and that writes to the destination are immediately visible to any subsequent reads within the same execution context.

Correctness and Invariant Maintenance

The correctness of the routine rests on the careful initialization and preservation of loop invariants. At the inception of the routine, the invariant,

$$\forall i \text{ such that } 0 \leq i < k, \quad dst[i] = src[i],$$

is trivially satisfied with $k = 0$. During each iteration, the byte at index k is copied from src to dst, and the invariant is updated to encompass the new index. This systematic verification ensures that upon termination, when $k = n$, the property

$$\forall i \in [0, n), \quad dst[i] = src[i]$$

is maintained. This methodical preservation of the invariant affirms that the memory copy operation is performed correctly and efficiently, with no inadvertent omissions or unintended data modifications.

Performance Considerations

The efficiency of the memory copy routine is directly correlated with its linear traversal of the memory block, leading to a time complexity of $O(n)$. Each iteration performs a constant number of operations, thereby ensuring that the total execution time scales linearly with the size of the memory region. Although the routine described herein employs a simple per-byte transfer mechanism, it forms the conceptual basis for more sophisticated techniques that preemptively leverage architectural features such as wider registers and pipeline optimizations. Under the assumption that each memory access consumes a fixed amount of time, the routine achieves optimal performance for the fundamental task of memory copying in environments where hardware-specific optimizations are either unavailable or deliberately eschewed in favor of general applicability.

x64 Assembly Code Snippet

```
; --------------------------------------------------------------
; Memory Copy Routine (memcpy equivalent)
;
; Description:
;    This routine copies 'n' bytes from the memory location pointed
↪   to by
;    RSI (source) to the memory location pointed to by RDI
↪   (destination).
;    It follows a simple per-byte copying strategy using pointer
↪   arithmetic.
;
; Invariant:
;    At the beginning of each iteration, for every index i in [0, k):
;        dst[i] = src[i]
;    where k is the current number of bytes copied.
;
; Calling Convention (System V AMD64):
;    RDI - Pointer to destination buffer (dst)
;    RSI - Pointer to source buffer (src)
;    RDX - Number of bytes to copy (n)
```

```
;
; Returns:
;    The routine simply returns to the caller with the destination
↪    pointer
;    unmodified.
;--------------------------------------------------------------------

section .text
global memcpy

memcpy:
    ; Check if the byte count (n) is zero. If so, skip copying.
    test    rdx, rdx         ; Set flags based on rdx.
    jz      memcpy_done      ; If n == 0, jump to function end.

copy_loop:
    ; Load one byte from the source pointed by RSI into AL.
    mov     al, byte [rsi]
    ; Store the byte in AL into the destination pointed by RDI.
    mov     byte [rdi], al

    ; Increment the source and destination pointers.
    inc     rsi
    inc     rdi

    ; Decrement the counter.
    dec     rdx

    ; If the counter is not zero, continue looping.
    jnz     copy_loop

memcpy_done:
    ret
```

Chapter 16

Memory Set Routine

Formal Problem Specification

Consider a contiguous block of memory represented by an array of bytes, denoted by dst. Given an integer $n > 0$ representing the number of bytes and a specified byte value v, the objective is to initialize each memory location in the block such that for every index i satisfying $0 \le i < n$, the equality

$$dst[i] = v$$

holds. This operation, equivalent in functionality to the standard library routine analogous to memset, assumes that the memory region is valid and non-overlapping, and it operates within a byte-addressable memory model. The specification mandates that the complete initialization be accomplished with strict adherence to the established invariant over the indices of the memory block.

Algorithmic Foundation and Invariant Analysis

The underpinning method employed in this routine is the sequential iteration over the n memory locations. Define an index variable k that is initialized to zero and is incremented after each assignment. At the onset, the invariant

$$\forall\, i \in [0, k), \quad dst[i] = v$$

is trivially satisfied with $k = 0$. During each iteration, the algorithm assigns the byte value v to the memory location indexed by k, subsequently updating the invariant to include the new index, so that

$$\forall\, i \in [0, k+1), \quad dst[i] = v.$$

This meticulous and systematic update of the invariant assures that upon termination, when $k = n$, the invariant

$$\forall\, i \in [0, n), \quad dst[i] = v$$

is fully maintained. The algorithm employs pointer arithmetic to traverse the memory block, ensuring that each successive memory location is accessed in constant time. The iterative process thereby establishes correctness for every single memory write, while also ensuring that the block is completely and uniformly initialized.

Memory Model Considerations and Data Alignment

The operation presupposes a memory architecture in which the memory is accessed as a contiguous sequence of bytes. The addressing scheme obligates that each byte is uniquely identifiable and directly accessible via pointer arithmetic. Although the algorithm is presented in its most general form using per-byte operations, the discussion of potential optimizations is predicated on architectural features such as data alignment. When both the starting address of dst and the size n conform to the natural alignment boundaries of the processor, it becomes feasible to leverage wider registers for parallel assignments. However, in the generalized formulation under consideration, the algorithm maintains its validity irrespective of the alignment of the memory region, thereby guaranteeing a robust and universally applicable solution to the memory initialization problem.

Performance Trajectory and Efficiency Analysis

The operational efficiency of the memory set routine is predominantly characterized by its linear time complexity, denoted by $O(n)$. Each iteration performs a constant number of operations, specifically the assignment of the byte value v to one memory cell and the subsequent adjustment of the pointer or index variable. The linear traversal of the memory block ensures that the overall execution time scales proportionally with the size of the memory region, a property that is essential for applications involving large data structures. The algorithm's design is minimalistic in overhead, isolating the memory assignment as the core operation. This facilitates a predictable performance trajectory, particularly important in contexts where deterministic timing is paramount. The capability to conduct this operation in a highly regular fashion further underscores its applicability in systems requiring both reliability and efficiency in memory manipulation tasks.

x64 Assembly Code Snippet

```
; -----------------------------------------------------------------
; Function: memset_asm
; Purpose: Set a contiguous block of memory to a specified byte
↪    value.
;
; Arguments (using System V AMD64 calling convention):
;    rdi - Pointer to the destination memory block (dst)
;    rsi - Integer containing the value v; only the lower 8 bits
↪    (sil) are used
;    rdx - Number of bytes to set (n)
;
; Precondition:
;    - The memory block pointed to by rdi is valid and writable.
;    - n > 0.
;
; Postcondition:
;    - For every index i in [0, n), the memory content at dst[i] is
↪    set to v.
;
; Algorithm Overview:
;    1. Test if the count in rdx is zero. If yes, return immediately.
;    2. Move the fill byte from rsi (using sil) into al.
;    3. Iterate over the memory block:
;          - Store the byte value in al at the address pointed by rdi.
;          - Increment rdi to advance to the next byte.
;          - Decrement rdx (the remaining count).
;          - Loop until rdx is zero.
;
;    Invariant:
;       At the start of each loop iteration, for all indices i in [0,
↪    k),
;          the condition dst[i] = v holds.
;
```

```asm
;------------------------------------------------------------------

global memset_asm
memset_asm:
    ; Check if number of bytes to set is zero.
    test    rdx, rdx
    jz      .done

    ; Since v is provided in rsi, move its lower 8-bit value (sil)
    ↪  into al.
    mov     al, sil

.loop:
    ; Store the value in al into the memory location pointed to by
    ↪  rdi.
    mov     byte ptr [rdi], al

    ; Advance the destination pointer to the next byte.
    inc     rdi

    ; Decrement the remaining byte count.
    dec     rdx

    ; Continue loop if the counter has not reached zero.
    jnz     .loop

.done:
    ret
```

Chapter 17

Memory Comparison Routine

Formal Problem Specification

Let two contiguous memory regions be represented by pointers s_1 and s_2, with a prescribed length of n bytes. The objective is to perform a bytewise comparison between the two regions. For each index i, where $0 \leq i < n$, the routine examines the bytes $s_1[i]$ and $s_2[i]$ and determines whether the corresponding values are equal. In the event of a discrepancy, the procedure is designed to compute and return a difference value that differentiates $s_1[i]$ from $s_2[i]$, which reflects their lexicographical ordering. If no mismatches are found throughout the entire range, the function returns zero, thereby signifying the equivalence of the two memory blocks. This formal specification is directly analogous to the standard memcmp operation found in various system libraries, and it is crucial that the memory regions are valid, contiguous, and accessible in a byte-addressable memory model.

Algorithmic Framework and Invariant Analysis

The algorithm utilizes an iterative process based on pointer arithmetic to traverse the memory regions. An index variable, denoted by k, is initialized to zero, and it governs the progression of the comparison. The following invariant is maintained throughout the execution of the routine:

$$\forall\, i \in [0, k), \quad s_1[i] = s_2[i].$$

At each iteration, the algorithm retrieves the byte at position k from both s_1 and s_2 and executes a comparison operation. Should these bytes differ, the algorithm computes the numerical difference between the two, thereby providing an order relationship that can be used to determine the relative magnitudes of the two memory contents. In cases where the bytes remain identical, the invariant is maintained by incrementing k, and the process is repeated until $k = n$. The successful termination of the loop with $k = n$ is indicative of the complete equivalence of the memory regions. This meticulous maintenance of the invariant ensures that the correctness of the algorithm can be rigorously established by applying inductive reasoning on the sequence of comparisons.

Memory Model and Data Alignment Considerations

The implementation is predicated on a memory architecture in which data is accessed as individual bytes via pointer arithmetic. As both memory regions are assumed to be contiguous and properly allocated, each byte is uniquely addressable. Although the primary algorithm iterates over single bytes to guarantee correctness in every scenario, considerations related to data alignment can become pertinent in optimized implementations. In contexts where the pointers s_1 and s_2 are aligned on natural word boundaries, it is theoretically feasible to extend the comparison operation to larger data units; however, for the foundational memcmp-like routine, the bytewise approach is favored for its simplicity and reliability. This method is robust in that it does not require any assumptions about the alignment or wider register support beyond the minimal requirements of the processor's instruction set.

Efficiency Analysis and Complexity Considerations

The performance characteristics of this routine are primarily determined by its linear time complexity, which is denoted by $O(n)$. In the worst-case scenario, the algorithm performs n comparisons—each involving the retrieval and evaluation of corresponding bytes from s_1 and s_2. The constant time operations within the loop guarantee that, aside from the number of bytes compared, the overall computational overhead remains minimal. In instances where a discrepancy occurs prior to comparing all n bytes, the algorithm exhibits early termination, thereby potentially reducing the average-case execution time. The simplicity of the loop structure, with its reliance on fundamental processor instructions for memory access and byte comparison, ensures that the routine is well-suited for implementation in performance-critical contexts where deterministic behavior is paramount.

x64 Assembly Code Snippet

```
;
↪    --------------------------------------------------------------------
; Function: memcmp
; Description:
;    Compares two contiguous memory regions byte-by-byte, similar to
;    the standard memcmp routine. It takes pointers to the first
↪    bytes
;    of the two regions (s1 and s2) and an integer n representing the
;    number of bytes to compare. If a mismatching byte is found, it
↪    returns
;    the numerical difference (s1[i] - s2[i]); otherwise, if no
↪    differences
;    are found throughout all n bytes, it returns 0.
;
; Calling Convention (SysV AMD64):
;    RDI -> pointer to memory region s1
;    RSI -> pointer to memory region s2
;    RDX -> number of bytes (n) to compare
; Return Value:
;    EAX contains the result of the comparison.
;
; Algorithm Description:
;    1. If n is zero, immediately return 0.
;    2. Initialize the loop invariant: for all i in [0, k), s1[i]
↪    equals s2[i].
;    3. For the current byte, load s1[k] and s2[k] into registers.
;    4. If the bytes differ, compute and return the difference.
;    5. Otherwise, increment pointers and decrement the counter.
;    6. Continue until all n bytes have been compared.
;
;
↪    --------------------------------------------------------------------
```

```nasm
        global memcmp           ; Declare entry point for the linker

memcmp:
        ; Prologue: establish a stack frame (if needed for debugging)
        push    rbp
        mov     rbp, rsp

        ; Check if n (RDX) is zero - if so, return 0 immediately.
        test    rdx, rdx
        je      .return_zero

.loop:
        ; Load one byte from memory region s1 into AL
        movzx   eax, byte [rdi]
        ; Load one byte from memory region s2 into CL
        movzx   ecx, byte [rsi]

        ; Compare the loaded bytes.
        cmp     al, cl
        ; If the bytes differ, jump to the section that computes the
        ↪  difference.
        jne     .found_difference

        ; Maintain loop invariant: s1[i] == s2[i] for the current index.
        ; Move to the next byte in both regions.
        inc     rdi
        inc     rsi

        ; Decrement the counter (n bytes remaining).
        dec     rdx
        ; If there are still bytes to compare, repeat the loop.
        jne     .loop

.return_zero:
        ; All compared bytes are identical, so return 0.
        xor     eax, eax
        jmp     .epilogue

.found_difference:
        ; The first mismatching byte has been found.
        ; The invariant is broken here, so compute:
        ;    difference = (unsigned value in s1) - (unsigned value in s2)
        ; AL and CL already contain these values.
        ; EAX already holds the zero-extended byte from s1,
        ; and ECX holds the zero-extended byte from s2.
        sub     eax, ecx

.epilogue:
        ; Epilogue: restore previous stack frame and return.
        pop     rbp
        ret
```

Chapter 18

Numeric String to Integer Conversion

Formal Problem Specification

Let S denote a contiguous sequence of characters encoding a numerical value in a predetermined radix, typically base 10. The task is to map the character sequence $S = \{s_0, s_1, \ldots, s_{L-1}\}$, where L constitutes the length of the string, to an integer value I in accordance with the digits represented. In this context, the character set is assumed to include only valid digits, with the potential inclusion of a leading sign indicator. Each character s_i in the domain pertaining to digits is assumed to be a member of the set $\{48, 49, \ldots, 57\}$ in terms of its ASCII value. The conversion procedure involves the extraction of the numerical content of each character and its incorporation into the cumulative computation of I. If a sign character is present, its effect is applied to the final numerical outcome.

Mathematical Model and Digit Extraction

Let the digit characters in S be denoted by s_i, where $0 \leq i < L$, and assume that any non-digit symbols have been appropriately handled in a prior validation phase. The extraction of the numerical value from each ASCII-coded digit is performed by subtracting the value 48 (i.e., the ASCII code for the character 0) from s_i, thereby yielding the digit value $d_i = s_i - 48$, where $0 \leq d_i \leq 9$. The integer I is then computed as an accumulation of these digit values, weighted by their respective positional values. Formally, assuming the most significant digit is encountered first,

$$I = \sum_{i=0}^{L-1} d_i \times 10^{(L-1-i)},$$

which represents the value of the numeral in its natural base-10 decomposition. Should the string include a negative sign as its initial character, the computed integer I is subsequently negated.

Algorithmic Considerations and Digit Accumulation

The conversion process is predicated on iteratively updating an accumulator variable. Initially, the accumulator I is set to 0. For each digit d_i extracted from the character sequence, the accumulator is updated by performing a multiplication by 10 (corresponding to the radix) followed by the addition of d_i. This procedure may be expressed incrementally as:

$$I_{k+1} = I_k \times 10 + d_k,$$

for $k = 0, 1, \ldots, L - 1$, with the starting condition $I_0 = 0$. This formulation directly accounts for the positional weighting of each digit, ensuring that the original numerical representation is preserved. The algorithmic structure inherently supports early cessation if the string incorporates any invalid digit; however, under the assumption of well-formed input, the process proceeds until all L digits have been processed.

Complexity and Operational Analysis

The conversion algorithm operates in linear time, with the time complexity being $O(L)$, where L represents the number of characters in the numeric string. Each iteration involves a constant amount of work: the extraction of a digit (via subtraction and evaluation), multiplication of the accumulator by 10, and an addition operation. In formal terms, for each index i, the operations performed involve arithmetic computations that are constant in time. This guarantees that the overall procedure is both efficient and predictable in terms of runtime. Furthermore, the algorithm is memory efficient, employing only a fixed number of registers or variables for the accumulator, the current digit extraction, and intermediate results.

The rigor of the transformation from a numeric string to an integer is underpinned by the invariant that, at the beginning of each iteration, the accumulator I correctly represents the numerical value of the substring consisting of the first k digit characters. This invariant, maintained across the iterative process, ensures the soundness of the final result upon completion of the digit accumulation procedure.

x64 Assembly Code Snippet

```
; Numeric String to Integer Conversion in x64 Assembly (NASM syntax)
; This program converts a null-terminated numeric string, which may
↪  start
; with a '+' or '-' sign, into its corresponding 64-bit integer
↪  value.
; The algorithm uses an accumulator to perform: I = I*10 +
↪  digit_value,
; and applies the sign at the end. The computed integer is then
↪  returned
; as the exit code (for demonstration purposes in a Linux
↪  environment).

global main

section .data
    ; Define a sample numeric string (with a negative sign in this
    ↪  example)
    numStr  db  "-1234567890", 0    ; null-terminated string

section .bss
    ; No uninitialized data needed for this example

section .text
main:
    ; Initialize registers:
    ; rsi will point to the current character in the string.
    ; rax will serve as the accumulator for the final integer value.
    ; rbx will hold the sign multiplier (1 for positive, -1 for
    ↪  negative).
    mov     rsi, numStr         ; Load address of the numeric string
    ↪  into rsi
    xor     rax, rax            ; Clear rax, setting the accumulator
    ↪  to 0
```

```
        mov     rbx, 1              ; Default sign multiplier is +1

        ; Check for an optional sign at the beginning of the string.
        mov     dl, byte [rsi]      ; Load the first character into dl
        cmp     dl, '-'             ; Compare with '-' (negative sign)
        je      handle_negative     ; Jump if negative sign found
        cmp     dl, '+'             ; Compare with '+' (positive sign)
        je      handle_plus         ; Jump if positive sign found
        jmp     convert_loop        ; Otherwise, proceed with conversion

handle_negative:
        mov     rbx, -1             ; Set sign multiplier to -1
        inc     rsi                 ; Increment pointer to skip the '-'
        ↪ character
        jmp     convert_loop

handle_plus:
        ; For a plus sign, simply skip the character without changing
        ↪ rbx.
        inc     rsi                 ; Increment pointer to skip the '+'
        ↪ character
        jmp     convert_loop

convert_loop:
        ; Loop to process each digit until the null terminator is
        ↪ encountered.
.loop:
        mov     dl, byte [rsi]      ; Load current character into dl
        cmp     dl, 0               ; Check if it's the null terminator
        je      finished_conversion

        ; Convert the ASCII code in dl to its numeric value by
        ↪ subtracting '0' (48).
        sub     dl, '0'             ; Now, dl holds the digit value (0 to
        ↪ 9)

        ; Multiply the accumulator (rax) by 10 to shift its decimal
        ↪ place.
        imul    rax, rax, 10        ; rax = rax * 10

        ; Add the current digit to the accumulator.
        movzx   rcx, dl             ; Zero-extend dl into rcx
        add     rax, rcx            ; rax = rax + (current digit)

        ; Move to the next character in the string.
        inc     rsi
        jmp     .loop

finished_conversion:
        ; Apply the sign multiplier to the computed integer value.
        imul    rax, rbx            ; rax now holds the signed integer
        ↪ result
```

```
; For demonstration, exit the program returning the computed
↪  integer
; (Note: Only the lower 8 bits are used by the Linux exit code).
mov    rdi, rax         ; Move the result into rdi (exit
↪  status)
mov    rax, 60          ; syscall number for exit in Linux x64
syscall                 ; Invoke the kernel to exit the
↪  program
```

Chapter 19

Integer to Numeric String Conversion

Formal Problem Specification

Let $N \in \mathbb{Z}$ denote the integer value subject to conversion. The objective is to transform N into its corresponding sequence of characters that constitutes its textual representation in base 10. The resulting string must encode each numerical digit in accordance with the standard ASCII encoding, whereby the digit 0 is represented by the code 48, 1 by 49, and so forth up to 9 corresponding to 57. For negative integers, the representation shall be prefixed with the minus sign, denoted by the character $-$, while non-negative integers are represented directly by their digit sequence. This specification mandates that the conversion is both unambiguous and fully reversible.

Mathematical Framework and Digit Extraction

Consider the integer N. In cases where $N < 0$, the operation commences with the determination of its absolute value, denoted by $|N|$. For the instance where $|N| = 0$, the string representation is uniquely defined as the character corresponding to 0. For $|N| > 0$, the conversion process is predicated on the successive extraction of the least significant digit. Formally, let

$$d = |N| \mod 10,$$

where d is an element of the set $\{0, 1, \ldots, 9\}$. This digit is then mapped to its ASCII equivalent via the transformation

$$c = d + 48.$$

Subsequently, the reduced magnitude is updated by performing an integer division:

$$|N| \leftarrow \lfloor |N|/10 \rfloor.$$

This iterative procedure decomposes the integer into its constituent digits, each extracted in order from the least significant to the most significant position. The mathematical description inherently implies a base-10 expansion of N, fulfilling the conventional numeral system representation.

Algorithmic Process and Structural Considerations

The assembly-level routine for integer to numeric string conversion is formulated as an iterative series of operations. The routine initially examines the sign of N. In the event of a negative number, a flag is set and the conversion continues on $|N|$. The subsequent sequence of operations proceeds as follows:

1. Compute the remainder

$$d_i = |N| \mod 10,$$

    thereby isolating the current least significant digit.

2. Convert the digit to its ASCII representation by calculating

$$c_i = d_i + 48.$$

3. Update the value of $|N|$ by the operation

$$|N| \leftarrow \lfloor |N|/10 \rfloor.$$

Since the iterative process yields the digits in reverse order, a reordering step is implemented subsequent to the iterative extraction. This reversal operation realigns the digit sequence so that the most significant character occupies the initial position of the string. The overall algorithm thus exhibits a temporal complexity that scales linearly with the number of digits in N, while managing special cases such as $N = 0$ through dedicated condition checks.

Implementation Considerations in Assembly

In the context of assembly language implementation, the conversion algorithm necessitates precise management of the processor's arithmetic and control registers. The division and remainder operations, commonly executed using instructions such as DIV or $IDIV$, must account for potential side effects including register overwrites. The algorithm typically employs a buffer or allocates a dedicated region on the stack to temporarily store the extracted digit characters. This temporary storage facilitates the subsequent reversal of the digit sequence, ensuring accurate ordering in the final string. Additionally, the detection of a negative integer requires conditional logic to record and ultimately prepend the minus sign to the assembled string. Addressing the edge case where $N = 0$ mandates a direct assignment of the character corresponding to 0, circumventing the iterative digit extraction loop. The intricacies of register allocation and memory organization are critical to ensure that the routine operates correctly and efficiently in a low-level programming environment.

Invariant and Correctness Properties

The correctness of the conversion routine is substantiated through the maintenance of several key invariants throughout its execution. At the commencement of each iteration, the invariant is that the temporary buffer contains the ASCII representations of the digits corresponding to the processed portion of N, albeit in reverse order. Formally, after processing k digits, if the temporary sequence is denoted by

$$C = c_0 c_1 \ldots c_{k-1},$$

then the following relation holds:

$$N = \left(\sum_{i=0}^{k-1} (c_i - 48) \times 10^i \right) + Q,$$

where Q is the remaining quotient derived from the reduction of $|N|$. This invariant indicates that the unprocessed portion Q and the reversed partial result together reconstruct the original value prior to the reversal step. The final reordering operation restores the natural digit order, and the subsequent incorporation of the sign (if required) culminates in a complete and correct string representation of N. The rigorous preservation of these invariant conditions throughout the iterative process guarantees that the assembly routine accurately implements the integer-to-string conversion as specified.

x64 Assembly Code Snippet

```
; Function: itoa
; Description:
;    Converts an integer (in RDI) to its ASCII string representation,
;    storing the result as a null-terminated string in the buffer
↪   pointed by RSI.
;    For a negative number, a '-' is prefixed.
;    The conversion is performed by extracting digits in reverse
↪   order and then reversing them.
;
; Calling Convention:
;    Input:
;      RDI - The integer value to be converted.
;      RSI - Pointer to the output buffer (must be large enough to
↪   hold the result).
;    Output:
;      The output buffer pointed by RSI contains the null-terminated
↪   ASCII string.
;
; Registers Used:
;    Volatile: RAX, RCX, RDX, R8, R9, R10, R11
;    Callee-Saved: RBX, R12
;
; Note: This routine assumes SysV AMD64 calling conventions.
;
global itoa
section .text
itoa:
    ; Prologue: set up the stack frame and preserve callee-saved
    ↪   registers.
```

```
        push    rbp
        mov     rbp, rsp
        push    rbx             ; Preserve RBX (callee-saved).
        push    r12             ; Preserve R12 (callee-saved).

        ; Move the input integer from RDI to RAX.
        mov     rax, rdi        ; RAX = N.
        cmp     rax, 0
        jne     .process_num
        ; Special case: if N is zero, store "0" and terminate.
        mov     byte [rsi], '0'
        mov     byte [rsi+1], 0
        jmp     .done

.process_num:
        ; Copy the input number into RBX for processing.
        mov     rbx, rax        ; RBX will hold the absolute value of N.
        mov     r8, 0           ; R8 will act as the sign flag (0 for
        ↪ non-negative, 1 for negative).
        cmp     rax, 0
        jge     .prepare_conversion
        ; If N is negative, negate it and set the sign flag.
        neg     rax
        mov     rbx, rax
        mov     r8, 1

.prepare_conversion:
        ; Reserve space on the stack for a temporary buffer to hold
        ↪ digits in reverse order.
        sub     rsp, 32         ; Allocate 32 bytes (sufficient for a
        ↪ 64-bit integer conversion).
        mov     r9, rsp         ; R9 points to the temporary digit
        ↪ buffer.
        xor     rcx, rcx        ; RCX will count the number of digits
        ↪ extracted.

.convert_loop:
        ; Loop: extract each digit until the number (in RBX) becomes 0.
        cmp     rbx, 0
        je      .conversion_done
        ; Use division to extract the least significant digit.
        mov     rax, rbx        ; Move current number into RAX.
        xor     rdx, rdx        ; Clear RDX for the division.
        mov     r10, 10         ; Divisor = 10.
        div     r10             ; RAX = quotient, RDX = remainder.
        ; Convert the remainder (digit) to its ASCII equivalent by
        ↪ adding 48.
        add     dl, 48          ; DL now holds the ASCII code for the
        ↪ digit.
        ; Store the ASCII digit in the temporary buffer.
        mov     [r9+rcx], dl
        inc     rcx             ; Increment the digit count.
        ; Update RBX with the quotient for the next iteration.
```

```
        mov     rbx, rax
        jmp     .convert_loop

.conversion_done:
        ; At this point, RCX holds the number of digits (in reverse
        ↪ order).
        ; Prepare the output buffer pointer.
        mov     r11, rsi        ; R11 is used to write the final string.
        ; If the original number was negative, output the '-' sign.
        cmp     r8, 1
        jne     .reverse_digits
        mov     byte [r11], '-'
        inc     r11

.reverse_digits:
        ; Reverse the digits from the temporary buffer into the output
        ↪ buffer.
        mov     r12, rcx        ; R12 is the digit counter.
.reverse_loop:
        cmp     r12, 0
        je      .null_terminate
        dec     r12
        mov     al, [r9 + r12]  ; Retrieve digit from the temporary
        ↪ buffer.
        mov     [r11], al
        inc     r11
        jmp     .reverse_loop

.null_terminate:
        ; Null-terminate the string.
        mov     byte [r11], 0
        ; Deallocate the temporary buffer.
        add     rsp, 32

.done:
        ; Epilogue: restore callee-saved registers and the stack frame.
        pop     r12
        pop     rbx
        pop     rbp
        ret
```

Chapter 20

Implementing a Basic Sorting Algorithm

Formal Problem Specification

The task is to design a routine that reorders an array of numerical elements into nondecreasing order. Let the array be denoted by A, with n elements where $n \in \mathbb{N}$. The goal is to ensure that for every index i in the interval $1 \le i < n$, the condition

$$A[i] \le A[i+1]$$

is satisfied when the sorting process is complete. The sorting algorithm is intended to operate directly on memory-stored data, using a sequence of elementary operations provided by the instruction set in assembly language. The design must consider in-place modifications, minimal auxiliary storage, and adherence to the constraints imposed by low-level data movement and control flow operations.

Algorithmic Description and Structural Design

A basic sorting algorithm such as bubble sort is considered for this implementation due to its simplicity and didactic value. Bubble sort operates by repeatedly traversing the array and comparing adjacent elements. Within each pass, for every pair of indices $(i, i+$

1) where $1 \leq i < n$, the algorithm performs a comparison. If

$$A[i] > A[i + 1],$$

a swap operation is executed to exchange the positions of the two elements. This process is iterated until a complete pass is made with no swap operations performed, indicating that the array is in sorted order.

The structure of the algorithm is inherently iterative. An outer loop manages successive passes across the array while an inner loop carries out comparisons and conditional exchanges. During each pass, the largest unsorted element is consequently shifted toward its final position at the right end of the array. This property ensures that after k passes, the final k elements of the array conform to the sorted order. The algorithm terminates once the number of required passes reduces such that no further swaps become necessary.

Mathematical Invariants and Correctness Analysis

The correctness of the bubble sort algorithm is underpinned by a series of mathematical invariants. During any given pass, an invariant can be stated as follows: after completing one full traversal of the array, the maximum element present in the unsorted portion of A is relocated to position $A[n - k]$, where k is the number of passes executed so far. Formally, after pass k, it holds that

$$A[i] \leq A[i + 1] \quad \text{for all} \quad 1 \leq i < n - k.$$

This invariant ensures that the partially sorted sequence progressively expands from the right end of the array toward the left. Moreover, during each comparison and subsequent swap, the preservation of local order within the traversed segment of the array contributes to a globally sorted outcome. The algorithm exhibits a worst-case time complexity on the order of $\mathcal{O}(n^2)$, where n is the number of elements in the array. Notwithstanding its inefficiency for large data sets, the simplicity of bubble sort renders it particularly suitable for illustrating fundamental sorting concepts at the assembly language level.

Assembly Implementation Considerations

In an assembly language implementation, various considerations must be balanced to faithfully reproduce the bubble sort algorithm. The routine must allocate registers to serve as index counters for the outer and inner loops, in addition to registers for holding intermediate values during comparisons and swap operations. Memory addressing must be managed meticulously so that each element of the array is correctly loaded into a register for evaluation.

Conditional branching instructions form the backbone of the decision-making process required for conditional swaps. These instructions are used to compare values and to direct flow control based on the outcome of each comparison. The swap operation itself typically involves the use of a temporary register to hold one of the operands, ensuring that data is not lost during the exchange. Furthermore, the implementation must account for potential hazards such as register overwrites and the intricacies of addressing modes pertinent to the target processor architecture.

Temporal Analysis and Data Movement Considerations

The bubble sort algorithm, when implemented at the assembly level, emphasizes two main operational aspects: iterative comparisons and data movement. Given an array of n elements, the worst-case scenario requires nearly $n - 1$ full passes through the data, leading to a quadratic number of comparisons in total. Each comparison is immediately followed, conditionally, by a swap that involves a sequence of data movement instructions.

In the context of assembly, data movement is achieved through carefully orchestrated memory load and store operations. The optimization of these instructions is critical, as even a marginal inefficiency in register utilization or memory access patterns can compound over the course of multiple iterations. Analysis of data dependencies and the scheduling of memory operations are essential to maintain acceptable performance within the constraints imposed by the architecture. The trade-off between clarity and efficiency is evident in the bubble sort routine, which, while not optimal in terms of algorithmic complexity, provides a clear and instructive model for understanding low-level data processing and control flow.

x64 Assembly Code Snippet

```
; Bubble Sort implementation in x64 Assembly
; This example uses the System V AMD64 ABI (Linux) to sort an array
↪  of 32-bit integers.
; The algorithm repeatedly traverses the array, swapping adjacent
↪  elements if they are out of order.
; When a full pass completes with no swaps, the array is sorted in
↪  nondecreasing order.

    section .data
; Define an unsorted array of 10 integers
array:      dd  5, 3, 8, 1, 9, 0, 2, 7, 4, 6
n_elements: equ 10

    section .text
    global main


;-------------------------------------------------------
; bubble_sort:
;   Sorts an array of 32-bit integers in-place using Bubble Sort.
;   Input:
;       rdi - pointer to the first element of the array
;       rsi - number of elements in the array
;   The routine repeatedly compares and swaps adjacent elements.
;   It stops when a full pass completes without any swaps.
;-------------------------------------------------------
bubble_sort:
    push rbp
    mov rbp, rsp
    push rbx                ; Preserve rbx (callee-saved register)

outer_loop:
    ; Initialize swapped flag in r8d to 0.
    ; r8d = 0 means no swap has occurred in this pass.
    mov r8d, 0

    ; Set inner loop index: rbx = 0
    xor rbx, rbx

inner_loop:
    ; Check if we have reached the end of the unsorted portion:
    ; Compare current index (rbx) with (n - 1).
    mov rax, rsi
    dec rax                 ; rax = n - 1
    cmp rbx, rax
    jge after_inner     ; If rbx >= n-1, exit inner loop

    ; Load current element A[i] and next element A[i+1].
    mov eax, dword ptr [rdi + rbx*4]
    mov ecx, dword ptr [rdi + rbx*4 + 4]
```

104

```
    ; Compare A[i] and A[i+1]. If already in order, skip swap.
    cmp eax, ecx
    jle next_inner

    ; Swap A[i] and A[i+1]:
    ; Use edx as temporary storage.
    mov edx, eax        ; edx := A[i]
    mov eax, ecx        ; eax := A[i+1]
    mov [rdi + rbx*4], eax
    mov [rdi + rbx*4 + 4], edx

    ; Mark that a swap has occurred.
    mov r8d, 1

next_inner:
    ; Move to the next pair in the array.
    inc rbx
    jmp inner_loop

after_inner:
    ; If no swaps were made during the inner loop, the array is
    ↪ sorted.
    cmp r8d, 0
    je finished
    ; Otherwise, repeat the outer loop for another pass.
    jmp outer_loop

finished:
    ; Restore registers and exit the bubble_sort routine.
    pop rbx
    pop rbp
    ret

;----------------------------------------------------------
; main:
;    Program entry point.
;    Calls bubble_sort to sort the array and then exits.
;----------------------------------------------------------
main:
    ; Load the address of the array and the number of elements.
    mov rdi, array
    mov rsi, n_elements
    call bubble_sort

    ; Exit the program using the Linux syscall (exit code 0).
    mov rax, 60         ; Syscall number for exit
    xor rdi, rdi        ; Exit code 0
    syscall
```

Chapter 21

Linear Search in Arrays

Formal Problem Specification

Let an array be defined as

$$A = \{a_1, a_2, \ldots, a_n\},$$

where $n \in \mathbb{N}$ represents the total number of elements. Given a target element denoted by x, the objective is to determine whether there exists an index i, with $1 \leq i \leq n$, for which

$$a_i = x.$$

The absence of such an index implies that x is not present in A. The equality between elements is assumed to be well-defined, and the search is conducted by examining each element of A in sequence.

Algorithmic Strategy

The linear search algorithm proceeds by sequentially traversing the array A. At each iteration, for index i in the interval $1 \leq i \leq n$, the element a_i is accessed and compared with the target x. If the condition

$$a_i = x$$

is satisfied, the algorithm immediately identifies a match and may return the corresponding index. Otherwise, the search continues until all elements have been examined. This sequential scanning method leverages the straightforward structure of the array, relying on direct comparisons rather than any form of pointer arithmetic or divide-and-conquer approach.

Invariant and Correctness Analysis

During the execution of the algorithm, a key invariant is maintained: at the beginning of the ith iteration, none of the elements in the set

$$\{a_1, a_2, \ldots, a_{i-1}\}$$

is equal to x. This invariant guarantees that if a match exists in the array, it has not been overlooked prior to reaching position i. Upon termination, two possibilities exist. Either a match is found, implying the existence of an index k such that

$$a_k = x,$$

or the invariant has been upheld for all iterations, leading to the conclusion that

$$\forall i \in \{1, 2, \ldots, n\}, \quad a_i \neq x.$$

This exhaustive and systematic examination of each element confirms the correctness of the linear search routine.

Temporal and Computational Complexity Analysis

The linear search algorithm requires a single comparison for each element in the array. In the worst-case scenario, when x is either absent in A or present at the last position, exactly n comparisons are performed. Thus, the worst-case time complexity is expressed as

$$O(n).$$

Statistical models based on a uniform probability distribution of x within A suggest that the average-case performance also adheres to linear complexity scaling. This linear growth in computational effort underscores the intrinsic relationship between the number of elements and the amount of work required by the algorithm.

Memory and Data Movement Considerations

The operation of a linear search routine presupposes that the array A is stored in a contiguous block of memory, such that the memory address of any element a_i can be computed as an offset from a base address. Each iteration of the search involves the loading of an element from memory, followed by a comparison with the target x. The efficiency of this process is inherently tied to the underlying memory architecture, whereby cache utilization and the sequential nature of memory accesses can have a significant influence on performance. The algorithm is characterized by its minimal auxiliary storage requirements, limiting the need for additional registers or temporary memory beyond those necessary for indexing and comparison variables.

x64 Assembly Code Snippet

```
; Linear Search in Arrays - x64 Assembly Implementation
; This function implements the linear search algorithm as described
↪   in the chapter.
; It sequentially scans through an integer array looking for the
↪   target value and returns
; the index (0-based) of the first occurrence. If the target is not
↪   found in the array,
; the function returns -1.
;
; Function Signature (System V AMD64 Calling Convention):
;   Input:
;     RDI - Pointer to the first element of the integer array (int
↪   *array)
;     RSI - Number of elements in the array (n)
;     RDX - Target integer value to search for (x)
;   Output:
;     RAX - Index of the target element if found (0-based), or -1 if
↪   not found.
;
; Algorithm Overview:
;   1. Check if the number of elements (n) is zero. If so, jump to
↪   return -1.
;   2. Initialize an index counter (i) to 0.
;   3. Loop: Compare the array element at index i with the target.
;     - If a match is found, return the current index.
;     - Otherwise, increment the index.
;   4. If the loop completes without a match, return -1.
;
```

```asm
; Loop Invariant:
;    At the start of each iteration, none of the elements in the
↪    array positions [0, i-1]
;    is equal to the target x.
;
; Time Complexity:
;    O(n) in the worst case, since each element is examined
↪    sequentially.

      .global linear_search
      .type linear_search, @function

linear_search:
      ; Prologue: Set up the stack frame.
      push    rbp
      mov     rbp, rsp

      ; Check if the array has any elements.
      cmp     rsi, 0
      je      return_not_found    ; If n == 0, no elements to search.

      ; Initialize the index counter (i = 0).
      xor     rcx, rcx            ; rcx will serve as our loop index
↪    (0-based).

search_loop:
      ; Terminate the loop if index >= n.
      cmp     rcx, rsi
      jge     return_not_found

      ; Load the element at array[i].
      ; Assuming each element is a 32-bit integer, multiply index by
↪    4.
      mov     eax, dword ptr [rdi + rcx*4]

      ; Compare the current element with the target value, x.
      cmp     eax, edx
      je      found_element       ; If equal, the target is found.

      ; Maintain loop invariant: All indices before 'rcx' have been
↪    checked.
      inc     rcx                 ; i = i + 1
      jmp     search_loop

found_element:
      ; The target x has been found at index 'rcx'.
      ; Return the index in RAX.
      mov     rax, rcx
      jmp     cleanup_and_return

return_not_found:
      ; If the target is not found after checking all array elements,
      ; set the return value to -1.
```

```
        mov     rax, -1

cleanup_and_return:
        ; Epilogue: Restore the previous stack frame and return.
        mov     rsp, rbp
        pop     rbp
        ret
```

Chapter 22

Binary Search in Arrays

Formal Problem Specification

Let a sorted array be denoted by

$$A = \{a_1, a_2, \ldots, a_n\},$$

with the ordering constraint

$$a_1 \leq a_2 \leq \cdots \leq a_n.$$

Given a target element x, the task is to determine an index k, where $1 \leq k \leq n$, such that

$$a_k = x.$$

If no such index exists, the routine must indicate the absence of x in A. The assumption of a total order on the elements of A ensures that comparisons are well defined, providing a framework within which an effective search strategy may be formulated.

Algorithmic Paradigm and Divide-and-Conquer Strategy

The binary search algorithm exploits the inherent order in A by employing a divide-and-conquer approach. Initially, two indices,

l and r, are established to represent the lower and upper bounds of the search interval, respectively, with $l = 1$ and $r = n$. The midpoint of this interval is computed through

$$m = \left\lfloor \frac{l+r}{2} \right\rfloor.$$

A comparison is then conducted between the target x and the array element a_m. If the equality

$$a_m = x$$

is satisfied, the search terminates successfully. If, instead, $x < a_m$, then for all indices $i \geq m$, the condition $a_i \geq a_m$ implies that x cannot reside in the subarray $\{a_m, a_{m+1}, \ldots, a_n\}$; hence, the upper bound is adjusted to $r = m - 1$. Conversely, if $x > a_m$, the lower bound is updated to $l = m + 1$. This process of halving the search interval continues iteratively, thereby achieving an exponential reduction in the problem size. The method is emblematic of an efficient divide-and-conquer strategy that leverages the sorted order of the array to minimize the number of comparisons required.

Invariant and Correctness Analysis

A fundamental invariant maintained throughout the execution of the binary search routine is that, if the target x is present in A, then it necessarily lies within the interval

$$[a_l, a_r],$$

where l and r denote the current lower and upper bounds, respectively. At the onset of each iteration, the invariant ensures that

$$x \in \{a_l, a_{l+1}, \ldots, a_r\}$$

if x is present in the array. The algorithm's progression involves judiciously updating the bounds based on a rigorous comparison at the midpoint. This guarantee, coupled with the maintenance of the invariant across each iteration, underpins the logical correctness of the routine. Upon termination, the algorithm either identifies an index k such that

$$a_k = x,$$

or it ascertains that the search interval has been exhausted, thereby confirming that $x \notin A$. The correctness proof is inherently tied to the properties of the sorted array and the systematic reduction of the search interval.

Temporal and Computational Complexity Analysis

The efficiency of binary search is evidenced by its time complexity characterization. In the worst-case scenario, each iteration precisely halves the search interval, resulting in a maximum number of iterations equal to

$$\lceil \log_2 n \rceil.$$

Thus, the time complexity of the algorithm is

$$O(\log n).$$

This logarithmic growth in computational cost is a direct consequence of the divide-and-conquer strategy, where the systematic elimination of half the potential search space in each step leads to a highly efficient resolution of the problem.

Memory and Data Movement Considerations

The binary search algorithm operates on an array A that is stored in contiguous memory, a characteristic that facilitates rapid access to any element via simple offset calculations from a base address. The computation of the midpoint index relies on efficient arithmetic operations, often implemented using instructions that combine addition and bit-shift operations in assembly language. The contiguous storage of the array enhances spatial locality, which in turn improves cache performance by reducing memory latency during element access. Additionally, the minimal auxiliary storage requirements of binary search allow for a compact register allocation and efficient branch management. These attributes are critical when implementing divide-and-conquer routines at the assembly level, where orchestrating data movement and leveraging hardware-specific optimizations can have a measurable impact on overall performance.

x64 Assembly Code Snippet

```
; Binary Search Implementation in x64 Assembly (System V AMD64
↪   Calling Convention)
; This routine searches for a target value in a sorted array.
; Formal Problem:
;   Given a sorted array A = {a0, a1, ..., a(n-1)} in memory,
;   and a target value held in RDX, the routine returns the 0-based
↪   index
;   of the target if it exists or -1 if the target is not found.
;
; Parameters:
;   RDI - pointer to the beginning of the array (each element is 8
↪   bytes)
;   RSI - number of elements in the array (n)
;   RDX - target value to be searched
;
; Returns:
;   RAX - index of the target value if found (0-based);
;         -1 if the target does not exist in the array.
;
; The algorithm uses the divide-and-conquer method calculating:
;   mid = low + ((high - low) >> 1)
; and adjusts the search boundaries accordingly based on:
;   if A[mid] == target --> found;
;   if target < A[mid]  --> high = mid - 1;
;   if target > A[mid]  --> low = mid + 1;
;
; Global declaration for the linker
global binary_search

section .text

binary_search:
    ; Check for an empty array: if (n == 0) then return -1
    test    rsi, rsi
    jz      return_not_found

    ; Initialize search bounds:
    ; low = 0 (stored in r8)
    ; high = n - 1 (stored in r9)
    xor     r8, r8          ; r8 = low = 0
    mov     r9, rsi         ; r9 = n
    dec     r9              ; r9 = high = n - 1

binary_search_loop:
    ; While (low <= high) do:
    cmp     r8, r9
    jg      return_not_found  ; If low > high then the target is not
    ↪   found

    ; Compute mid = low + ((high - low) >> 1)
```

```
        mov     r10, r9         ; r10 = high
        sub     r10, r8         ; r10 = high - low
        shr     r10, 1          ; r10 = (high - low) / 2
        add     r10, r8         ; r10 = mid index

        ; Calculate the address of array[mid]:
        ; element_address = base_address + (mid * 8)
        mov     r11, r10
        shl     r11, 3          ; r11 = mid * 8 (byte offset)
        mov     r12, [rdi + r11]   ; r12 = A[mid] (load 64-bit element)

        ; Compare the element A[mid] with the target stored in RDX
        cmp     r12, rdx
        je      found_target    ; if A[mid] == target, branch to
        ↪  found_target

        ; If target is less than array[mid], update high = mid - 1
        jl      adjust_high

        ; Else, target is greater than array[mid]:
        ; Update low = mid + 1
        mov     r8, r10
        inc     r8
        jmp     binary_search_loop

adjust_high:
        mov     r9, r10
        dec     r9
        jmp     binary_search_loop

found_target:
        ; Element found: return the index (0-based) in r10
        mov     rax, r10
        ret

return_not_found:
        ; Element not found: return -1 in RAX
        mov     rax, -1
        ret
```

Chapter 23

Implementing a Simple Stack Data Structure

Structural and Operational Semantics

The design of a simple stack data structure is predicated on the abstract model of a Last-In-First-Out (LIFO) container. Within this model, the structure is characterized by two primary operations: the insertion of an element at the top of the stack, commonly referred to as a push operation, and the removal of the most recently inserted element, known as a pop operation. These operations are defined mathematically by considering a sequence $S = \langle s_1, s_2, \ldots, s_k \rangle$, where an element s_{k+1} is added by a push, yielding the new sequence $S' = \langle s_1, s_2, \ldots, s_k, s_{k+1} \rangle$, and a pop operation removes s_{k+1} under the condition $k \geq 1$. In the absence of elements, the stack is said to be empty and the pop operation must be handled with appropriate error detection. The maintenance of the invariant that the order of elements in S remains strictly LIFO is essential in ensuring the correctness of stack operations at the assembly level.

Assembly-Level Design Considerations

At the level of assembly language, the functional implementation of a stack demands an intricate interplay between instruction sequencing and manual memory management. The stack is typically implemented as a contiguous block of memory allocated either statically or dynamically. A dedicated pointer, often maintained in a general-purpose register, denotes the current top of the stack. The push operation involves writing an element to the address indicated by the top pointer and then updating the pointer to reflect the new top position. Conversely, the pop operation entails decrementing the top pointer, prior to reading the element from memory. This approach relies on precise arithmetic manipulations, generally implemented using integer addition or subtraction, and on bit-shift operations to compute offsets accurately. Moreover, explicit checks to preempt conditions such as stack overflow or underflow are critical, given the absence of hardware-enforced protections in a bare-metal context.

Manual Memory Management and Data Movement

Memory allocation for the stack is a central concern in a manual memory management regime, particularly when the implementation is carried out in an environment devoid of higher-level memory management utilities. The allocated memory region must satisfy alignment constraints to leverage efficient access patterns and ensure reliability in arithmetic computations. The design must account for the initial establishment of a base address, from which all subsequent elements are accessed by calculating offsets. These offsets are derived by multiplying the size of an individual element by an index, with the multiplication often realized through scaled register addressing or shift operations. The careful orchestration of memory reads and writes, coupled with deliberate pointer arithmetic, underpins the data movement strategy integral to an efficient stack implementation. The management of this memory resource is explicit, requiring programmers to authenticate the validity of addresses during both push and pop operations.

Register Utilization and Instruction Scheduling

The implementation at the assembly level necessitates the judicious allocation of processor registers to distinguish between the base address, the current top pointer, and temporary operands used in arithmetic operations. Typically, one register is designated as the pointer to the base of the pre-allocated memory block, while another register holds the current index or address corresponding to the top of the stack. Assembly instructions such as addition, subtraction, and bit-shift operations are used to modify the top pointer, ensuring that element insertion and removal operations are performed with minimal latency. The sequence of instructions must be carefully scheduled to avoid pipeline stalls and to optimize branch prediction, thereby maintaining the high throughput expected from low-level routines. The adherence to a well-defined operational invariant, namely that the pointer always accurately reflects the most recent modification state of the stack, constitutes a critical aspect of this design. The precision in register utilization ultimately ensures that the stack data structure operates with predictable performance characteristics while being responsive to the demands of manual memory management.

x64 Assembly Code Snippet

```
; Simple Stack Implementation in x64 Assembly for Linux
; This code demonstrates a basic stack data structure with push and
↪   pop operations.
; Each stack element is assumed to be a 64-bit integer.
; The stack is implemented in a statically allocated memory block.
;
; The stack is modeled as a sequence S = (s1, s2, ..., sk).
; The push operation adds an element s(k+1) at the end:
;     S' = (s1, s2, ..., sk, s(k+1))
; The pop operation removes the last element s(k+1) (provided k   1).
;
; The pointer arithmetic used here computes the offset as:
;     offset = index * sizeof(qword)   ; here, sizeof(qword) = 8
↪   bytes
;
; Registers used:
;    rbx  : Base address of the stack memory region.
;    r12  : Current index (number of elements currently in the
↪   stack).
;    rax  : Used for value passing (input to push; returned value
↪   from pop).
;
; Error conditions:
; - Stack Overflow: When trying to push an element after 256
↪   entries.
; - Stack Underflow: When trying to pop from an empty stack.
;
```

```
; Linux system calls are used for error reporting (sys_write) and
↪   program exit (sys_exit).

global _start

section .data
    stack_overflow_error db "Error: Stack Overflow!", 10, 0
    stack_underflow_error db "Error: Stack Underflow!", 10, 0

section .bss
    ; Reserve memory for the stack: maximum 256 qword elements (8
    ↪   bytes each)
    stack resq 256

section .text

_start:
    ; Initialize the stack:
    ; rbx holds the base address of the stack memory.
    ; r12 is used as the index (number of elements) and starts at
    ↪   zero.
    mov rbx, stack        ; Base address of our stack.
    xor r12, r12          ; r12 = 0, no elements in the stack
    ↪   initially.

    ; --- Demonstration of stack operations ---
    ; Push example values onto the stack.

    ; Push the value 10.
    mov rax, 10
    call push

    ; Push the value 20.
    mov rax, 20
    call push

    ; Push the value 30.
    mov rax, 30
    call push

    ; Pop one element (expected value: 30).
    call pop
    ; At this point, rax holds the popped value (30).

    ; Push the value 40.
    mov rax, 40
    call push

    ; Pop two elements consecutively (expected values: 40 then 20).
    call pop      ; Pops 40 into rax.
    call pop      ; Pops 20 into rax.

    ; Conclude demonstration: exit program with code 0.
```

119

```
        mov rdi, 0           ; Exit code 0.
        call exit_syscall

;-------------------------------------------------------------
; Procedure: push
; Description:
;     Pushes a 64-bit value onto the stack.
;     Input: value to push is in rax.
;     Uses global variables:
;        rbx : base address of the stack.
;        r12 : current stack size / index.
push:
        ; Check for stack overflow: if r12 >= 256, signal error.
        cmp r12, 256
        jae push_overflow

        ; Calculate destination address:
        ;    dest_address = rbx + (r12 * 8)
        mov rcx, r12
        shl rcx, 3          ; Multiply index by 8.
        add rcx, rbx        ; rcx now points to the target memory
        ↪   location.

        ; Store the value from rax into the computed memory location.
        mov [rcx], rax

        ; Increment the stack index.
        inc r12

        ret

push_overflow:
        ; Handle stack overflow error.
        ; rdi is set to point to the error message.
        mov rdi, stack_overflow_error
        call print_and_exit

;-------------------------------------------------------------
; Procedure: pop
; Description:
;     Pops the top 64-bit value from the stack.
;     Returns the value in rax.
pop:
        ; Check for stack underflow: if r12 is zero, no elements to pop.
        cmp r12, 0
        je pop_underflow

        ; Decrement the stack index to point to the top element.
        dec r12

        ; Calculate source address:
        ;    source_address = rbx + (r12 * 8)
        mov rcx, r12
```

```
    shl rcx, 3        ; Multiply index by 8.
    add rcx, rbx      ; rcx now points to the memory holding the top
    ↪ element.

    ; Retrieve the value from memory.
    mov rax, [rcx]

    ret

pop_underflow:
    ; Handle stack underflow error.
    mov rdi, stack_underflow_error
    call print_and_exit
```

```
;--------------------------------------------------------------
; Procedure: print_and_exit
; Description:
;    Prints an error message and exits the program.
;    Input: rdi must point to a null-terminated error string.
print_and_exit:
    ; First, compute the length of the error message.
    mov rsi, rdi      ; rsi will point to our error string.
    call strlen       ; Returns length in rdx.

    ; Write the error message to standard output (stdout file
    ↪ descriptor 1).
    mov rax, 1        ; Syscall number for sys_write.
    mov rdi, 1        ; File descriptor 1 (stdout).
    syscall

    ; Exit the program with error code 1.
    mov rax, 60       ; Syscall number for sys_exit.
    mov rdi, 1        ; Exit error code.
    syscall
```

```
;--------------------------------------------------------------
; Procedure: strlen
; Description:
;    Calculates the length of a null-terminated string.
;    Input: rsi points to the string.
;    Returns: rdx contains the length of the string.
strlen:
    xor rdx, rdx      ; Clear rdx (length counter).
.len_loop:
    cmp byte [rsi + rdx], 0
    je .len_done
    inc rdx
    jmp .len_loop
.len_done:
    ret
```

```
;--------------------------------------------------------------
; Procedure: exit_syscall
```

```asm
; Description:
;    Exits the program using a Linux system call.
exit_syscall:
    mov rax, 60          ; Syscall number for sys_exit.
    syscall
```

Chapter 24

Implementing a Queue Data Structure

Structural and Operational Semantics

The queue is formally modeled as an ordered sequence $Q = \langle q_1, q_2, \ldots, q_n \rangle$, where the element q_1 represents the head of the queue and q_n the tail. The foundational invariant inherent to a queue is the strict adherence to the first-in-first-out (FIFO) discipline. Enqueue operations extend the sequence by appending an element q_{n+1} at the tail, thereby transforming Q into $Q' = \langle q_1, q_2, \ldots, q_n, q_{n+1} \rangle$. Conversely, the dequeue operation extracts the head element q_1, reducing the sequence to $Q'' = \langle q_2, \ldots, q_n \rangle$. Consideration of exceptional states is critical; for instance, an empty queue is characterized by the absence of any elements, and the execution of a dequeue operation in such an instance necessitates rigorous error detection and handling. The preservation of the ordering invariant serves as the cornerstone for the consistent behavior of the queue at the assembly level.

Enqueue and Dequeue Operations

The primary operations that underpin the functionality of the queue consist of the enqueue and dequeue processes. The enqueue operation is responsible for the insertion of a new element at the tail, ensuring that the new element becomes the most recently added item. In contrast, the dequeue operation withdraws the element situated at the head, thereby ensuring that the element that has resided in the queue for the longest duration is the one removed. This duality of operations embodies the FIFO concept, which is mathematically defined through the transformation of the sequence Q as detailed previously. In implementations where the queue is bounded, it is imperative to consider both the overflow scenario—resulting from an attempt to enqueue an element when the maximum capacity has been reached—and the underflow scenario, which arises when a dequeue operation is attempted on an empty queue. Correctness in these operations is maintained by strictly updating the head and tail pointers in a manner that reflects the intrinsic order of the elements.

Memory Layout and Data Movement

A robust implementation of a queue at a low level mandates a meticulously orchestrated memory layout. Typically, the queue is allocated as a contiguous block of memory, and its logical structure is superimposed onto this physical memory region. The positions corresponding to the head and tail are managed through pointer arithmetic. For instance, indexes corresponding to the head and tail are scaled by the size of an individual data element, such that the effective address is computed as the base address plus the product of the element size and the index. In many scenarios, the size of a word is encapsulated by the constant $sizeof(qword)$, and arithmetic operations such as bit-shift instructions are employed to facilitate rapid multiplication by powers of two. Additionally, when implementing a circular buffer variant of the queue, modulo arithmetic is used to wrap the tail index around to the start of the memory region, represented by an update such as $tail = (tail + 1)$ mod N, where N denotes the fixed capacity of the queue. Such precise control over memory addresses and data movement is essential for ensuring both performance and reliability in manual memory management contexts.

Register Allocation and Instruction Scheduling

Within an assembly language framework, registers assume a pivotal role in managing the state of the queue. Typically, separate registers are designated to hold the pointers to the head and tail positions, thereby delineating the boundaries of the active queue. The enqueue operation necessitates the use of a register to advance the tail pointer after a new element has been inserted, while the dequeue operation requires decrementing or advancing the head pointer following the removal of an element. The arithmetic instructions involved, such as addition or modulo operations, must be scheduled with careful consideration to avoid pipeline hazards and to optimize the utilization of the processor's resources. Attention to such details ensures that the operations maintain the FIFO invariant without incurring performance penalties due to contention or misaligned instruction execution. The rigorous allocation of registers and the precise timing of arithmetic and data movement instructions serve to reinforce the structural integrity and operational correctness of the queue data structure at the assembly level.

x64 Assembly Code Snippet

```
; x64 Assembly Implementation of a Circular Queue Data Structure
; This implementation demonstrates the key equations and algorithms:
;   - Next index calculation: next_index = (current_index + 1) mod
↪  QUEUE_SIZE
;   - Memory address computation: element_address = base_address +
↪  (index * sizeof(qword))
;   - FIFO behavior through enqueue and dequeue operations.
;
; Assemble with NASM for Linux x64.
;-------------------------------------------
; Constants
%define QUEUE_SIZE 8    ; Maximum number of elements in the queue
;-------------------------------------------

section .data
    ; (No static data required for this example)

section .bss
    head:   resq 1      ; 64-bit head index (initially 0)
    tail:   resq 1      ; 64-bit tail index (initially 0)
    queue:  resq QUEUE_SIZE   ; Memory for QUEUE_SIZE qwords (8
    ↪  bytes each)

section .text
    global _start

;-------------------------------------------
; _start - Program Entry Point
```

```
;--------------------------------------------
_start:
    ; Initialize head and tail indices to 0
    mov qword [head], 0
    mov qword [tail], 0

    ; Example Operations:
    ; Enqueue three elements: 10, 20, 30
    mov rdi, 10
    call enqueue

    mov rdi, 20
    call enqueue

    mov rdi, 30
    call enqueue

    ; Dequeue one element (expected to be 10)
    call dequeue
    ; Returned value is now in rax (can be used for further
    ↪  processing)

    ; Enqueue another element: 40
    mov rdi, 40
    call enqueue

    ; Dequeue again (expected to be 20)
    call dequeue

    ; Exit the program (using Linux syscall exit)
    mov rdi, 0           ; Exit status 0
    mov rax, 60          ; syscall: exit
    syscall

;--------------------------------------------
; Function: enqueue
; Description: Inserts a new element into the queue.
; Parameter: rdi - The 64-bit value to enqueue.
; Returns:   rax - 0 on success, -1 if the queue is full.
; Algorithm:
;    1. Retrieve current tail and head indices.
;    2. Compute next tail index = (tail + 1) mod QUEUE_SIZE.
;    3. If next tail equals head, the queue is full (overflow
↪  condition).
;    4. Otherwise, store the new element at the tail address and
↪  update the tail index.
;--------------------------------------------
enqueue:
    push rbp
    mov rbp, rsp
    push rbx                ; Preserve rbx

    ; Preserve the value to be enqueued in r8.
```

```
        mov r8, rdi

        ; Load tail and head indices from memory.
        mov rbx, [tail]     ; Current tail index in rbx.
        mov rcx, [head]     ; Current head index in rcx.

        ; Compute next tail index: rdx = tail + 1.
        mov rdx, rbx
        inc rdx
        cmp rdx, QUEUE_SIZE
        jne .no_wrap
        mov rdx, 0          ; Wrap around if at boundary.
.no_wrap:
        ; Check for overflow: if (next tail == head) then the queue is
        ↪ full.
        cmp rdx, rcx
        je enqueue_full

        ; Calculate memory address to store the new element.
        ; Each element is 8 bytes, so: address = queue + (tail * 8)
        lea rdi, [queue + rbx*8]
        mov [rdi], r8       ; Store the enqueued value.

        ; Update tail with the new index.
        mov [tail], rdx

        ; Return success code 0.
        mov rax, 0
        pop rbx
        pop rbp
        ret

enqueue_full:
        ; Queue is full. Return error code -1.
        mov rax, -1
        pop rbx
        pop rbp
        ret

;--------------------------------------------
; Function: dequeue
; Description: Removes and returns the head element from the queue.
; Returns:   rax - The dequeued element, or -1 if the queue is
↪ empty.
; Algorithm:
;   1. Check if the queue is empty (head == tail).
;   2. If not empty, load the element at the head.
;   3. Update head index = (head + 1) mod QUEUE_SIZE.
;--------------------------------------------
dequeue:
        push rbp
        mov rbp, rsp
        push rbx           ; Preserve rbx
```

```
    ; Load current head and tail indices.
    mov rbx, [head]      ; Current head index in rbx.
    mov rcx, [tail]      ; Current tail index in rcx.

    ; Check for empty queue: if head == tail.
    cmp rbx, rcx
    je dequeue_empty

    ; Calculate the memory address for the head element.
    lea rdx, [queue + rbx*8]
    mov rax, [rdx]       ; Load the dequeued element into rax.

    ; Update head index: head = (head + 1) mod QUEUE_SIZE.
    inc rbx
    cmp rbx, QUEUE_SIZE
    jne .update_head
    mov rbx, 0           ; Wrap around if at boundary.
.update_head:
    mov [head], rbx

    pop rbx
    pop rbp
    ret

dequeue_empty:
    ; Queue is empty. Return error code -1.
    mov rax, -1
    pop rbx
    pop rbp
    ret
```

Chapter 25

Linked List Traversal

Data Layout and Node Addressing

A linked list is characterized by its non-contiguous memory allocation where each node is dynamically allocated and comprises at least one data field and a pointer field that links to the successor node. Each node is typically organized as a composite data structure, with the pointer field positioned at a specific memory offset. The pointer, expressed as an address in memory (denoted by p), serves as the sole mechanism for establishing connectivity between nodes. In an assembly language context, this field is explicitly managed, with the address of the next node computed via register-based arithmetic. Notably, the physical arrangement of the nodes is decoupled from their logical structure; that is, the ordering inherent to the linked list is solely preserved by the contents of the pointer field rather than by contiguous memory placement.

Pointer Integrity and Dynamic Linking

Pointer manipulation in assembly necessitates rigorous management to ensure the integrity of dynamic links between nodes. Each pointer, when loaded into a register, must be treated as an opaque reference to a memory location. The pointer obtained from the current node, p_{next}, must undergo validation in order to bypass any inadvertent dereferencing of a null or corrupted address. Assembly operations involve explicitly loading the pointer value from the memory location associated with p_{next}, followed by the appropriate arithmetic adjustments to account for any possible offset. Consequently, absolute care must be exercised during pointer arithmetic to guarantee that any manipulation preserves the invariants of the linked list structure—namely, that p_{next} accurately reflects the address of the subsequent node or the termination indicator, typically represented by the null pointer (0).

Traversal Algorithms in Assembly

Traversal of a linked list in assembly is achieved through an iterative algorithm that exploits the pointer contained in each node. The process commences with the loading of the head pointer, denoted as p_{head}, into a register dedicated to tracking the current node. Iteration is implemented by repeatedly dereferencing p_{head} to fetch the pointer p_{next}, which is then reloaded into the same register. This loop continues until p_{head} is found to equal 0, signaling the end of the list. The assembly-level routine must ensure that at each iteration, the value stored at the memory location addressed by p_{head} is processed according to the required operation. This processing may involve data manipulation, condition checks, or further pointer arithmetic. The algorithm rests upon the invariant that each node's pointer maintains an unbroken chain from the head to the terminal node, thereby enabling a systematic and sequential visit to all nodes.

Practical Considerations in Assembly-Level Linked List Operations

Assembly implementations of linked list traversal must contend with several pragmatic factors. Foremost is the management of registers that hold the pointers; registers must be allocated efficiently to prevent inadvertent clobbering of pointer values during successive load and store operations. Memory alignment is another critical consideration, as proper alignment ensures that dereference operations execute with maximal efficiency on the given hardware. Additionally, the manual management required by assembly language imposes an explicit scrutiny of potential pathological cases such as circular lists or the presence of nodes with invalid pointer references. The systematic use of explicit branch instructions and conditional moves in the traversal loop provides a means to safe-

guard the algorithm against such aberrations. In this context, pointer arithmetic is performed with fine control, typically involving multiplication by a constant representing the size of a node structure (commonly
$textttsizeof(node)$) to accurately compute the effective address for each dereference operation. Robust error detection mechanisms and boundary verification protocols enhance the reliability of the traversal, ensuring that the pointer chain is maintained without interruption throughout the lifetime of the process.

x64 Assembly Code Snippet

```
;  --------------------------------------------------------
;  x64 Assembly Code Snippet for Linked List Traversal
;
;  This program demonstrates the linked list traversal algorithm as
↪  described
;  in the chapter. Each node is a 16-byte structure containing:
;     - an 8-byte pointer to the next node (p_next)
;     - an 8-byte data field.
;  The traversal loop begins at the head node and continues until a
↪  NULL pointer
;  is encountered.
;
;  Environment: Linux x64 using NASM syntax.
;  --------------------------------------------------------


section .data
    ; Define three nodes of the linked list.
    ; Node structure:
    ;     Offset 0: dq (8 bytes) pointer to next node
    ;     Offset 8: dq (8 bytes) data value

    node3:
        dq 0                    ; p_next = NULL (end of list)
        dq 0x33333333           ; data: example value for node3

    node2:
        dq node3                ; p_next = address of node3
        dq 0x22222222           ; data: example value for node2

    node1:
        dq node2                ; p_next = address of node2 (head node)
        dq 0x11111111           ; data: example value for node1

    ; A label holding the head pointer of the list.
    head_ptr:
        dq node1
```

```asm
section .bss
    ; (No uninitialized data is needed for this example)

section .text
    global main

;-------------------------------
; traverse_list:
;
; Traverses a linked list given a pointer to the head node.
; Input:
;     RDI - pointer to the head node of the list.
; Operation:
;     1. Validate that the current node pointer is non-NULL.
;     2. Load the data field from the current node (for
↪   demonstration).
;     3. Read the pointer to the next node and update the pointer.
;     4. Repeat until a NULL pointer is encountered.
;-------------------------------

traverse_list:
    push rbp                    ; Save base pointer
    mov rbp, rsp                ; Establish stack frame

    mov rax, rdi                ; rax will hold the current node
    ↪   pointer

.loop_start:
    test rax, rax               ; Check if current node pointer is
    ↪   NULL
    jz .loop_end                ; If NULL, exit the loop

    ; --------------------------------------------------------
    ; Process the current node.
    ; --------------------------------------------------------
    ; The node structure is as follows:
    ;     [rax]        : pointer to next node (p_next)
    ;     [rax + 8]    : current node data
    ;
    ; Load the data field; this could be any processing routine.
    mov rbx, [rax + 8]          ; Load data from the current node
    ↪   into RBX

    ; (Placeholder for additional processing of the node's data)
    nop

    ; --------------------------------------------------------
    ; Fetch the next node pointer.
    ; --------------------------------------------------------
    mov rcx, [rax]              ; Load pointer to next node from
    ↪   current node
```

```asm
        ; Validate pointer integrity: the next pointer should be
        ↪  non-NULL
        test rcx, rcx               ; Check if next pointer is NULL
        jz .loop_end                ; If yes, then we have reached the
        ↪  end

        ; In some cases, pointer arithmetic might be needed if nodes are
        ↪  part of a
        ; contiguous block with a fixed size. For example, if the
        ↪  pointer stored
        ; were an index offset, you would need to multiply by
        ↪  sizeof(node) (16 bytes).
        ; In our design, the absolute address is stored, so no
        ↪  multiplication is required.
        ;
        ; Example (commented out):
        ;   mov rdx, 16
        ;   imul rcx, rdx           ; Adjust pointer if necessary

        ; Update the current node pointer and iterate.
        mov rax, rcx
        jmp .loop_start

.loop_end:
        pop rbp                     ; Restore base pointer
        ret                         ; Return from subroutine


;--------------------------------
; main:
;
; Application entry point.
; Loads the head pointer from the data section and initiates the
↪  linked list
; traversal. Upon completion, the program exits via the Linux system
↪  call.
;--------------------------------

main:
        ; Load the head pointer from the label "head_ptr"
        mov rdi, [rel head_ptr]     ; rdi now contains the address of the
        ↪  head node
        call traverse_list          ; Traverse the linked list

        ; Exit the program using the Linux syscall interface.
        mov rax, 60                 ; syscall number for exit
        xor rdi, rdi                ; exit status 0
        syscall                     ; invoke system call to exit
```

Chapter 26

Simple File Reading Operation

System Call Interface for File I/O

File input operations at the assembly level are orchestrated through the operating system's system call interface. This mechanism allows the program to request kernel services by placing predefined values in designated registers before invoking the interrupt or trap instruction. In the context of file reading, two principal system calls come into play: the call to *open*, which establishes a connection to a file via a file descriptor, and the call to *read*, which transfers data from the file into a user-provided memory buffer. The operation of these calls relies on a well-defined convention whereby the system call number, passed in a specific register, signals the desired operation, and subsequent registers convey parameters such as file paths, flag options, and data buffer addresses. This methodology abstracts the physical details of the hardware from software-level file manipulation, permitting a controlled and secure interface between user programs and the kernel.

File Descriptor Acquisition and Management

The process of opening a file culminates in the acquisition of a file descriptor, commonly denoted by the symbol fd. This descriptor is a nonnegative integer that serves as an abstract handle for the file, encapsulating system-level information regarding the file's state and access mode. The *open* system call performs both the resolution of the file pathname and the verification of access permissions, yielding a descriptor that permits subsequent operations. The intrinsic properties of the file descriptor include the maintenance of an internal file offset and mode flags, which directly influence the behavior of the subsequent *read* operations. Effective management of these descriptors is paramount, for improper handling could lead to resource exhaustion or erroneous operations that may compromise the integrity of the file system.

Operational Details of the File Read Mechanism

Once a valid file descriptor has been obtained, the *read* system call is employed to transfer file contents into a pre-allocated memory buffer. The call takes as arguments the file descriptor fd, the starting address of the buffer, and the maximum number of bytes to be read during the transaction. The operation is characterized by its synchronous nature, meaning that the call will block until the requested data becomes available or an end-of-file condition is encountered. Integral to the operation is the maintenance of proper pointer arithmetic; the address passed to the *read* call must be aligned as required by the architecture, and the buffer size must correspond to the constraints of both the underlying hardware and the operating system. The return value of this call signifies the actual number of bytes successfully read, a figure that may differ from the requested number owing to factors such as the terminal state of the file or resource limitations at the time of the call.

Error Handling and Resource Management in File I/O

Robust error checking is an essential aspect of system call-based file reading. When invoking either *open* or *read*, the operating system returns a negative value to indicate an error state. Such errors may arise from a variety of conditions, including but not limited to insufficient permissions, non-existent file paths, or transient hardware failures. The numerical error codes associated with these failures, which are stored in a dedicated error variable (commonly referenced as *errno*), provide a quantitative measure of the failure's root cause. Careful examination of the return values ensures that the process can distinguish between valid read operations and those that terminate unexpectedly. In parallel with error detection, meticulous management of system resources is critical. The file descriptor, once its function has been fulfilled, must be relinquished appropriately to prevent resource leakage. Although the act of closing the file is typically managed in a separate routine, the verification of correct descriptor acquisition and subsequent validation of the data transfer via *read* remain core to ensuring the reliability and efficiency of file-based input operations.

Architectural Considerations and Performance Implications

The performance characteristics of file reading operations are influenced by the nuances of the underlying hardware and the architectural conventions of the operating system. The proper alignment of memory buffers is imperative; misaligned buffers may incur performance penalties or even lead to access violations on certain architectures. Moreover, the efficiency of the *read* operation is interlinked with the granularity of data transfer. Reading data in sizable, architecturally optimal chunks can ameliorate the latency introduced by system calls and decrease the frequency of transitions between user mode and kernel mode. Additionally, the caching behavior of the operating system plays a fundamental role in determining the effective data throughput. The system's internal file cache, when leveraged appropriately, can serve to significantly reduce the perceived latency of disk I/O operations. Consequently, detailed empirical analysis and judicious resource management are paramount in harnessing the full capabilities of the hardware and ensuring that the simple file reading operation meets the rigorous performance standards expected in high-assurance computing environments.

x64 Assembly Code Snippet

```
; This x64 assembly program demonstrates a simple file reading
↪   operation
; using Linux system calls (openat, read, close, and exit). It opens
↪   a file
; named "input.txt", reads up to 128 bytes into a buffer, and
↪   properly handles
; errors by exiting with an appropriate error code if any issues
↪   occur.

SECTION .data
    fileName    db   "input.txt", 0      ; Null-terminated file name
    ↪   string

SECTION .bss
    buffer      resb 128                  ; Reserve a 128-byte buffer
    ↪   for file data

SECTION .text
    global  _start

_start:
    ;-------------------------------------------------
    ; Open the file using the openat system call.
    ;-------------------------------------------------
    ; sys_openat parameters:
    ;   RAX = 257            (syscall number for openat)
    ;   RDI = -100           (AT_FDCWD: use the current working
    ↪   directory)
    ;   RSI = pointer to filename (address of fileName)
    ;   RDX = flags          (O_RDONLY = 0 for read-only)
    ;   R10 = mode           (ignored for read-only, set to 0)
    mov     rax, 257             ; syscall number: openat
    mov     rdi, -100            ; AT_FDCWD (-100) represents the
    ↪   current working directory
    lea     rsi, [rel fileName]  ; load effective address of
    ↪   fileName into RSI
    mov     rdx, 0               ; flags: O_RDONLY = 0
    mov     r10, 0               ; mode: not required for read-only
    ↪   files
    syscall                      ; invoke openat system call

    ; Check for error in file open (negative value in RAX indicates
    ↪   an error)
    cmp     rax, 0
    js      open_error           ; jump to error handler if file open
    ↪   fails

    ; Store the valid file descriptor (nonnegative number) in r12
    ↪   for future use
    mov     r12, rax             ; r12 now holds the file descriptor
```

```
;--------------------------------------------------
; Read the file contents into the buffer.
;--------------------------------------------------
; sys_read parameters:
;    RAX = 0                   (syscall number for read)
;    RDI = file descriptor   (from r12)
;    RSI = pointer to buffer (address of buffer)
;    RDX = number of bytes to read (128)
mov     rax, 0          ; syscall number: read
mov     rdi, r12        ; file descriptor obtained from
↪ openat
lea     rsi, [rel buffer]   ; load effective address of buffer
↪ into RSI
mov     rdx, 128        ; number of bytes to read from the
↪ file
syscall                 ; invoke read system call

; Check if read was successful (negative return indicates an
↪ error)
cmp     rax, 0
js      read_error      ; jump to error handler if read
↪ fails
; On success, RAX contains the number of bytes read and the
↪ buffer is filled.

;--------------------------------------------------
; Close the file descriptor to release the resource.
;--------------------------------------------------
; sys_close parameters:
;    RAX = 3                   (syscall number for close)
;    RDI = file descriptor   (stored in r12)
mov     rax, 3          ; syscall number: close
mov     rdi, r12        ; close the file descriptor stored
↪ in r12
syscall                 ; invoke close system call

;--------------------------------------------------
; Exit the program successfully.
;--------------------------------------------------
; sys_exit parameters:
;    RAX = 60                  (syscall number for exit)
;    RDI = 0                   (exit code 0 for success)
mov     rax, 60         ; syscall number: exit
xor     rdi, rdi        ; set exit code to 0 (successful
↪ termination)
syscall                 ; invoke exit system call

;--------------------------------------------------
; Error Handling Routines
;--------------------------------------------------
open_error:
```

```
    ; Handle file open error by exiting the program with exit code
    ↪   1.
    mov     rax, 60             ; syscall number: exit
    mov     rdi, 1              ; exit code 1 (indicating error in
    ↪   opening file)
    syscall                     ; invoke exit system call

read_error:
    ; Handle file read error:
    ; First, attempt to close the file, then exit with exit code 1.
    mov     rax, 3              ; syscall number: close
    mov     rdi, r12            ; file descriptor in r12
    syscall                     ; close file (ignore any potential
    ↪   error here)
    mov     rax, 60             ; syscall number: exit
    mov     rdi, 1              ; exit code 1 (indicating error in
    ↪   reading file)
    syscall                     ; invoke exit system call
```

Chapter 27

Simple File Writing Operation

System Call Interface for File Output

Assembly-level file output operations are mediated through the operating system's system call interface. This interface stipulates that registers are loaded with specific values, such as the system call number and associated parameters, to transition control from user space to the kernel. In the context of writing data to a file, the process typically involves system calls such as *open*, *write*, and *close*. The *open* call is responsible for generating a file descriptor that uniquely identifies the file within the system, while the *write* call transfers data from a pre-allocated memory buffer into the file. The subsequent *close* call terminates the association between the file descriptor and kernel resources, ensuring that any buffers or state information held by the operating system are properly flushed and released.

Acquisition and Configuration of the Write Handle

The initial phase of file writing involves the generation of a file descriptor through the *open* system call. This call accepts parameters that include the pathname of the target file, a set of flags denoting write-oriented access (such as O_WRONLY or a combination involving O_CREAT), and, when relevant, file mode specifications to determine the permissions if a new file is created. The file descriptor returned encapsulates the state of the file, including its internal offset and access permissions. Sensitive to both the state of the file system and the calling program, this handle constitutes the gateway through which all subsequent output operations are performed.

Operational Semantics of the File Output Mechanism

The process of writing output data to a file is governed by the *write* system call, which is invoked with the file descriptor, a pointer to the memory buffer containing the data, and a count representing the number of bytes intended for transfer. The system call interfaces with the underlying I/O subsystem in a synchronous manner, ensuring that control is not returned to the program until the designated number of bytes has been processed or an anomaly has been detected. Integral to this operation is the adherence to pointer arithmetic and memory alignment requirements imposed by the system architecture, as improper alignment can degrade performance or trigger access violations. The actual number of bytes written is returned by the *write* call, and may differ from the requested count due to factors such as hardware limitations or internal buffering strategies enforced by the operating system.

Error Handling Procedures and Resource Finalization

Robustness in file writing operations necessitates stringent error handling routines. The return value provided by the *write* system call serves as the primary indicator of operational success, with a negative value signaling an error condition. Such error codes facilitate the diagnosis of issues ranging from inadequate permissions to transient device failures. Consistent with best practices in system-level programming, each system call must be accompanied by checks that ensure the integrity of the process state. In addition, once a file output operation has been concluded—irrespective of whether it has completed successfully or encountered an error—the file descriptor must be closed via the *close* system call. This operation guarantees that kernel resources allocated for the file are duly released, thereby forestalling resource leakage and maintaining the overall stability of the system.

Architectural Implications and Performance Considerations

The invocations of system calls such as *write* are intrinsically linked with architectural characteristics and performance overheads. Each transition from user mode to kernel mode incurs a context switch that can impose latency on write operations. Consequently, the optimization of file output routines requires careful consideration of the buffer sizes and the frequency of write operations. Memory alignment and the granularity of data transfers must be calibrated according to the hardware specifications and the caching policies of the operating system. In scenarios where high throughput is desired, batching write requests and aligning buffers to the system's preferred boundaries can yield significant performance improvements. Such architectural considerations underscore the necessity for a meticulous approach when implementing file output functionalities at the assembly level.

x64 Assembly Code Snippet

```
; This program demonstrates a simple file writing operation in x64
↪    Assembly
; using the Linux system call interface. The program opens a file
↪    for writing,
; writes a message to it, and then closes the file descriptor while
↪    performing
; basic error handling.


;-------------------------------------------------------
; Data Section: Define the filename and the message to be written
;-------------------------------------------------------
SECTION .data
    filename:   db "output.txt", 0          ; Null-terminated file
    ↪   name
    message:    db "Hello, x64 Assembly File Output!", 0xA
                                            ; Message to write
                                            ↪    followed by a
                                            ↪    newline
```

```
msg_len:    equ $ - message                ; Calculate the length
↪   of the message

;--------------------------------------------------------
; Text Section: The main code of the program starts here
;--------------------------------------------------------
SECTION .text
    global _start

_start:
    ;------------------------------------------------
    ; Step 1: Open the file using sys_open.
    ;        System call parameters:
    ;        RAX = 2           (sys_open)
    ;        RDI = pointer to filename
    ;        RSI = flags: O_WRONLY (0x01) | O_CREAT (0x40) = 0x41
    ;        RDX = mode: 0644 permissions (0x1A4)
    ;------------------------------------------------
    mov    rax, 2                    ; sys_open system call number
    lea    rdi, [rel filename]       ; address of filename string
    mov    rsi, 0x41                 ; flags: write only (0x01) |
    ↪   create if not exist (0x40)
    mov    rdx, 0x1A4                ; file mode 0644 (octal) =>
    ↪   permissions: rw-r--r--
    syscall

    ; Check if the file was opened successfully.
    ; A negative return value in RAX indicates an error.
    cmp    rax, 0
    js     open_error                ; jump if error (sign flag set)
    mov    r12, rax                  ; save the returned file
    ↪   descriptor in r12


    ;------------------------------------------------
    ; Step 2: Write to the file using sys_write.
    ;        System call parameters:
    ;        RAX = 1           (sys_write)
    ;        RDI = file descriptor (from open)
    ;        RSI = pointer to data buffer (message)
    ;        RDX = number of bytes to write (msg_len)
    ;------------------------------------------------
    mov    rax, 1                    ; sys_write system call number
    mov    rdi, r12                  ; file descriptor obtained
    ↪   earlier
    lea    rsi, [rel message]        ; pointer to the message
    mov    rdx, msg_len              ; length of the message in
    ↪   bytes
    syscall

    ; Verify the result of the write operation.
    cmp    rax, 0
    js     write_error               ; jump to write error handling
    ↪   if negative
```

143

```
;--------------------------------------------
; Step 3: Close the file using sys_close.
;          System call parameters:
;             RAX = 3          (sys_close)
;             RDI = file descriptor
;--------------------------------------------
        mov     rax, 3                  ; sys_close system call number
        mov     rdi, r12                ; file descriptor to close
        syscall


;--------------------------------------------
; Step 4: Exit the program successfully.
;          System call parameters:
;             RAX = 60         (sys_exit)
;             RDI = exit code (0 for success)
;--------------------------------------------
        mov     rax, 60                 ; sys_exit system call number
        xor     rdi, rdi                ; set exit code to 0
        syscall

;-------------------------------------------------------------
; Error Handling Routines
;-------------------------------------------------------------

open_error:
        ; If opening the file fails, exit with error code 1.
        mov     rax, 60                 ; sys_exit
        mov     rdi, 1                  ; exit code 1 indicating open
        ↪  error
        syscall

write_error:
        ; If write fails, attempt to close the file descriptor (if
        ↪  valid)
        ; and then exit with error code 2.
        mov     rax, 3                  ; sys_close
        mov     rdi, r12                ; file descriptor to close
        syscall
        mov     rax, 60                 ; sys_exit
        mov     rdi, 2                  ; exit code 2 indicating write
        ↪  error
        syscall
```

Chapter 28

Command-Line Argument Parsing

Initialization and Argument Retrieval

Upon process invocation, the operating system allocates a structured memory region that encapsulates the count of command-line arguments alongside a contiguous array of pointers. This memory arrangement typically commences with an integer value, denoted as *argc*, which indicates the number of command-line parameters provided. Immediately succeeding this count lies an array of pointers, conventionally referenced as *argv*, where each pointer directs to a null-terminated string representing an individual argument. Within the confines of an assembly program, a careful examination of this layout is essential; the extraction of these pointers requires precise pointer arithmetic and a thorough understanding of the underlying memory model. The retrieval process involves reading the initial count from memory and subsequently iterating through the pointer array to access each corresponding string.

Examination of Memory Layout and Pointer Arithmetic

The memory layout associated with command-line arguments is defined by a sequential arrangement that renders each program parameter accessible from a predetermined offset relative to the stack pointer. This fixed structure necessitates that the assembly program employs low-level arithmetic operations to isolate and process the address of every argument contained within the array. The alignment of pointers and the corresponding strings is governed by the system architecture, mandating that arithmetic computations respect both the inherent data sizes and the alignment constraints. In practice, the program must account for the precise increment required to transit from one pointer to the next, ensuring that every argument is accurately dereferenced and interpreted. An erroneous calculation at this stage can result in the misinterpretation of adjacent memory regions, thereby compromising the integrity of dynamic input handling.

Dynamic Input Handling and Argument Validation

In scenarios demanding dynamic input management, the operation of parsing command-line arguments evolves into a critical phase that intertwines extraction with rigorous validation. Each argument, once identified, must undergo verification to confirm its adherence to expected formatting rules, such as proper null-termination and avoidance of extraneous characters. This validation step is imperative, as the operational semantics of the program often depend on the integrity of the input data. Should discrepancies between the declared count *argc* and the actual memory layout occur, they must be detected through subsequent comparisons and verifications. Moreover, the parsing mechanism is tasked with converting the raw input—often represented as ASCII characters—into a format that is amenable to subsequent computational procedures, all while ensuring that the bounds of the supplied memory are not overstepped.

Considerations in Assembly-Level Argument Processing

The assembly-level handling of command-line arguments encapsulates a multifaceted process that is intimately linked with system calling conventions and low-level memory management. The extraction of parameters is not merely a sequential access of data; it demands a nuanced understanding of register utilization, as the initial argument pointers are typically accessed using predefined registers or explicit stack pointers established during program startup. The critical elements of this process include meticulous pointer arithmetic, careful management of temporary storage registers to prevent inadvertent overwrites, and adherence to memory alignment constraints prescribed by the hardware. Additionally, robust error detection mechanisms must be employed at every stage of the parsing process to ensure that the dynamic input is accurately and efficiently accommodated by the assembly program's internal logic.

x64 Assembly Code Snippet

```
;-------------------------------------------------------------
; x64 Assembly Example: Command-Line Argument Parsing
; This program demonstrates:
;   - Retrieving argc and argv from the process stack
;   - Using pointer arithmetic to access each null-terminated
↪   argument string
;   - Validating each argument pointer before processing
;   - Calculating string length and printing each argument via the
↪   sys_write syscall
;
; Note: This code is intended for Linux (System V AMD64 ABI).
;-------------------------------------------------------------

global _start

section .data
    newline:        db 0xA              ; Newline character (LF)
    newline_len:    equ $ - newline     ; Length of newline
    ↪   character

section .text

_start:
    ;-------------------------------------------------------------
    ; Retrieve argc and argv from the stack.
    ; At process startup, the stack is laid-out as:
    ;   [rsp]           -> argc (number of arguments)
    ;   [rsp+8]         -> pointer to argv[0] (program name)
    ;   [rsp+16]        -> pointer to argv[1]
    ;   ... and so on.
    ;-------------------------------------------------------------
    mov rbx, [rsp]          ; rbx = argc
    cmp rbx, 0
    jle _exit               ; If no arguments, exit
```

```asm
        lea rsi, [rsp + 8]      ; rsi points to the first argv pointer
        xor rcx, rcx            ; Initialize loop counter: rcx = 0

process_next_arg:
        cmp rcx, rbx            ; Compare counter with argc
        jge _exit               ; If all arguments processed, exit

        ;-----------------------------------------------------------
        ; Load the pointer to the current argument string.
        ; Each pointer is 8 bytes (64 bits) long.
        ; Equation: address = base + (index × 8)
        ;-----------------------------------------------------------
        mov rax, [rsi + rcx*8]  ; rax now holds the pointer to argv[rcx]
        test rax, rax
        jz skip_arg             ; If null pointer, skip this argument

        ; Preserve registers that may be modified by the call.
        push rcx                ; Save current index counter
        push rsi                ; Save base pointer of argv array

        ; Call the string printing routine.
        mov rdi, rax            ; Pass pointer to string in rdi
        call print_string

        ; Print a newline after the argument.
        mov rax, 1              ; sys_write syscall number
        mov rdi, 1              ; File descriptor: stdout
        mov rsi, newline        ; Address of newline character
        mov rdx, newline_len    ; Number of bytes to write
        syscall

        pop rsi                 ; Restore rsi
        pop rcx                 ; Restore rcx

skip_arg:
        inc rcx                 ; Move to the next argument
        jmp process_next_arg

_exit:
        ; Exit the program with status 0.
        mov rax, 60             ; sys_exit syscall number
        xor rdi, rdi            ; Exit status 0
        syscall

;-----------------------------------------------------------------
; print_string:
;   Prints a null-terminated string to stdout.
;   It calculates the length of the string by iterating until
;   a null byte (0) is encountered, then uses sys_write.
;   Input: rdi = pointer to the string.
;-----------------------------------------------------------------
print_string:
```

148

```
    push rbx                ; Save rbx (will be used for pointer
    ↪   storage)
    mov rbx, rdi            ; Copy original string pointer into rbx
    xor rcx, rcx            ; rcx will serve as the length counter

find_null:
    mov al, byte [rbx + rcx] ; Load byte from string into al
    cmp al, 0
    je  do_write            ; If null terminator found, end loop
    inc rcx                 ; Increment length counter
    jmp find_null

do_write:
    ; Use sys_write to print the string.
    mov rax, 1              ; sys_write syscall number
    mov rdi, 1              ; File descriptor: stdout
    mov rsi, rbx            ; Pointer to the string
    mov rdx, rcx            ; String length calculated in rcx
    syscall

    pop rbx                 ; Restore rbx
    ret
```

Chapter 29

Dynamic Memory Allocation

Dynamic Memory Allocation Mechanisms

The process of dynamic memory allocation at the assembly level involves the explicit request to the operating system for a contiguous block of memory that can be utilized during runtime. In this context, the assembly program leverages the system call interface to transition from static, compile-time memory assumptions to a dynamic model that permits memory expansion or contraction. The initiation of a dynamic memory request is mediated through specialized system-level routines, whereby the programmer must set up appropriate registers and parameters in accordance with the underlying calling convention. A typical dynamic allocation scenario entails the specification of the desired memory size, which is often expressed in multiples of the system's page size (e.g., 4096 bytes), ensuring that both alignment constraints and performance considerations are addressed in a single operation.

Dynamic Memory Request via System-Level Calls

The integration between assembly routines and the operating system is characterized by a well-defined interface that translates a memory allocation request directly into a kernel invocation. This section delineates the internal protocol without relying on higher-level abstractions. Assembly programs commonly specify parameters such as the allocation size, memory access permissions, and potential mapping flags. The use of dedicated registers to pass these parameters is governed by the platform's application binary interface, thereby necessitating precise register management and adherence to calling conventions. When the system call is executed, the kernel performs internal verifications and may return either a valid memory address indicating the successful allocation or an error code signaling failure. In this regard, the process incorporates initial error checking and validation, ensuring that subsequent operations on dynamically allocated memory are built upon a correctly established memory region.

Memory Management and Allocation Strategies

Following a successful memory allocation request, the management of the received memory segment becomes paramount. The allocated memory region is typically organized into segments that conform to system alignment requirements, a factor that influences both access efficiency and compatibility with the memory management unit. Assembly-level programmers must employ meticulous pointer arithmetic to track the boundaries of allocated memory, enabling manual management of the free list or other auxiliary data structures designed to monitor memory usage. Strategies for dynamic allocation are further complicated by the potential issue of fragmentation; hence, methods for coalescing adjacent free memory blocks or splitting larger blocks into suitably sized partitions are often implemented. The theoretical underpinnings of these strategies are supported by concepts from data structure management and algorithmic efficiency, with an emphasis on maintaining access invariants that preserve data integrity across successive allocation and deallocation cycles.

Error Detection and Resource Deallocation

The robustness of dynamic memory allocation is heavily dependent on rigorous error detection and resource deallocation mechanisms.

Assembly routines that request memory dynamically must incorporate systematic verification of kernel responses, vigilantly examining status codes returned by system calls to ascertain whether the allocation has been fulfilled. This verification is coupled with a comprehensive strategy for resource deallocation, whereby memory is explicitly relinquished once its operational utility has been exhausted. Deallocation not only involves the restoration of memory back to the pool managed by the kernel but also requires the careful update of internal tracking structures within the assembly program. Such processes mitigate the risk of memory leaks and the subsequent degradation of system performance. The precise orchestration of these tasks underlines the importance of error-handling protocols in maintaining the stability and predictability of runtime memory management.

Interplay Between Application Logic and Memory Allocation

The dynamic allocation of memory in an assembly program is integrally linked with the broader logic of application execution. Memory requests are closely synchronized with key operational phases, wherein the temporal existence of an allocation is dictated by the specific requirements of the computing task at hand. This section examines the delicate balance between the transient nature of dynamic memory and the sustained demands of program logic. In instances where memory is allocated for localized computational routines or temporary data storage, the timely deallocation of such memory is essential to prevent resource exhaustion. The nuanced coordination between allocation initiation, operational use, and subsequent release is further constrained by the hardware's memory management policies and the finite nature of available system memory. Consequently, an in-depth comprehension of the interplay between runtime program flow and dynamic memory management is essential for the design of resilient, high-performance assembly applications.

x64 Assembly Code Snippet

```
; x64 Assembly Code Snippet for Dynamic Memory Allocation Example
; This example demonstrates:
```

```
;   1. Requesting dynamic memory via the mmap system call,
;   2. Initializing the allocated memory with a constant pattern,
;   3. Computing a simple checksum over the memory region, and
;   4. Releasing the memory using the munmap system call.
;
; The code adheres to the Linux x64 syscall interface and uses the
↪  following:
;   - mmap syscall (number 9): Allocate memory.
;   - munmap syscall (number 11): Free allocated memory.
;   - exit syscall (number 60): Terminate the program.
;
; Registers for mmap parameters:
;   rdi = addr (0: let kernel choose)
;   rsi = length (e.g., 4096 bytes)
;   rdx = prot (PROT_READ | PROT_WRITE = 3)
;   r10 = flags (MAP_PRIVATE | MAP_ANONYMOUS = 0x22)
;   r8  = file descriptor (-1 for anonymous mapping)
;   r9  = offset (0)
;
; Error checking is performed immediately after the mmap syscall.
; Upon successful allocation, the memory is initialized, processed,
↪  and finally released.

        section .data
alloc_size:  dq 4096         ; Desired allocation size (in bytes)

        section .text
        global _start

_start:
        ;---------------------------------------------
        ; 1. Dynamic Memory Allocation via mmap
        ;---------------------------------------------
        mov     rax, 9              ; syscall number: mmap
        xor     rdi, rdi            ; addr = 0 (NULL, let kernel decide)
        mov     rsi, [alloc_size]   ; length = 4096 bytes
        mov     rdx, 3              ; prot = PROT_READ | PROT_WRITE
        ↪   (1|2)
        mov     r10, 0x22           ; flags = MAP_PRIVATE |
        ↪   MAP_ANONYMOUS (0x02 | 0x20)
        mov     r8, -1              ; file descriptor = -1 (not used)
        xor     r9, r9             ; offset = 0
        syscall                     ; invoke mmap

        ; Check for error: a negative return value indicates failure.
        test    rax, rax
        js      allocation_failed
        ; Save the returned pointer in rbx for further use.
        mov     rbx, rax


        ;---------------------------------------------
        ; 2. Memory Initialization
```

```
; Fill the allocated memory region with the QWORD constant
↪ 0xAAAAAAAAAAAAAAAA.
;-----------------------------------------------
mov     rcx, 4096/8          ; Number of 8-byte chunks (512
↪ QWORDs)
mov     rdi, rbx             ; rdi points to allocated memory
mov     rax, 0xAAAAAAAAAAAAAAAA ; QWORD pattern
cld                          ; Clear direction flag (ensure
↪ forward direction)
init_loop:
stosq                        ; Store rax into [rdi] and update
↪ rdi (rdi += 8)
loop    init_loop


;-----------------------------------------------
; 3. Compute Checksum over Allocated Memory
; Sum all 8-byte values to calculate a simple checksum.
;-----------------------------------------------
xor     rsi, rsi             ; Clear rsi: accumulator for
↪ checksum
mov     rcx, 4096/8          ; Number of QWORDs: 512 iterations
mov     rdi, rbx             ; Reset pointer to start of
↪ allocated memory
checksum_loop:
lodsq                        ; Load a QWORD from [rdi] into rax
↪ (rdi += 8)
add     rsi, rax             ; Add the loaded value to checksum
↪ accumulator in rsi
loop    checksum_loop
; The computed checksum now resides in rsi.


;-----------------------------------------------
; 4. Deallocate Memory via munmap
;-----------------------------------------------
mov     rdi, rbx             ; Base address of allocated memory
mov     rsi, [alloc_size]    ; Length of the memory block to
↪ unmap (4096 bytes)
mov     rax, 11              ; syscall number: munmap
syscall                      ; release memory


;-----------------------------------------------
; 5. Program Termination
;-----------------------------------------------
mov     rax, 60              ; syscall number: exit
xor     rdi, rdi             ; exit status: 0 (successful
↪ termination)
syscall

allocation_failed:
;-----------------------------------------------
; Error Handling: Memory Allocation Failed
;-----------------------------------------------
mov     rax, 60              ; syscall number: exit
```

154

```
mov     rdi, 1              ; exit status: 1 (indicates an error
↪   occurred)
syscall
```

Chapter 30

Multiprecision Arithmetic Operations

Representation of Multiprecision Numbers

In modern computer architectures, numbers exceeding the width of a single register are represented as sequences of fixed-size words. A large integer, denoted by N, is typically expressed in the form

$$N = \sum_{i=0}^{k-1} x_i \cdot 2^{w \cdot i},$$

where each x_i represents an individual word, w is the word size (for example, 64), and k is the number of registers involved in the representation. This decomposition enables the extension of the numerical range far beyond the intrinsic limitation of a single register. The choice of base, here 2^w, aligns naturally with the binary structure of digital hardware, thereby ensuring that arithmetic operations can be partitioned into sequences of operations on standard machine words.

Addition and Subtraction in Multiprecision Arithmetic

Arithmetic operations on multiprecision numbers require algorithms that operate in a digit-by-digit manner, treating each machine word as an individual digit and handling inter-word interactions through the propagation of carry or borrow bits.

1 Digit-by-Digit Computation and Carry Propagation

Multiprecision addition is executed by performing word-level additions starting from the least significant word. At each step, the sum of corresponding words, together with any carry from the previous addition, produces a result that may again yield a carry. The process involves computing individual sums of the form

$$s_i = x_i + y_i + c_i,$$

where x_i and y_i are the ith words of the two numbers and c_i denotes the incoming carry. The carry out from this addition is then propagated to the next word, thereby ensuring correctness across the entire sequence of registers.

2 Borrow Management in Multiprecision Subtraction

In the subtraction of multiprecision numbers, each word is subtracted in conjunction with any borrow that may have been generated by a previous operation. If a particular subtraction yields a negative result in the context of the word size, a borrow is generated and carried into the subsequent word subtraction. The computation adheres to the form

$$d_i = x_i - y_i - b_i,$$

with the borrow b_i being set when the difference is negative, and then applied to the next higher word. This systematic propagation of borrow ensures that each individual subtraction contributes to the final difference without loss of significance.

Multiplication of Multiprecision Numbers

Multiplication in the context of multiprecision arithmetic is substantially more complex than word-level operations. The algorithm typically involves the generation of partial products that arise from multiplying individual words of the operands. Each partial product, computed as

$$p_{i,j} = x_i \cdot y_j,$$

must be shifted by an appropriate multiple of w bits before it is added into the cumulative result. The summation of these partial products is performed with care, as the addition of overlapping terms demands rigorous management of carry propagation. The accumulation process is inherently nested, where an outer loop iterates over the digits of one operand and an inner loop computes the contributions from the corresponding digits of the second operand.

Division and Remainder Computations

Division of multiprecision numbers demands a comprehensive algorithm that extends the principles of long division to an environment where operands are partitioned across multiple registers. Such algorithms establish a quotient and a remainder by iteratively estimating the division of the upper segments of the dividend by the divisor. At each iteration, a provisional quotient digit is generated, and the corresponding multiple of the divisor is subtracted from the current remainder. The iterative nature of this algorithm necessitates precise alignment and shifting operations to ensure that each digit is correctly computed and incorporated into the final result.

Internal Mechanisms for Carry, Overflow, and Register Coordination

The correctness of multiprecision arithmetic relies upon the internal handling of carry and borrow signals. The arithmetic unit must coordinate between successive register operations in a manner that preserves the integrity of the calculation. The overflow resulting from a word-level addition is captured through dedicated processor flags, which in turn inform subsequent word operations. This inter-register coordination is critical in ensuring that the multiprecision algorithm produces an accurate result across all registers involved. Each operation is designed to detect, propagate, and resolve the presence of excess bits beyond the capacity of a single word.

Algorithmic Complexity and Efficiency Considerations

The computational complexity of multiprecision arithmetic routines is a subject of both theoretical and practical importance. For instance, the naive multiplication algorithm presents a complexity of $O(n^2)$, where n represents the number of words employed in the representation. However, the inherent parallelism available at the word level and the judicious management of register operations can mitigate computational overhead. Efficiency gains are achieved by minimizing inter-register data transfers and by optimizing the sequence of low-level additions, multiplications, and subtractions. The intricate balance among these operations demands an integrated approach that harmonizes algorithmic theory with the architectural specifics of the underlying hardware, thereby maximizing performance while ensuring correctness in the manipulation of numbers spanning multiple registers.

x64 Assembly Code Snippet

```
; This x64 Assembly code snippet demonstrates multiprecision
↪   arithmetic operations:
;   - Representation of multiprecision numbers using arrays of 64-bit
↪   words.
;   - Multiprecision addition with digit-by-digit computation and
↪   carry propagation.
;   - Multiprecision subtraction with borrow management.
;   - Multiprecision multiplication using a nested loop for partial
↪   products.
;
; NASM syntax is used and the code is targeted for Linux x86-64.
;
; For demonstration purposes, we work with 4-word (256-bit) numbers.
; The result array for addition reserves an extra word for potential
↪   carry.
; The multiplication routine produces an 8-word result.

section .data
    ; Define two 256-bit (4×64-bit words) multiprecision numbers.
```

```
num1:    dq 0x12345678ABCDEF00, 0x0FEDCBA987654321,
↪    0x1111111111111111, 0x2222222222222222
num2:    dq 0xAAAAAAAAAAAAAAAA, 0xBBBBBBBBBBBBBBBB,
↪    0xCCCCCCCCCCCCCCCC, 0xDDDDDDDDDDDDDDDD

; Reserve a 5-word space for addition/subtraction result (extra
↪    word for carry/borrow).
result:  dq 0, 0, 0, 0, 0

section .bss
    ; Reserve space for the multiplication result: 4-word × 4-word →
    ↪    8 words.
    mult_result: resq 8

section .text
    global _start

;-----------------------------------------------------------
; Routine: multi_add
; Description: Perform multiprecision addition.
;              result = num1 + num2 (each 4-word number).
; Algorithm:   For each word (starting from the least-significant),
;              the routine adds corresponding words and uses ADC to
;              include any carry from the previous addition.
;-----------------------------------------------------------
multi_add:
    push    rbp
    mov     rbp, rsp
    mov     rcx, 4          ; number of 64-bit words
    clc                     ; clear carry flag
    mov     rdi, num1       ; pointer to num1
    mov     rsi, num2       ; pointer to num2
    mov     rdx, result     ; pointer to result array
.add_word:
    mov     r8, [rdi]       ; load word from num1
    add     r8, [rsi]       ; add corresponding word from num2
    adc     r8, 0           ; add carry (if any) from previous
    ↪    addition
    mov     [rdx], r8       ; store the sum
    add     rdi, 8          ; move to next word in num1
    add     rsi, 8          ; move to next word in num2
    add     rdx, 8          ; move to next storage location in
    ↪    result
    loop    .add_word
    ret


;-----------------------------------------------------------
; Routine: multi_sub
; Description: Perform multiprecision subtraction.
;              result = num1 - num2 (each 4-word number).
; Algorithm:   For each word, subtract the corresponding word of
↪    num2 from num1,
```

160

```
;                  using SBB to include any borrow from previous
↪   subtraction.
;-------------------------------------------------------
multi_sub:
    push    rbp
    mov     rbp, rsp
    mov     rcx, 4          ; number of 64-bit words
    clc                     ; clear carry flag (used as borrow flag)
    mov     rdi, num1       ; pointer to num1
    mov     rsi, num2       ; pointer to num2
    mov     rdx, result     ; pointer to result array
.sub_word:
    mov     r8, [rdi]       ; load word from num1
    sub     r8, [rsi]       ; subtract corresponding word from num2
    sbb     r8, 0           ; subtract borrow (if any) from previous
    ↪   subtraction
    mov     [rdx], r8       ; store the difference
    add     rdi, 8
    add     rsi, 8
    add     rdx, 8
    loop    .sub_word
    ret


;-------------------------------------------------------
; Routine: multi_mul
; Description: Perform multiprecision multiplication.
;             mult_result = num1 * num2, where each operand is 4
↪   words.
; Algorithm:  Uses a nested loop to multiply each word of num1 by
↪   each word of num2.
;             The partial product for digits i and j is added into
↪   the position (i+j)
;             of the result with proper shifting and carry
↪   propagation.
;-------------------------------------------------------
multi_mul:
    push    rbp
    mov     rbp, rsp

    ; Zero out mult_result array (8 words) before accumulation.
    mov     rdi, mult_result
    mov     rcx, 8
    xor     rax, rax
.zero_loop:
    mov     [rdi], rax
    add     rdi, 8
    loop    .zero_loop

    ; Initialize outer loop index (i).
    xor     r11, r11        ; r11 will hold the index i (0 to 3)

.outer_mul:
    cmp     r11, 4
```

161

```
        jge     .end_multi_mul
        ; Load digit i of num1.
        mov     rax, [num1 + r11*8]

        ; Initialize inner loop index (j) to 0.
        xor     r12, r12        ; r12 holds the inner index j

.inner_mul:
        cmp     r12, 4
        jge     .next_outer
        ; Load digit j of num2.
        mov     rdx, [num2 + r12*8]
        ; Multiply: unsigned 64-bit multiplication.
        ; Result: RDX:RAX contains the 128-bit product.
        mul     rdx             ; Multiply: RAX * [num2+j] -> RDX:RAX

        ; Compute the destination address for the partial product.
        ; The low 64-bit product goes into mult_result[i+j].
        mov     r8, mult_result
        add     r8, (r11 + r12)*8
        ; Add the low part with carry propagation.
        add     qword [r8], rax

        ; Propagate carry:
        ; If the addition of RAX produced a carry, ADC will add it along
        ↪  with the high half.
        ; Adjust the pointer to the next word.
        mov     r8, mult_result
        add     r8, (r11 + r12 + 1)*8
        adc     rdx, 0          ; incorporate carry flag into high part
        add     qword [r8], rdx

        inc     r12
        jmp     .inner_mul

.next_outer:
        inc     r11
        jmp     .outer_mul

.end_multi_mul:
        pop     rbp
        ret


;-------------------------------------------------------
; _start: Program entry point.
; Description: Demonstrates call to multiprecision addition.
;              (For testing, multi_sub and multi_mul routines are
↪  available.)
;-------------------------------------------------------
_start:
        ; Call multiprecision addition routine.
        call multi_add
```

162

```asm
; Exit the program.
mov     rax, 60         ; syscall: exit
xor     rdi, rdi
syscall
```

Chapter 31

Bit Counting Routine

Problem Statement and Formalization

Consider an unsigned integer x represented in binary form with a fixed word size w. The objective is to define a bit counting routine that computes the number of bits set to 1 in the binary expansion of x. Formally, if x is expressed as

$$x = \sum_{i=0}^{w-1} b_i \cdot 2^i,$$

where each coefficient $b_i \in \{0, 1\}$ denotes the state of the ith bit, the desired count $C(x)$ is given by

$$C(x) = \sum_{i=0}^{w-1} b_i.$$

This calculation, often referred to as the population count or Hamming weight, serves as a foundational operation in various bit-level applications and algorithmic contexts.

Algorithmic Paradigms

Multiple paradigms exist for designing a bit counting routine. One conceptual approach employs a digit-by-digit examination of the binary representation of x. In this iterative framework, each bit is evaluated in sequence, and a counter is incremented whenever a bit is determined to be set. This method provides an intuitive mapping between the binary form of x and the accumulated result, albeit with a linear dependency on the word size w.

An alternative method exploits the properties of binary arithmetic by iteratively removing the least significant set bit from x. Given the identity

$$x \,\&\, (x - 1),$$

which effectively clears the lowest set bit of x, the routine may be structured to count iterations until x becomes zero. This paradigm tends to perform fewer iterations, especially when x has relatively few set bits, and hence can offer performance benefits on average.

Analytical Complexity and Resource Utilization

The efficiency of a bit counting routine is subject to analysis based on the number of operations executed relative to the word size. The digit-by-digit approach entails a worst-case computational complexity of $\mathcal{O}(w)$, since each of the w bits must be inspected. In contrast, the bit-clearing technique has a worst-case complexity of $\mathcal{O}(C(x))$, where $C(x)$ is the number of set bits in x, and this is particularly advantageous when $C(x) \ll w$.

Within a formal analysis, each bit-level operation is considered to have a constant time cost, and the overall resource utilization is dictated by the number of iterations required. Optimization efforts in hardware-level implementations often focus on reducing the dependency on w by parallelizing bit evaluations or utilizing specialized instructions.

Hardware Considerations and Architectural Implications

Modern processor architectures frequently incorporate dedicated instructions designed to perform population counts, thus offloading the computational burden from software routines. These instructions exploit the inherent parallelism present in hardware to compute $C(x)$ efficiently within a single or a few clock cycles. When such facilities are unavailable, the routine must rely on a series of fundamental bitwise operations, shifts, and arithmetic instructions, each contributing to the overall execution time.

The interaction between the routine and the register file is critical; the efficient extraction and manipulation of individual bits relies on low-level operations that interact closely with the processor's data paths and pipeline architecture. Considerations such as instruction latency, throughput, and the effects of processor caching are paramount when analyzing the performance of a bit counting routine within a multiprecision arithmetic framework.

x64 Assembly Code Snippet

```
;--------------------------------------------------------------
; x64 Assembly Implementation of a Bit Counting Routine
;
; This routine computes the population count (Hamming weight) of the
; unsigned 64-bit integer provided in RDI. It implements the
↪   algorithm
; that iteratively clears the least significant set bit using the
↪   identity:
;
;     x = x & (x - 1)
;
; The number of times this operation is performed before x becomes
↪   zero
; is equal to the number of 1s in the binary representation of x.
;
; Input:
;   RDI  - unsigned 64-bit integer 'x'
;
; Output:
;   RAX  - population count, i.e., number of bits set to 1 in x
;
; Calling Convention: System V AMD64
;--------------------------------------------------------------

global popcount
section .text

popcount:
      ; Copy input number from RDI into RAX for processing
      mov     rax, rdi        ; rax = x
      xor     rcx, rcx        ; clear counter (rcx = 0)

bit_count_loop:
      test    rax, rax        ; check if x is 0
      jz      count_done      ; if x==0, jump to done
```

```asm
    ; Compute x & (x - 1) to clear the lowest set bit:
    mov     rdx, rax        ; copy current x to rdx
    dec     rdx             ; rdx = x - 1
    and     rax, rdx        ; update x = x & (x - 1)

    inc     rcx                 ; increment count (found one set bit)
    jmp     bit_count_loop  ; repeat the loop

count_done:
    ; Move the population count into RAX as the return value
    mov     rax, rcx
    ret
```

Chapter 32

Bit Field Extraction and Manipulation

Bit Field Representation and Mathematical Foundations

Let a register be represented by a fixed-width binary number x, where

$$x = \sum_{i=0}^{w-1} 2^i \, b_i,$$

with each coefficient $b_i \in \{0, 1\}$ indicating the state of the ith bit. A bit field is defined as a contiguous subset of these bits. Given an offset k and a field width m, the bit field can be described by the set $\{b_k, b_{k+1}, \ldots, b_{k+m-1}\}$. The extraction of this field from x is mathematically formalized as

$$F = \frac{x}{2^k} \mod 2^m,$$

which is equivalent to the operation that first right-shifts x by k positions and then applies a mask to isolate the subsequent m bits. This model establishes the foundation for algebraic manipulation of bit fields.

Techniques for Bit Field Extraction

The extraction process begins by aligning the bits of interest to the least significant bit positions. This is typically achieved by a right-shift operation, expressed as

$$x' = x \gg k,$$

where the notation $\gg$ denotes the right-shift by k positions. Thereafter, a bit mask M is defined to select the m consecutive bits, where

$$M = 2^m - 1.$$

The isolated bit field F is then obtained by computing the bitwise conjunction

$$F = x' \wedge M.$$

This operation ensures that any bits outside of the desired field are set to zero, resulting in a value that precisely represents the selected subset. The systematic use of bitwise shifts and logical operations in this context forms the basis of efficient bit extraction methodologies.

Modification and Reassembly of Bit Fields

Once a bit field has been extracted, it is often necessary to modify its value before reintegration into the original register. Consider a modified field denoted by F' that is intended to replace the original bit field in x. The process first involves the construction of a mask M aligned with the target field by left-shifting the base mask to the appropriate offset,

$$M = (2^m - 1) \ll k,$$

where $\ll$ denotes the left-shift operation. The register x is then cleared in the positions corresponding to the bit field by applying the complement of M,

$$x_{\text{cleared}} = x \wedge (\sim M).$$

Subsequently, the modified field F' is aligned into the correct position using a left-shift,

$$F'_{\text{aligned}} = F' \ll k.$$

The final reassembly of the modified register is accomplished by merging the cleared register with the shifted modified field via the bitwise OR operation,

$$x_{\text{modified}} = x_{\text{cleared}} \lor F'_{\text{aligned}}.$$

This sequence of operations allows for the precise alteration of selected bits without affecting the remaining data, thereby maintaining the overall integrity of the register while updating the target bit field.

Efficient Data Handling through Bit Field Manipulation

The manipulation of bit fields is integral to efficient data handling in contemporary digital systems. By operating at the granularity of individual bits, data representations can be compacted, and specialized operations can be performed with minimal computational overhead. The extraction, modification, and reassembly processes leverage elementary bitwise operations, which are inherently parallelizable and can be executed rapidly by dedicated hardware.

The mathematical rigor underlying these operations—as encapsulated in the expressions

$$F = (x \gg k) \land (2^m - 1),$$

$$x_{\text{cleared}} = x \land (\sim ((2^m - 1) \ll k)),$$

and

$$x_{\text{modified}} = x_{\text{cleared}} \lor (F' \ll k)$$

—provides a framework for analyzing both the correctness and the computational efficiency of bit field manipulation techniques. This formalism is essential in applications such as data compression, digital signal processing, and cryptography, where the compactness of data representations and the speed of operations are of paramount importance.

x64 Assembly Code Snippet

```
; --------------------------------------------------------
; x64 Assembly Code for Bit Field Extraction and Modification
```

170

```
;
; This code demonstrates:
; 1. Extraction of a bit field from a 64-bit register (x in RAX)
;    using an offset (k) and field width (m) based on the formula:
;          F = (x >> k) & ((1 << m) - 1)
;
; 2. Clearing the original bit field in x and inserting a new field
↪  F'
;    using the steps:
;          x_cleared = x & ~( ((1 << m) - 1) << k )
;          x_modified = x_cleared | ((F' & ((1 << m) - 1)) << k)
;
; Input:
;   RAX = original 64-bit value x.
;   R11 = new bit field value F' (only lower m bits are
↪  significant).
;
; Constants used:
;   k = 8  (bit field offset)
;   m = 8  (bit field width)
;
; Output:
;   RAX = modified value x with the updated bit field.
;-----------------------------------------------------------

global modify_bitfield
section .text

modify_bitfield:
    ; Function prologue
    push   rbp
    mov    rbp, rsp

    ; Set bit field parameters: k (offset) and m (width)
    mov    r12, 8          ; r12 holds k = 8 (offset)
    mov    r13, 8          ; r13 holds m = 8 (width)

    ; Compute mask = (1 << m) - 1
    ; This mask has its m least significant bits set to 1.
    mov    r14, 1          ; r14 = 1
    mov    cl, r13b        ; cl = m (from r13)
    shl    r14, cl         ; r14 = 1 << m
    dec    r14             ; r14 = (1 << m) - 1, i.e., 0xFF for m =
↪  8

    ; Optional: Extract the original bit field F from x for
↪  demonstration.
    ; F = (x >> k) & mask
    mov    r15, rax        ; copy original x into r15
    mov    cl, r12b        ; cl = k (offset from r12)
    shr    r15, cl         ; r15 = x >> k
    and    r15, r14        ; r15 now contains the extracted bit
↪  field F
```

```
; Clear the targeted bit field in x:
; Compute (mask << k) which selects the bit field bits
mov     r8, r14          ; r8 = mask (0xFF)
mov     cl, r12b         ; cl = k
shl     r8, cl           ; r8 = mask << k (bit field position
↪  mask)
not     r8               ; r8 = ~(mask << k) to clear the field
and     rax, r8          ; clear the bit field in x

; Prepare the new bit field value F':
; Ensure that F' (in R11) fits into m bits: F' = F' & mask.
and     r11, r14         ; limit F' to m bits
mov     cl, r12b         ; cl = k (offset)
shl     r11, cl          ; shift F' into the proper bit field
↪  position

; Merge the new field into the cleared x:
or      rax, r11         ; x = x with the new bit field inserted

; Function epilogue
mov     rsp, rbp
pop     rbp
ret
```

Chapter 33

Binary to Hexadecimal Conversion

Overview of Numeral Systems

The binary numeral system is a base-2 representation in which any number x is expressed as

$$x = \sum_{i=0}^{n-1} b_i \, 2^i,$$

where each coefficient $b_i \in \{0, 1\}$ denotes the state of the ith bit. In contrast, the hexadecimal numeral system is a base-16 representation. A number H in hexadecimal is written as

$$H = \sum_{j=0}^{k-1} h_j \, 16^j,$$

with each h_j assuming an integer value in the range 0 to 15, conventionally represented by the symbols $0, 1, 2, \ldots, 9$ and A, B, C, D, E, F for values 10 through 15. The intrinsic relationship between these numeral systems is derived from the fact that each hexadecimal digit corresponds exactly to four binary digits. This correspondence facilitates the condensation of lengthy binary strings into a more succinct and readily interpretable format.

Mathematical Framework for the Conversion Process

Consider a binary number x represented in the form

$$x = \sum_{i=0}^{n-1} b_i\, 2^i.$$

The conversion to a hexadecimal representation leverages the natural grouping of binary digits into segments of four. When the total number of binary digits n is not a multiple of four, zero-padding is introduced at the most significant end to form complete quartets. Each quartet, or nibble, is defined by

$$N_k = \sum_{j=0}^{3} b_{4k+j}\, 2^j,$$

for an appropriate index k. A bijective mapping function

$$f : \{0, 1, \ldots, 15\} \rightarrow \{0, 1, 2, 3, 4, 5, 6, 7, 8, 9, A, B, C, D, E, F\},$$

associates the numerical value of each nibble N_k with its corresponding hexadecimal digit. Consequently, the hexadecimal representation of x can be formally expressed as

$$H = \sum_{k=0}^{K-1} f\left(\sum_{j=0}^{3} b_{4k+j}\, 2^j \right) 16^k,$$

where K represents the total number of nibbles constituting the padded binary number. This formulation delineates a rigorous framework for the numeric transformation, ensuring that the conversion is mathematically sound and uniquely defined.

Analytical Approach to Grouping and Mapping

The conversion process is analytically decomposed into two principal stages: grouping of binary digits and mapping of grouped values to hexadecimal symbols. Initially, the binary number is partitioned into contiguous four-bit segments. For each segment indexed by k, the corresponding nibble is constructed as follows:

$$N_k = \sum_{j=0}^{3} b_{4k+j}\, 2^j.$$

If the binary number's length n does not satisfy $n \equiv 0 \pmod 4$, leading zeros are appended to the most significant nibble, a procedure that preserves the numerical value of x. Following the grouping, each nibble N_k is translated to its hexadecimal equivalent by employing the mapping f, yielding

$$h_k = f(N_k).$$

The final hexadecimal string representation is obtained by sequencing the digits in a manner that reflects the original binary order, thus achieving a compact and efficient conversion. This analytical methodology underscores the significance of the four-to-one correspondence between binary digits and hexadecimal digits, which streamlines both the computational and human interpretation of binary data.

x64 Assembly Code Snippet

```
; This x64 Assembly program demonstrates the conversion of a 64-bit
↪    binary
; number into its hexadecimal string representation. The conversion
↪    follows
; the analytic framework described in the chapter, where a binary
↪    number:
;
;        x = (i=0)^(n-1) b_i * 2^i
;
; is divided into nibbles of 4 bits each:
;
;        N_k = (j=0)^3 b_(4k+j) * 2^j
;
; and then each nibble is mapped to its hexadecimal digit using the
↪    mapping:
;
;        f(N_k) =  (if N_k <= 9 then N_k + 48, else N_k + 55)
;
; The 16 hexadecimal digits are stored in the output string in order
↪    from the
; Most Significant Nibble (MSN) to the Least Significant Nibble
↪    (LSN).
```

175

```
;
; Assemble and link (Linux x64 using NASM):
;   nasm -f elf64 binary_to_hex.asm -o binary_to_hex.o
;   ld binary_to_hex.o -o binary_to_hex
; Then run: ./binary_to_hex

section .data
    ; Sample 64-bit binary input number (you may change this value
    ↪  to test)
    input:      dq 0xDEADBEEFCAFEBABE
    ; Buffer to hold the resulting hexadecimal string (16 hex digits
    ↪  plus null terminator)
    hex_buffer: times 17 db 0
    ; Newline character for output formatting
    newline:    db 10

section .text
    global _start

_start:
    ; Load the 64-bit binary number into rsi.
    ; This number remains constant throughout the conversion.
    mov rsi, [input]

    ; Initialize rdi as our nibble index, starting at 15 (MSN) down
    ↪  to 0 (LSN).
    mov rdi, 15

convert_loop:
    ; ---------------------------------------------------------
    ; Compute the shift amount as: shift = (nibble index) * 4.
    ; This aligns with the nibble extraction formula:
    ;     N_k = (x >> (4*k)) & 0xF
    ; ---------------------------------------------------------
    mov r8, rdi         ; r8 = current nibble index (k)
    imul r8, 4          ; r8 = k * 4

    ; ---------------------------------------------------------
    ; Extract the nibble from the binary number:
    ;   1. Copy the original number from rsi to r9.
    ;   2. Shift r9 right by the amount in cl (r8b) so that the
    ↪  target nibble
    ;      is in the least significant 4 bits.
    ;   3. AND with 0xF to isolate the nibble.
    ; ---------------------------------------------------------
    mov r9, rsi
    mov cl, r8b         ; Use the lower 8 bits of r8 as the shift
    ↪  count.
    shr r9, cl          ; r9 = rsi >> (k*4)
    and r9, 0xF         ; r9 now holds the nibble value N_k (0 <=
    ↪  N_k <= 15)

    ; ---------------------------------------------------------
```

```
; Map the nibble to its hexadecimal ASCII character.
; According to the mapping:
;     If N_k <= 9, then ASCII = N_k + 48 ('0'-'9')
;     Else, ASCII = N_k + 55 ('A'-'F') because 65 - 10 = 55.
; ----------------------------------------------------------
cmp r9, 9
jbe digit_conversion     ; If nibble is between 0 and 9, jump to
↳ digit_conversion.
add r9, 55               ; For values 10-15, add 55 to convert to
↳ ASCII ('A'... 'F')
jmp store_digit

digit_conversion:
add r9, 48               ; For values 0-9, add 48 to convert to
↳ ASCII ('0'-'9')

store_digit:
; ----------------------------------------------------------
; Calculate the storage index in the hex_buffer.
; The digit from nibble index k (where k ranges from 15 down to
↳ 0)
; should be stored at position (15 - k) to maintain the natural
↳ order
; (MSN first, LSN last) in the resulting string.
; ----------------------------------------------------------
mov r10, 15
sub r10, rdi             ; r10 = (15 - k)

; Store the resulting ASCII character into the buffer.
mov byte [hex_buffer + r10], r9b

; Decrement rdi to move to the next nibble and loop until all 16
↳ nibbles are processed.
dec rdi
cmp rdi, -1
jge convert_loop

; Append a null terminator at the end of the hexadecimal string.
mov byte [hex_buffer + 16], 0

; ----------------------------------------------------------
; Output the resulting hexadecimal string to stdout.
; Using the Linux sys_write system call:
;     syscall number: 1 (sys_write)
;     rdi: file descriptor (1 for stdout)
;     rsi: pointer to the hex_buffer
;     rdx: number of bytes (16, not counting the null terminator)
; ----------------------------------------------------------
mov rax, 1               ; sys_write
mov rdi, 1               ; stdout file descriptor
mov rsi, hex_buffer      ; pointer to our hexadecimal string
mov rdx, 16              ; we output 16 characters
syscall
```

```asm
; Write a newline character to stdout for better output
↪  formatting.
mov rax, 1              ; sys_write
mov rdi, 1              ; stdout
mov rsi, newline        ; pointer to newline character
mov rdx, 1              ; 1 byte
syscall


; ----------------------------------------------------------
; Exit the program cleanly using the sys_exit system call:
;    syscall number: 60 (sys_exit)
;    rdi: exit code (0 for success)
; ----------------------------------------------------------
mov rax, 60             ; sys_exit
xor rdi, rdi            ; exit code 0
syscall
```

Chapter 34

Hexadecimal to Binary Conversion

Representation and Notational Conventions

A hexadecimal numeral is expressed as a string composed of digits selected from the set $\{0, 1, 2, \ldots, 9, A, B, C, D, E, F\}$. In this notation, the symbols A, B, C, D, E, and F represent the decimal values 10, 11, 12, 13, 14, and 15, respectively. Any hexadecimal string $H = d_0 d_1 \cdots d_{k-1}$ is interpreted by assigning positional weights according to the power of 16, such that the numerical value is given by

$$x = \sum_{i=0}^{k-1} \varphi(d_i) \cdot 16^{k-1-i},$$

where $\varphi : \{0, 1, \ldots, 9, A, B, C, D, E, F\} \rightarrow \{0, 1, \ldots, 15\}$ is the mapping that assigns to each hexadecimal digit its corresponding integer value.

Mathematical Formulation of the Conversion Process

The conversion from hexadecimal to binary leverages the intrinsic property that the base 16 is equivalent to 2^4. This property establishes a bijective correspondence between each hexadecimal digit and a block of four binary digits (a nibble). Formally, define the function

$$\psi : \{0, 1, \ldots, 15\} \to \{0000, 0001, \ldots, 1111\},$$

which maps an integer in the range 0 through 15 to its four-bit binary representation. Consequently, for a hexadecimal string $H = d_0 d_1 \cdots d_{k-1}$, the complete binary representation can be regarded as the concatenation of the four-bit sequences

$$\psi\big(\varphi(d_0)\big),\ \psi\big(\varphi(d_1)\big),\ \ldots,\ \psi\big(\varphi(d_{k-1})\big).$$

Alternatively, the binary value corresponding to H may be computed directly as

$$x = \sum_{i=0}^{k-1} \varphi(d_i) \cdot 2^{4(k-1-i)}.$$

This formulation encapsulates both the weight assigned by the hexadecimal positional notation and the underlying four-to-one mapping to binary digits.

Parsing Methodology and Digit Extraction

The initial phase in the conversion process involves the rigorous parsing of the hexadecimal string. Each character d_i in the string $H = d_0 d_1 \cdots d_{k-1}$ undergoes an interpretation that isolates only those characters that conform to the defined symbol set. The mapping function φ converts every accepted character into its corresponding integer value in $\{0, 1, \ldots, 15\}$. Special attention is accorded to the handling of any extraneous characters such as leading spaces or punctuation; only the valid hexadecimal symbols participate in the subsequent transformation. This digit extraction process ensures the fidelity of the input, establishing a precise correspondence between the textual representation and the mathematical quantification required for binary reconstruction.

Aggregation of Binary Nibbles and Reconstruction of the Binary Value

Subsequent to the extraction and individual conversion of hexadecimal digits, each integer value is transformed into its corresponding four-bit binary sequence by means of the function ψ. The process thereafter involves the careful aggregation of the binary nibbles. This aggregation is performed by concatenating the resulting four-bit blocks in the same order as encountered in the hexadecimal string to preserve the inherent positional significance. Denoting the binary representation of the ith hexadecimal digit as $\beta_i = \psi\big(\varphi(d_i)\big)$, the complete binary representation is obtained as

$$B = \beta_0\|\beta_1\|\cdots\|\beta_{k-1},$$

with $\|$ representing the concatenation operator. Equivalently, the aggregated binary value is accurately computed by evaluating

$$x = \sum_{i=0}^{k-1} \varphi(d_i) \cdot 2^{4(k-1-i)},$$

thus unifying the digit-wise mapping with the corresponding positional weights. This dual perspective—concatenation of individual nibbles and direct numerical synthesis—provides a robust and mathematically rigorous approach to the conversion of hexadecimal strings into their corresponding binary values.

x64 Assembly Code Snippet

```
section .data
    ; Example hexadecimal input string (null-terminated)
    hexString db "1A3F", 0
    ; Output message for printf. Using %llx to print a 64-bit number
    ↪   in hexadecimal.
    outputMsg db "Converted binary value (hex): %llx", 10, 0

section .bss
    ; No uninitialized data required for this example

section .text
    global main
    extern printf

main:
    ; Initialize the aggregated result to zero.
    xor rax, rax            ; RAX will store the computed integer
    ↪   value (the binary equivalent)

    ; Set RSI to point to the beginning of the hexadecimal string.
    mov rsi, hexString
```

```
convert_loop:
    ; Load the current character from the hex string.
    mov bl, byte [rsi]
    cmp bl, 0
    je conversion_done      ; Exit loop when null terminator is
    ↪  encountered.

    ; Convert the ASCII character to its numerical value.
    cmp bl, '0'
    jl check_letter         ; If below '0', check if it's a valid
    ↪  letter.
    cmp bl, '9'
    jle digit_numeric       ; Digit is between '0' and '9'.

check_letter:
    cmp bl, 'A'
    jl check_lowercase      ; Character might be a lowercase letter.
    cmp bl, 'F'
    jle digit_upper         ; Digit is between 'A' and 'F'.
check_lowercase:
    cmp bl, 'a'
    jl invalid_hex          ; Not a valid hexadecimal character.
    cmp bl, 'f'
    jle digit_lower         ; Digit is between 'a' and 'f'.
    jmp invalid_hex         ; Otherwise, it's an invalid character.

digit_numeric:
    ; Convert ASCII '0'-'9' to integer value 0-9.
    sub bl, '0'
    jmp process_digit

digit_upper:
    ; Convert ASCII 'A'-'F': subtract 'A' then add 10.
    sub bl, 'A'
    add bl, 10
    jmp process_digit

digit_lower:
    ; Convert ASCII 'a'-'f': subtract 'a' then add 10.
    sub bl, 'a'
    add bl, 10

process_digit:
    ; Multiply the current result by 16 (i.e., shift left by 4 bits)
    ↪  to set positional weight.
    shl rax, 4
    ; Zero-extend the digit value in BL and add it to RAX.
    movzx rcx, bl
    add rax, rcx

    ; Move to the next character in the hex string.
    inc rsi
    jmp convert_loop
```

```
invalid_hex:
    ; If an invalid character is encountered, load a recognizable
    ↪ error value.
    mov rax, 0xFFFFFFFFFFFFFFFF
    jmp conversion_done

conversion_done:
    ; At this point, RAX contains the complete binary value computed
    ↪ using:
    ;   x = sum_{i=0}^{k-1} (d_i) * 2^(4*(k-1-i))
    ; where each hexadecimal digit is processed via a 4-bit (nibble)
    ↪ conversion.

    ; Print the resulting value using the printf function.
    mov rdi, outputMsg      ; First argument: format string.
    mov rsi, rax            ; Second argument: the computed binary
    ↪ value.
    xor rax, rax            ; Clear RAX for variadic function call
    ↪ (SysV ABI requirement).
    call printf

    ; Exit the program gracefully.
    mov rax, 60             ; Syscall number for exit.
    xor rdi, rdi            ; Exit code 0.
    syscall
```

Chapter 35

Floating Point Arithmetic: Basic Operations

Floating Point Number Format

Floating point numbers are typically represented in a normalized form that encapsulates both magnitude and precision while accommodating a vast dynamic range. A canonical representation is expressed as

$$(-1)^s \times 1.m \times 2^{e-b},$$

where s denotes the sign bit, m is the fractional part of the significand (mantissa), e represents the stored exponent, and b is the bias defined by the chosen standard. This form permits the encoding of both very small and very large numbers within a fixed number of bits. The implicit leading bit (typically 1 in normalized numbers) is understood to exist prior to the binary point and aids in maximizing the precision available for the remaining fraction. The design of the representation ensures that arithmetic operations can be performed in a systematic and predictable manner regardless of the wide range of numerical values encountered.

Addition and Subtraction

The implementation of floating point addition and subtraction involves several rigorous stages that guarantee the preservation of numerical accuracy and adherence to the format's constraints. Initially, operands must be aligned by comparing their exponents. The number with the smaller exponent is right-shifted so that both numbers share a common exponent value, thereby facilitating the correct arithmetic combination of the significands. Given two normalized numbers,

$$(-1)^{s_1} \times 1.m_1 \times 2^{e_1-b} \quad \text{and} \quad (-1)^{s_2} \times 1.m_2 \times 2^{e_2-b},$$

exponent alignment transforms the significands such that the scale of both is identical. Once aligned, the operation—whether addition or subtraction—is performed on the significands, while the signs dictate the algebraic sign of the operation. Post arithmetic, the resultant value is generally not normalized; a normalization process is applied to restore the condition where the significand begins with a leading digit of one. Finally, the rounding procedure is executed according to the prescribed rounding mode, which may be round-to-nearest or another specified mode, to ensure that the outcome fits within the limited precision available.

Multiplication

Multiplication of floating point numbers is executed by decomposing the operation into distinct manipulations of the sign, exponent, and significand components. The sign of the product is determined by the exclusive-or (XOR) of the sign bits of the multiplicands. For operands

$$(-1)^{s_1} \times 1.m_1 \times 2^{e_1-b} \quad \text{and} \quad (-1)^{s_2} \times 1.m_2 \times 2^{e_2-b},$$

the product is computed by first multiplying the normalized significands, yielding an intermediate result that may extend beyond the normalized range. Simultaneously, the exponents are added:

$$e_{\text{product}} = e_1 + e_2 - b.$$

If the multiplication of significands produces a result that exceeds the standard normalized range, an additional normalization step adjusts the significand and the exponent accordingly. The final step involves rounding the normalized product to conform to the precision restrictions defined by the floating point standard. This sequence of operations ensures that the multiplication process maintains both the integrity of the data and the efficiency required for high-performance computation.

Division

The division of floating point numbers is handled through a process that mirrors the structural decomposition applied in multiplication, albeit with adjusted algebraic operations. The quotient's sign is derived by applying the XOR operation to the sign bits of the dividend and the divisor. For two normalized numbers,

$$(-1)^{s_1} \times 1.m_1 \times 2^{e_1-b} \quad \text{and} \quad (-1)^{s_2} \times 1.m_2 \times 2^{e_2-b},$$

the exponent of the quotient is computed by subtracting the exponent of the divisor from that of the dividend and then adding the bias:

$$e_{\text{quotient}} = e_1 - e_2 + b.$$

The significands are divided, resulting in a value that often requires adjustment. Should the division of the significands, namely $1.m_1/1.m_2$, yield a result outside the normalized range, a normalization procedure is once again applied to correct the scale. The final quotient is then rounded in accordance with the rounding mode specified by the floating point standard. Throughout this procedure, exceptional cases—such as division by zero or the handling of subnormal numbers—are addressed by well-defined rules inherent to the floating point arithmetic paradigm.

x64 Assembly Code Snippet

```
; x64 Assembly Code Example: Floating Point Basic Operations
; This code demonstrates floating point addition, subtraction,
↪    multiplication,
; and division using the x87 FPU instructions.
; The operations correspond to the mathematical formulations
↪    discussed in the
; chapter for normalized floating point arithmetic. The FPU hardware
↪    automatically
; handles exponent alignment, normalization, and rounding according
↪    to IEEE standards.
```

```
;
; Assemble with: nasm -felf64 fp_ops.asm
; Link with: ld -o fp_ops fp_ops.o
; Run on a Linux x64 system.

section .data
    ; Double-precision (64-bit) floating point operands
    float_1     dq 3.141592653589793    ; First operand (e.g., )
    float_2     dq 2.718281828459045    ; Second operand (e.g.,
    ↪ e)

    ; Memory locations to store computation results
    result_add  dq 0.0                  ; Result of addition:  +
    ↪ e
    result_sub  dq 0.0                  ; Result of subtraction:
    ↪  - e
    result_mul  dq 0.0                  ; Result of
    ↪ multiplication:  * e
    result_div  dq 0.0                  ; Result of division:  /
    ↪ e

section .text
    global main
main:
    ; Initialize the x87 FPU; ensures that the status word and
    ↪ control word are set.
    finit


    ↪  ;-------------------------------------------------------------
    ; Floating Point Addition
    ; The x87 FPU automatically aligns exponents when performing
    ↪ addition.
    ; For two numbers: (-1)^s1 * 1.m1 * 2^(e1 - b) and (-1)^s2 *
    ↪ 1.m2 * 2^(e2 - b)
    ; the hardware adjusts the significands so that the exponents
    ↪ match.

    ↪  ;-------------------------------------------------------------
    fld     qword [float_1]     ; ST(0) = float_1 ()
    fld     qword [float_2]     ; ST(0) = float_2 (e), ST(1) =
    ↪ float_1
    faddp   st1, st0            ; ST(1) = ST(1) + ST(0); pop ST(0)
                                ; Now ST(0) contains ( + e)
    fstp    qword [result_add]  ; Store the addition result from
    ↪ ST(0) to result_add


    ↪  ;-------------------------------------------------------------
    ; Floating Point Subtraction
    ; Similar to addition, the FPU aligns exponents before
    ↪ subtracting the significands.
```

187

```
↳      ;-------------------------------------------------------------------
fld     qword [float_1]        ; ST(0) = float_1 ()
fld     qword [float_2]        ; ST(0) = float_2 (e), ST(1) =
↳  float_1
fsubp   st1, st0               ; ST(1) = ST(1) - ST(0); pop ST(0)
                               ; Now ST(0) contains ( - e)
fstp    qword [result_sub]     ; Store the subtraction result to
↳  result_sub


↳      ;-------------------------------------------------------------------
; Floating Point Multiplication
; In multiplication, the FPU multiplies the significands and
↳  adds the exponents.
; The product may need re-normalization if it falls outside the
↳  normalized range.
; These steps are inherently managed by the hardware.


↳      ;-------------------------------------------------------------------
fld     qword [float_1]        ; ST(0) = float_1 ()
fld     qword [float_2]        ; ST(0) = float_2 (e), ST(1) =
↳  float_1
fmulp   st1, st0               ; ST(1) = ST(1) * ST(0); pop ST(0)
                               ; Now ST(0) contains ( * e)
fstp    qword [result_mul]     ; Store the multiplication result
↳  to result_mul


↳      ;-------------------------------------------------------------------
; Floating Point Division
; For division, the FPU divides the significands and subtracts
↳  the exponents.
; If the quotient is not normalized, a normalization step is
↳  performed by hardware.


↳      ;-------------------------------------------------------------------
fld     qword [float_1]        ; ST(0) = dividend: float_1 ()
fld     qword [float_2]        ; ST(0) = divisor: float_2 (e),
↳  ST(1) =
fdivp   st1, st0               ; ST(1) = ST(1) / ST(0); pop ST(0)
                               ; Now ST(0) contains ( / e)
fstp    qword [result_div]     ; Store the division result to
↳  result_div


↳      ;-------------------------------------------------------------------
; Program Exit: Return 0 to the operating system.
; For Linux x64, use the exit syscall.


↳      ;-------------------------------------------------------------------
mov     rax, 60                ; Syscall number for exit (60)
xor     rdi, rdi               ; Exit code 0
```

188

syscall

Chapter 36

Floating Point Comparisons

Floating Point Representation in Comparative Analysis

Floating point numbers are encoded in a canonical form expressed as

$$(-1)^s \times 1.m \times 2^{e-b},$$

where s denotes the sign bit, m represents the fractional component of the significand, e is the stored exponent, and b is the bias inherent to the representation standard. The structure of this encoding necessitates that any comparative analysis must take into account the composite nature of the number. In assembly-level operations, the process of comparison is not a trivial bitwise operation. Instead, it requires an understanding of the impact of each component of the floating point number on the overall numerical value. A precise comparison involves the orchestration of sign, exponent, and significand, where even minor discrepancies due to rounding or representation precision can lead to variations in the outcome of a comparison.

Assembly Level Mechanisms for Floating Point Comparison

Assembly instructions that operate on floating point values execute comparisons by first ensuring that the operands are interpreted correctly under the rules of the floating point standard. The comparison instructions in a modern x64 architecture are designed to evaluate the relative ordering of two floating point numbers by setting condition flags or status bits within hardware registers. Such instructions perform evaluations that take into account the normalized form of the operands. The hardware determines the outcome by aligning the significands, comparing the exponents, and finally considering the sign bits; this series of actions results in a state where the processor flags accurately reflect the relationship between the operands. These operations are executed with an inherent accommodation for the peculiarities of floating point arithmetic, thereby ensuring that the assembled condition, whether indicating equality, inequality, or unordered conditions, is both robust and congruent with the IEEE specifications.

Special Cases and Unordered Conditions

The comparative process must also address circumstances in which standard numerical ordering does not apply. In particular, special values such as NaNs (Not a Number) introduce complexities that require careful consideration. When one or both operands are NaNs, the comparison yields an unordered result. The hardware recognizes such cases and sets the appropriate flags to indicate that a reliable numerical relationship does not exist. Similarly, infinities and subnormal numbers present unique challenges; the representation of these values, while conforming to the general format, may lead to conditions where their magnitude comparisons differ from those of regular normalized numbers. The ordered comparison instructions in assembly are designed to accommodate these exceptional scenarios, ensuring that any subsequent conditional logic can distinguish between ordered and unordered outcomes in a systematic manner.

Precision, Rounding, and Comparison Accuracy

The finite precision of floating point representations imposes limitations that can affect the outcome of comparisons. Due to the fixed number of bits allocated to the significand, rounding errors are an intrinsic consequence of floating point arithmetic. The selection of a rounding mode—commonly round-to-nearest or an alternative as specified by the floating point standard—plays a critical role in how these errors manifest when operands are compared. In assembly-level operations, the rounding mode in effect during the execution of a comparison can subtly influence the flags set by the comparison instruction when the operands are nearly equal or when their differences approach the limits of representational precision. This sensitivity necessitates that the comparative mechanisms embedded within the processor must handle rounding-induced discrepancies with a high degree of accuracy, thereby ensuring that the eventual decision regarding the ordering of the operands truly reflects their intended numerical relationship.

x64 Assembly Code Snippet

```
; Comprehensive x64 Assembly example for Floating Point Comparison
; This snippet demonstrates:
;   - Setting up the MXCSR control register for the floating point
↪  environment
;   - Loading two double-precision floating point values
;   - Using the SSE instruction UCOMISD for comparison
;   - Handling ordered and unordered outcomes (e.g., NaN cases)
;   - Exiting with distinct exit codes based on the comparison
↪  result

section .data
    new_mxcsr   dd 0x1F80       ; Default MXCSR value:
    ↪  round-to-nearest mode, no flush-to-zero
    value1      dq 1.234        ; First operand (double precision)
    value2      dq 2.345        ; Second operand (double precision)

section .text
    global _start

_start:
    ; Set up the floating point control/status register (MXCSR)
    ldmxcsr [new_mxcsr]
```

```asm
; Load the double precision values from memory into SSE
↪   registers
movsd xmm0, [value1]        ; Load first operand into xmm0
movsd xmm1, [value2]        ; Load second operand into xmm1

; Perform an unordered comparison of xmm0 and xmm1.
; The UCOMISD instruction sets the CF, ZF, and PF flags
↪   accordingly.
ucomisd xmm0, xmm1

; Check for unordered condition (e.g., one or both operands are
↪   NaN)
jp unordered_result         ; Jump if parity is set indicating
↪   unordered comparison

; Check for equality (ZF flag set)
je equal_result             ; Jump if operands are equal

; Check if xmm0 is less than xmm1 (CF flag set)
jb less_than_result

; If not less-than, equal, or unordered, then xmm0 must be
↪   greater than xmm1
greater_than_result:
    ; Handle case where value1 > value2.
    ; For demonstration, exit with code 2.
    mov rax, 60             ; syscall: exit
    mov rdi, 2             ; exit code 2 (greater-than condition)
    syscall

less_than_result:
    ; Handle case where value1 < value2.
    ; For demonstration, exit with code 1.
    mov rax, 60             ; syscall: exit
    mov rdi, 1             ; exit code 1 (less-than condition)
    syscall

equal_result:
    ; Handle case where value1 == value2.
    ; For demonstration, exit with code 0.
    mov rax, 60             ; syscall: exit
    mov rdi, 0             ; exit code 0 (equality)
    syscall

unordered_result:
    ; Handle unordered result (e.g., one or both operands is NaN).
    ; For demonstration, exit with code 3.
    mov rax, 60             ; syscall: exit
    mov rdi, 3             ; exit code 3 (unordered comparison)
    syscall

; End of Floating Point Comparison Code Snippet
```

Chapter 37

Decimal to Binary Conversion

Mathematical Underpinnings of Numeral Systems

The decimal numeral system, which is based on ten distinct symbols, and the binary numeral system, founded on two digits, exhibit a fundamental difference in radix. The conversion process relies on the well-established relationship expressed as

$$n = 2q + r,$$

where n is the original decimal integer, q is the quotient resulting from integer division by 2, and r, with $r \in \{0, 1\}$, is the remainder representing a binary digit. Iterative application of this division theorem yields a sequence of remainders which, when assembled in the reverse order of their computation, faithfully maps n onto its binary representation.

Iterative Division Algorithm and Reverse Accumulation

Conversion of a decimal integer into its binary string representation is predicated on the repeated application of the division algorithm. In detail, if the integer under consideration is nonzero, the process involves determining the remainder of division by 2, which identifies the least significant bit at each stage. This operation is mathematically delineated by the expression

$$r = n \mod 2,$$

followed by the update

$$n \leftarrow \lfloor n/2 \rfloor.$$

These operations are iterated until n reduces to zero. Notably, the order in which remainders are produced is inverse to the conventional significance of bits; therefore, the assembly of the final binary string necessitates a reversal of the recorded sequence. This reverse accumulation is indispensable to obtain a representation that aligns with the standard left-to-right hierarchical format.

Assembly-Level Implementation Considerations

At the assembly language level, the efficiency and correctness of the decimal-to-binary conversion algorithm are heavily dependent on the meticulous management of registers and memory. The pivotal division operation is executed via dedicated machine instructions that yield both the quotient and the remainder in a single operation. It is imperative that the processor registers employed for these operations are allocated in a way that preserves their contents across multiple iterations of the conversion loop. Additionally, the translation of each numerical remainder, which assumes a value of 0 or 1, into its corresponding character symbol (conforming to standard encoding such as ASCII) involves arithmetic transformations that must be integrated seamlessly within the instruction sequence. The algorithm's implementation must balance the constraints of minimal instruction latency, precise flag management, and strict adherence to the architecture's calling conventions.

Memory Organization and Data Structuring in Conversion

The orchestration of temporary data storage is central to the effective execution of the conversion procedure. Given that the iterative method inherently generates the binary digits in reverse order, a designated contiguous memory area—whether part of the processor's stack or an explicitly allocated buffer—is utilized to store these intermediate values. The data structure must support a final reversal operation, thereby rearranging the collected digits into the correct left-to-right order as expected in a conventional binary string. Given the absence of high-level memory management constructs in assembly programming, the design must ensure that memory reservations do not exceed the available bounds and that the management of read and write pointers is exacting. This careful data structuring underpins the overall fidelity of the conversion process, ensuring that every bit is accurately represented and positioned within the resultant string.

x64 Assembly Code Snippet

```
; Decimal to Binary Conversion in x64 Assembly
; --------------------------------------------------------------
; This program converts a given decimal number into its binary
↪   string
; representation using the iterative division algorithm based on:
;      n = 2q + r
; where the remainder r (0 or 1) is obtained via division by 2.
; The remainders are stored in reverse order and later reversed to
; produce the standard left-to-right binary representation.
;
; Assemble with:
;      nasm -f elf64 decimal_to_binary.asm -o decimal_to_binary.o
; Link with:
;      ld decimal_to_binary.o -o decimal_to_binary
; Run with:
;      ./decimal_to_binary
; --------------------------------------------------------------

section .data
    dec_num    dq 37              ; Decimal number to convert.
    newline    db 0xA, 0          ; Newline (LF) for output.

section .bss
    ; Allocate a buffer to hold the binary string.
    ; Maximum of 64 digits for a 64-bit number plus an extra byte
    ↪   for null-termination.
    bin_buffer resb 66

section .text
    global _start

_start:
    ; Load the decimal number from data into rdi.
```

196

```
    mov rdi, [dec_num]
    ; Set rsi to point to the binary buffer.
    lea rsi, [bin_buffer]
    ; Initialize index register rbx to 0 for storing characters.
    xor rbx, rbx

    ; Special-case: if the number is zero, output "0".
    cmp rdi, 0
    jne convert_loop
    mov byte [rsi], '0'
    mov byte [rsi+1], 0
    jmp print_result

;------------------------------------------------------------
; convert_loop: Iteratively divide the number by 2.
; Each iteration computes:
;     quotient = n / 2, remainder = n mod 2
; The remainder (after converting to ASCII) is stored in bin_buffer.
;------------------------------------------------------------
convert_loop:
.convert_loop_start:
    cmp rdi, 0
    je conversion_done

    ; Set up dividend in rax.
    mov rax, rdi
    xor rdx, rdx          ; Clear rdx before division.
    mov rcx, 2            ; Divisor = 2.
    div rcx               ; Divide rdx:rax by 2:
                          ;     quotient -> rax, remainder -> rdx

    ; Convert remainder to ASCII: '0' + remainder.
    add dl, '0'
    ; Store the resulting ASCII digit in bin_buffer at index rbx.
    mov [rsi + rbx], dl
    inc rbx               ; Increment index to point to next free
    ↪ byte.

    ; Update rdi with the quotient for the next iteration.
    mov rdi, rax
    jmp .convert_loop_start

conversion_done:
    ; Append null terminator to the reversed binary string.
    mov byte [rsi + rbx], 0

    ;------------------------------------------------------------
    ; Reverse the binary string in bin_buffer so that the
    ; most significant bit appears first.
    ; Set r8 as the start index and rcx as the end index.
    ;------------------------------------------------------------
    xor r8, r8            ; r8 = 0, start index.
    mov rcx, rbx
```

```
        dec rcx              ; rcx = rbx - 1 (last valid character index).

.reverse_loop:
    cmp r8, rcx
    jge reversal_done   ; If start index >= end index, our reversal
    ↪ is complete.
    ; Swap the characters at positions r8 and rcx.
    mov al, [rsi + r8]
    mov dl, [rsi + rcx]
    mov [rsi + r8], dl
    mov [rsi + rcx], al
    inc r8
    dec rcx
    jmp .reverse_loop
reversal_done:

;------------------------------------------------------------
; print_result: Write the binary string to stdout.
; Use the write system call (number 1) with:
;    rax = 1 (syscall number), rdi = 1 (stdout file descriptor),
;    rsi = pointer to the binary string, rdx = length of the string.
;------------------------------------------------------------
print_result:
    mov rdx, rbx         ; rdx = length of the binary string.
    mov rax, 1           ; Syscall number for write.
    mov rdi, 1           ; File descriptor 1 (stdout).
    syscall

    ; Write a newline.
    mov rax, 1           ; write syscall.
    mov rdi, 1           ; stdout.
    lea rsi, [newline]
    mov rdx, 1           ; Write one byte (newline character).
    syscall

    ; Exit the program.
    mov rax, 60          ; Syscall number for exit.
    xor rdi, rdi         ; Exit code 0.
    syscall
```

Chapter 38

Binary to Decimal Conversion

Mathematical Foundations for Conversion

A binary numeral is inherently defined by a sequence of digits, each of which represents a coefficient in a polynomial expansion with base two. Given a binary string of length n, the digit at position i (when indexed from zero, with 0 corresponding to the most significant digit) contributes to the overall value in accordance with its positional weight. In mathematical terms, if the binary string is expressed as

$$b_0 \, b_1 \, \ldots \, b_{n-1},$$

then its decimal equivalent, denoted by D, is given by

$$D = \sum_{i=0}^{n-1} b_i \cdot 2^{n-1-i}.$$

This formulation encapsulates the combinatorial significance of the binary numeral system, where each digit b_i (with $b_i \in \{0,1\}$) is scaled by the corresponding power of two and subsequently aggregated. The representation naturally aligns with the principles of polynomial evaluation, and it is amenable to transformation through iterative procedures such as Horner's method, wherein the polynomial is evaluated by successive multiplications by the base 2 followed by an additive incorporation of the next coefficient.

Iterative Accumulation Algorithm

The conversion from a binary string to its decimal value may be procedurally realized by an iterative accumulation strategy. In this approach, a running total, denoted by A, is initialized to zero and then updated sequentially for each binary digit. For a binary string presented in standard left-to-right order, the algorithm processes each digit using the recurrence relation

$$A_{i+1} = 2 \cdot A_i + d_i,$$

where $A_0 = 0$, and d_i represents the numerical value of the digit stored at the ith position. After processing all n digits, the final accumulated value A_n is equivalent to the full decimal conversion of the binary string. This iterative schema is both computationally efficient and numerically stable, as each successive multiplication by 2 is effectively a left-shift operation in binary arithmetic, and the addition of the current digit integrates the next lower order of significance. The methodology closely mirrors Horner's rule for polynomial evaluation, thereby leveraging a well-established numerical technique in the domain of digital arithmetic.

Data Structuring Considerations for Conversion Routine

The binary string, which is assumed to be stored in a contiguous block of memory, necessitates precise management when interfacing with the conversion routine. Conceptually, the string is traversed character by character, with each character being interpreted as a binary digit, following an arithmetic transformation that maps its symbolic representation to the numeric values 0 or 1. This mapping is fundamental to ensuring that the iterative accumulation accurately reflects the intended binary numeral. Special attention must be accorded to the termination of the string; a designated terminator, such as a null character, denotes the end of the input sequence, thereby providing a natural stopping point for the conversion process. Additionally, the routine must account for the potential presence of extraneous leading zeroes, ensuring that every digit is incorporated in the proper sequence as dictated by the positional significance of binary numerals. Memory management considerations include the maintenance of robust pointer arithmetic to accurately access each consecutive character in the string, thereby preserving the integrity of the accumulated decimal value through every iteration. The coupling of these data structuring principles with the iterative computational schema ultimately yields a reliable conversion strategy that accurately transforms a binary string into its decimal equivalent.

x64 Assembly Code Snippet

```
;****************************************************************
; Binary to Decimal Conversion using Iterative Accumulation
;
; This x64 Assembly program demonstrates the conversion of a
; null-terminated binary string into its decimal equivalent.
; The core algorithm follows the recurrence:
;     A[i+1] = 2 * A[i] + d_i
; where A[0] is initialized to 0 and d_i represents the binary digit
; (0 or 1) extracted from the input string.
;
; The conversion leverages a left-shift operation (SHL) to multiply
; the accumulator by 2, thus mirroring the polynomial evaluation
; (Horner's method) approach described in the chapter.
;
; The code is organized into three sections:
;    1. Data Section: Contains a sample binary string.
;    2. Text Section: Implements the conversion routine and the
;       program's _start entry point.
;    3. BSS Section: Reserved for uninitialized data (unused here).
;
; This example is written for Linux x86-64 using NASM syntax.
;****************************************************************

SECTION .data
    ; Example binary string: "1100101" (equals 101 in decimal)
    bin_string db "1100101", 0   ; Null-terminated string

SECTION .bss
    ; No uninitialized data required for this routine

SECTION .text
    global _start


;-------------------------------------------------------------
; Function: binary_to_decimal
; Description:
;    Converts a null-terminated binary string into its decimal
;    equivalent by iteratively processing each character.
;
; Input:
```

```
;   RDI - Pointer to the null-terminated binary string.
;
; Output:
;   RAX - The accumulated decimal value.
;         In case of an invalid character, RAX is set to -1.
;-----------------------------------------------------------------
binary_to_decimal:
    xor rax, rax            ; Initialize accumulator A = 0

.binary_loop:
    mov bl, byte [rdi]      ; Load current character from the string
    cmp bl, 0
    je .done_conversion     ; Terminate loop at null terminator

    ; Check if the character is '0' or '1'
    cmp bl, '0'
    je .process_zero
    cmp bl, '1'
    je .process_one

    ; If an invalid character is encountered,
    ; set the result to -1 and exit.
    mov rax, -1
    jmp .done_conversion

.process_zero:
    ; For binary digit '0': A = 2 * A + 0
    shl rax, 1              ; Multiply accumulator by 2 (equivalent to
    ↳ left shift)
    jmp .next_character

.process_one:
    ; For binary digit '1': A = 2 * A + 1
    shl rax, 1             ; Multiply accumulator by 2
    add rax, 1            ; Add 1 for the binary digit '1'
    jmp .next_character

.next_character:
    inc rdi                 ; Advance to the next character in the string
    jmp .binary_loop        ; Repeat the loop for the next digit

.done_conversion:
    ret                     ; Return with the result in RAX

;-----------------------------------------------------------------
; Entry Point: _start
; Description:
;   Loads the address of the binary string into RDI, calls the
;   conversion function, and then exits with the conversion
;   result as the exit code.
;
; Note:
;   The exit system call (syscall number 60) is used to terminate
```

```
;    the program, in compliance with Linux x86-64 conventions.
;---------------------------------------------------------------
_start:
    lea rdi, [rel bin_string]   ; Load pointer to the binary string
    ↪ into RDI
    call binary_to_decimal      ; Call conversion function (result in
    ↪ RAX)

    ; Exit the program, using the decimal conversion as the exit
    ↪ code
    mov rdi, rax                ; Set the exit code from the
    ↪ conversion result
    mov rax, 60                 ; Syscall number for exit (Linux
    ↪ x86-64)
    syscall                     ; Invoke kernel to exit the program
```

Chapter 39

Fixed-Point Arithmetic Simulation

Mathematical Foundations of Fixed-Point Representation

Fixed-point arithmetic constitutes a numerical representation in which real numbers are represented by integers scaled by a predetermined constant. In this formulation, a real number r is approximated by an integer x such that

$$r \approx \frac{x}{S},$$

where S is the scaling factor, often chosen as a power of two, e.g., $S = 2^F$, with F denoting the number of fractional bits. This approach permits the simulation of fractional numbers via integer math, leveraging the inherent efficiency of integer operations. The correspondence between the fixed-point representation and the underlying real value is defined by the transformation

$$x = \lfloor r \cdot S \rceil,$$

where $\lfloor \cdot \rceil$ denotes an appropriate rounding operation. The fidelity of this simulation is directly influenced by the choice of S, which determines the granularity of the fractional representation and the magnitude of quantization error.

Scaling Factor Considerations and Representation

The selection of a suitable scaling factor S is central to fixed-point arithmetic simulation. When S is chosen as a power of two, the transformation operations, such as multiplication by S or division by S, correspond to efficient bit-shift operations in hardware. The fixed-point number, often denoted as x_{fp}, thereby encodes the real value r with the relation

$$x_{\text{fp}} = r \cdot 2^F,$$

and the inverse conversion, retrieving r from x_{fp}, is accomplished by

$$r = \frac{x_{\text{fp}}}{2^F}.$$

In simulation, the scaling factor is not merely a multiplier; it governs the trade-off between range and precision. A higher value of F offers increased precision at the expense of a reduced dynamic range, while a lower value of F extends the range but compromises detail in the fractional component. The careful calibration of F is indispensable to ensure that the simulated arithmetic aligns with the targeted numerical properties.

Simulation of Fixed-Point Addition and Subtraction

Fixed-point addition and subtraction are conceptually analogous to their integer counterparts. When two fixed-point numbers, say x_{fp} and y_{fp}, share the same scaling factor S, the operations are defined by

$$x_{\text{fp}} + y_{\text{fp}} \quad \text{and} \quad x_{\text{fp}} - y_{\text{fp}},$$

which naturally preserve the scaling factor. The preservation of S obviates the need for rescaling after addition or subtraction, thereby maintaining consistency in the representation. However, careful attention must be directed to potential overflow conditions, as the summation or difference of the underlying integers might exceed the representable range, particularly in systems for which the fixed-point numbers are confined to bounded integer types.

Simulation of Fixed-Point Multiplication and Division

Fixed-point multiplication and division introduce additional layers of complexity, necessitating explicit manipulation of the scaling factors to ensure numerical accuracy. In fixed-point multiplication, the product of two fixed-point numbers x_{fp} and y_{fp} is initially computed as

$$P = x_{fp} \cdot y_{fp},$$

which yields a result scaled by S^2. To recover a fixed-point number that maintains the original scaling factor, it is requisite to perform a renormalization step:

$$x_{fp} \times y_{fp} \approx \frac{P}{S} = \frac{x_{fp} \cdot y_{fp}}{S}.$$

Division within the fixed-point framework is similarly treated. Given a dividend x_{fp} and a divisor y_{fp}, an intermediate product is formed by scaling the dividend:

$$Q = \frac{x_{fp} \cdot S}{y_{fp}},$$

which ensures that the quotient Q is expressed with the appropriate scaling. Both operations may involve rounding considerations, and the truncation of low-order bits must be carefully managed to mitigate the propagation of rounding errors through successive operations.

Error Propagation and Rounding Considerations

The simulation of fixed-point arithmetic via integer math intrinsically introduces errors arising from quantization and rounding operations. Each transformation from a real number r to its fixed-point counterpart x_{fp} involves a rounding procedure, which may lead to a quantization error

$$\epsilon = r - \frac{x_{fp}}{S}.$$

In iterative arithmetic operations, particularly in multiplication and division where a secondary scaling is applied, these errors can accumulate. A careful analysis of error propagation is warranted to ascertain the bounds of numerical accuracy. Techniques for error minimization, such as the implementation of rounding schemes (e.g., round-to-nearest), can ameliorate the adverse effects of these errors. Moreover, the potential for overflow and underflow must be contemplated, given that fixed-point arithmetic operates within a confined range determined by the underlying integer representation. The simulation framework must incorporate strategies for detecting and controlling such events, thereby preserving the integrity of numerical computations.

x64 Assembly Code Snippet

```
; --------------------------------------------------------
; x64 Assembly Code for Fixed-Point Arithmetic Simulation
;
; This snippet demonstrates the simulation of fixed-point arithmetic
; using integer math with a scaling factor S = 2^FCONST (here,
↪  FCONST = 16).
; A fixed-point number is represented as:
;     x_fp = real_value * SCALE
; where SCALE = 2^FCONST = 65536.
;
; The code performs the following operations:
;    1. Fixed-point Addition:    result = a_fp + b_fp
;    2. Fixed-point Subtraction: result = b_fp - a_fp
;    3. Fixed-point Multiplication:
;         result = (a_fp * b_fp) >> FCONST
;    4. Fixed-point Division:
;         result = (a_fp << FCONST) / b_fp
;
; Comments accompany each section to explain the computation
↪  process.
; --------------------------------------------------------

; Define constants and fixed-point numbers in the data section
SECTION .data
    FCONST      equ 16              ; Number of fractional bits
    SCALE       equ 1 << FCONST     ; Scaling factor: 2^16 =
    ↪  65536

    ; Define fixed-point representations of two sample real numbers:
    ; For example, let a = 1.5 and b = 2.25.
    ; Their fixed-point representations are computed as:
    ;    a_fp = 1.5 * SCALE = 1.5 * 65536 = 98304
    ;    b_fp = 2.25 * SCALE = 2.25 * 65536 = 147456
    a_fp        dq 98304            ; 64-bit fixed-point value of
    ↪  1.5
```

207

```
    b_fp        dq 147456              ; 64-bit fixed-point value of
    ↪  2.25

; Reserve space to store results of computations
SECTION .bss
    result_add  resq 1                 ; Result of addition
    result_sub  resq 1                 ; Result of subtraction
    result_mul  resq 1                 ; Result of multiplication
    result_div  resq 1                 ; Result of division

; Code section: performs fixed-point arithmetic computations
SECTION .text
    global _start

_start:
    ; ----------------------------
    ; Fixed-Point Addition:
    ;   Compute: result_add = a_fp + b_fp
    ; ----------------------------
    mov     rax, [a_fp]                ; Load fixed-point value of a
    ↪  into rax
    add     rax, [b_fp]                ; rax = a_fp + b_fp
    mov     [result_add], rax          ; Store the addition result


    ; ----------------------------
    ; Fixed-Point Subtraction:
    ;   Compute: result_sub = b_fp - a_fp
    ; ----------------------------
    mov     rax, [b_fp]                ; Load fixed-point value of b
    ↪  into rax
    sub     rax, [a_fp]                ; rax = b_fp - a_fp
    mov     [result_sub], rax          ; Store the subtraction result


    ; ----------------------------
    ; Fixed-Point Multiplication:
    ;   Compute: result_mul = (a_fp * b_fp) >> FCONST
    ;   The multiplication produces a 128-bit result in RDX:RAX.
    ;   To renormalize, shift the 128-bit product right by 16 bits.
    ; ----------------------------
    mov     rax, [a_fp]                ; Load a_fp into rax
    mov     rbx, [b_fp]                ; Load b_fp into rbx
    mul     rbx                        ; Unsigned multiply: RDX:RAX =
    ↪  a_fp * b_fp

    ; Perform a 128-bit right shift by FCONST (16) bits:
    ; The 64-bit result will be:
    ;     result = (RDX << (64 - 16)) OR (RAX >> 16)
    ; Since (RAX >> 16) provides the lower 48 bits and
    ; (RDX << 48) provides the upper 16 bits after shifting.
    mov     rdi, rdx                   ; Move high 64 bits to rdi
    shl     rdi, 48                    ; rdi = RDX << (64-16)  i.e.,
    ↪  shift left by 48 bits
    shr     rax, 16                    ; rax = RAX >> 16
```

208

```
or      rax, rdi              ; Combine to get the
↳   renormalized 64-bit result
mov     [result_mul], rax     ; Store the multiplication
↳   result

;   ---------------------------
; Fixed-Point Division:
;   Compute: result_div = (a_fp << FCONST) / b_fp
;   Shifting a_fp left by 16 bits adjusts for the fixed-point
↳   scaling.
;   ---------------------------
mov     rax, [a_fp]           ; Load a_fp into rax
shl     rax, FCONST           ; Multiply a_fp by SCALE (i.e.,
↳   left shift by 16 bits)
xor     rdx, rdx              ; Clear rdx to prepare for
↳   division (dividend is in RDX:RAX)
mov     rbx, [b_fp]           ; Load b_fp into rbx, the
↳   divisor
div     rbx                   ; Unsigned division: quotient in
↳   rax, remainder in rdx
mov     [result_div], rax     ; Store the division result

;   ---------------------------
; End of Computation: Exit Program
; Use Linux syscall to exit gracefully.
;   ---------------------------
mov     rax, 60               ; Syscall number for exit (60)
xor     rdi, rdi              ; Status code 0
syscall                       ; Invoke the kernel to exit
```

Chapter 40

Using SIMD for Vector Addition

Fundamental Concepts of SIMD Processing

SIMD (Single Instruction, Multiple Data) processing is a paradigm that enables the simultaneous execution of the same arithmetic operation across multiple data elements. In this model, wide vector registers and specialized execution units perform parallel operations, thereby reducing the number of individual instructions required for operations such as vector addition. Consider two vectors, $\mathbf{a} = \{a_0, a_1, \ldots, a_{n-1}\}$ and $\mathbf{b} = \{b_0, b_1, \ldots, b_{n-1}\}$. A SIMD vector addition computes the result vector $\mathbf{c} = \{c_0, c_1, \ldots, c_{n-1}\}$ such that

$$c_i = a_i + b_i, \quad \forall\, i \in \{0, 1, \ldots, n-1\}.$$

This formulation encapsulates the essence of data-level parallelism, where each component-wise addition is performed concurrently. The efficiency gained arises from the ability to handle several data elements in a single processor cycle, thus exploiting the full width of vector registers available in modern architectures.

Mathematical Foundations of Vector Addition

Vector addition as executed in a SIMD environment is founded upon elementary arithmetic extended to multidimensional data structures. Formally, let $\mathbf{a}, \mathbf{b} \in \mathbb{R}^n$. The addition operation is defined by the component-wise summation:

$$\mathbf{c} = \mathbf{a} + \mathbf{b} \quad \text{where} \quad c_i = a_i + b_i.$$

This operation is both associative and commutative:

$$a_i + b_i = b_i + a_i \quad \text{and} \quad (a_i + b_i) + d_i = a_i + (b_i + d_i),$$

for any vectors $\mathbf{a}, \mathbf{b}, \mathbf{d} \in \mathbb{R}^n$. Such properties ensure that the order of operations does not affect the correctness of the result, a characteristic that is critically important when employing parallel execution strategies. The mathematical succinctness of vector addition facilitates its mapping onto hardware levels where a single instruction can perform these multiple, independent arithmetic operations concurrently.

Architectural Considerations and Data Handling

The performance benefits of SIMD execution are closely tied to the organization of data in memory and the corresponding utilization of vector registers. Data must be arranged contiguously and aligned with respect to memory boundaries to allow for efficient vector loading. This minimizes memory access latency and maximizes throughput. Modern processors are equipped with advanced caching mechanisms and prefetching hardware that optimize the movement of data from memory to wide SIMD registers. In this context, the effective vector width—determined by the size of available SIMD registers—directly influences the degree of parallelism and the overall speedup achieved during vector addition.

Moreover, careful data partitioning ensures that the load and store operations for vector elements are optimally executed. For instance, when processing arrays of floating-point numbers, a SIMD register may hold multiple elements (e.g., four or eight) depending on the precision. This maximizes the number of simultaneous arithmetic operations and minimizes the overhead associated with repeatedly fetching data from memory. The architectural design thereby necessitates a harmonious balance between register size, memory bandwidth, and computational throughput to fully exploit the benefits of data-level parallelism in vector addition.

Performance Implications and Parallel Execution

The adoption of SIMD instructions for vector addition introduces a significant performance enhancement due to the intrinsic capacity for parallel processing. By executing multiple additions concurrently, SIMD-enabled systems decrease the total number of instruction cycles required relative to scalar processing. This reduction is most pronounced in applications that operate on large data sets where the overhead of instruction dispatch and the latency of sequential computation are substantially diminished.

Performance gains in SIMD vector addition are also influenced by the efficiency of the underlying execution pipeline and the ability of the processor to schedule operations without resource conflicts. The simultaneous utilization of multiple execution units—each capable of processing a segment of the vector—reduces the effective computational complexity. Consequently, the throughput of arithmetic operations is increased, providing a speedup that scales with the width of the SIMD registers as well as the efficiency of memory alignment and data preloading strategies. Such analysis is central to modern high-performance computing, where vectorized operations serve as a fundamental building block for a wide array of numerical and data-processing applications.

x64 Assembly Code Snippet

```
;----------------------------------------
; Function: simd_vector_add
; Description:
;   Performs SIMD vector addition on two arrays of single-precision
↪   floats.
;   It computes the result vector such that:
;       c[i] = a[i] + b[i]      for i = 0 to count-1
;   using AVX instructions to process 8 floats (32-bit each) per
↪   iteration.
;
```

```
;    Note:
;       - The total number of elements (in RCX) must be a multiple of
↪   8.
;       - The arrays are assumed to be stored in contiguous memory
↪   (unaligned loads
;         are used via vmovups, though alignment can improve
↪   performance if possible).
;
; Input (System V AMD64 Calling Convention):
;   RDI - Pointer to destination array (float *dest)
;   RSI - Pointer to first source array (float *a)
;   RDX - Pointer to second source array (float *b)
;   RCX - Number of elements in the vectors (must be divisible by 8)
;
; Registers Used:
;   YMM0, YMM1  - AVX registers used for vector loading and
↪   addition.
;   R8          - Loop counter for the number of iterations.
;
; Algorithm Overview:
;   1. Compute the number of iterations, where each iteration
↪   processes 8 consecutive
;       32-bit float elements.
;   2. In each loop iteration:
;         - Load 8 floats from the first and second vectors into YMM
↪   registers.
;         - Add the corresponding elements using the vaddps
↪   instruction.
;         - Store the resulting 8 floats into the destination array.
;   3. Advance the source and destination pointers and repeat until
↪   all elements are processed.
;
;   Mathematical formulation:
;         For each i where 0 <= i < count,
;               c[i] = a[i] + b[i]
;   which is executed in parallel for 8 successive elements per
↪   iteration via SIMD.
;-------------------------------------

global simd_vector_add
simd_vector_add:
    ; Calculate the number of AVX iterations (each processes 8
    ↪  floats)
    mov   r8, rcx          ; r8 = total number of floats in the
    ↪  vector
    shr   r8, 3            ; divide by 8 ==> r8 now contains (count /
    ↪  8)

    ; If no iterations needed, jump to end of function
    test  r8, r8
    jz    vector_add_end

vector_add_loop:
```

```asm
    ; Load 8 floats from the first source array (vector a) into YMM0
    vmovups ymm0, ymmword ptr [rsi]

    ; Load 8 floats from the second source array (vector b) into
    ↪  YMM1
    vmovups ymm1, ymmword ptr [rdx]

    ; Perform parallel addition: YMM0 = YMM0 + YMM1
    vaddps ymm0, ymm0, ymm1

    ; Store the computed 8 floats into the destination array (vector
    ↪  c)
    vmovups ymmword ptr [rdi], ymm0

    ; Advance pointers by 32 bytes (8 floats * 4 bytes each)
    add     rsi, 32
    add     rdx, 32
    add     rdi, 32

    ; Decrement the loop counter and iterate if not zero
    dec     r8
    jnz     vector_add_loop

vector_add_end:
    ; Use vzeroupper to clear upper portions of YMM registers,
    ; preventing performance penalties when transitioning between
    ↪  AVX and SSE code
    vzeroupper
    ret
```

Chapter 41

Implementing an XOR Cipher

Fundamental Properties of the XOR Operation

The XOR operation, denoted by $\oplus$, is defined on binary digits such that the resultant bit is set to 1 if and only if exactly one of the two operand bits is 1. Formally, for binary operands, the operation satisfies the following relationships:

$$0 \oplus 0 = 0, \quad 0 \oplus 1 = 1, \quad 1 \oplus 0 = 1, \quad 1 \oplus 1 = 0.$$

In addition to its basic definition, the XOR operation is characterized by critical algebraic properties. It is commutative, meaning that for any bits a and b, the equality

$$a \oplus b = b \oplus a$$

holds true. It is also associative:

$$(a \oplus b) \oplus c = a \oplus (b \oplus c).$$

A particularly salient feature of XOR is its self-inverting nature: for any bit x, applying XOR with another bit y twice returns the original value, that is,

$$(x \oplus y) \oplus y = x.$$

These properties form the mathematical foundation for its application in encryption schemes.

Algebraic Framework for XOR-Based Encryption

In the context of an XOR cipher, the encryption process is modeled by a simple binary operation applied element-wise to a plaintext sequence and a key sequence. Let $\mathbf{M} = \{m_0, m_1, \ldots, m_{n-1}\}$ represent the plaintext message encoded as a sequence of bits, and let $\mathbf{K} = \{k_0, k_1, \ldots, k_{n-1}\}$ denote the key sequence. The encryption is realized through the relation

$$\mathbf{C} = \mathbf{M} \oplus \mathbf{K},$$

where $\mathbf{C}$ is the resulting ciphertext. Owing to the self-inverting property of the XOR operation, decryption is performed identically:

$$\mathbf{M} = \mathbf{C} \oplus \mathbf{K}.$$

This framework elegantly encapsulates a symmetric cipher, wherein both encryption and decryption are achieved by the same binary operation, thus ensuring that the transformation is reversible provided the key remains unchanged.

Mechanism of the XOR Cipher

The operational mechanism of an XOR cipher is inherently straightforward. During encryption, each bit of the plaintext $\mathbf{M}$ is combined with the corresponding bit of the key $\mathbf{K}$ via the XOR operation. This process is repeated sequentially over the entire data set, resulting in the ciphertext $\mathbf{C}$. The process can be mathematically expressed on a per-element basis as

$$c_i = m_i \oplus k_i, \quad \text{for } i = 0, 1, \ldots, n - 1.$$

By virtue of the operation's commutativity and associativity, the order in which the bits are processed does not affect the outcome. Moreover, the decryption process utilizes the same operation, exploiting the identity

$$(m_i \oplus k_i) \oplus k_i = m_i,$$

to restore the original plaintext. This symmetry underscores the cipher's simplicity and computational efficiency.

Design Considerations in Cipher Construction

The implementation of an XOR cipher necessitates careful consideration of key selection and management. When the key $\mathbf{K}$ is chosen such that its bits are statistically independent and uniformly distributed, and the key length matches that of the plaintext, the resulting encryption can, in the idealized limit, attain information-theoretic security. This scenario is exemplified by the one-time pad, wherein each key bit is used exactly once. However, practical constraints often lead to the reuse of key material, which introduces vulnerabilities due to the linear characteristics of the XOR operation. Repeated key usage can give rise to detectable patterns in the ciphertext, thereby rendering the cipher susceptible to various forms of cryptanalysis.

The design must also account for the mode of operation in terms of data segmentation. The operation is applied discretely on blocks of bits; thus, aligning the data structure with the cipher's requirements is essential. Furthermore, an analysis of the entropy and statistical properties of both the key and the ciphertext is imperative to minimize the risk of exposure through frequency analysis or other linear attacks.

Analytical Perspective on XOR Cipher Security

From a cryptographic analysis viewpoint, the security of an XOR cipher is intrinsically linked to the properties of the key. When the key adheres to the ideal conditions of complete randomness and non-repetition, the ciphertext exhibits a uniform distribution akin to the key, obscuring any statistical inference regarding the plaintext. Conversely, deviations from these ideal conditions facilitate the application of linear cryptanalytic techniques. The inherent linearity of the XOR operation implies that the transformation does not introduce additional non-linearity, which is a desirable attribute in modern encryption schemes to frustrate adversaries exploiting statistical correlations.

The theoretical underpinnings of the XOR cipher are further illuminated by considerations of information theory. The mutual information between the plaintext and the ciphertext is minimized

217

when the key is random and unique, thereby ensuring minimal leakage of information. This analytical perspective provides a quantitative framework for evaluating the security parameters of the cipher and for devising strategies to mitigate potential vulnerabilities.

x64 Assembly Code Snippet

```
; -------------------------------
; x64 Assembly Implementation of an XOR Cipher
;
; This code implements a simple XOR encryption and decryption
↪   routine.
; The algebraic operations demonstrated are:
;
;   Encryption:   c[i] = m[i] XOR key
;   Decryption:   m[i] = c[i] XOR key     ; (Since (m XOR key) XOR
↪   key = m)
;
; The program performs the following steps:
; 1. Defines a plaintext message and a one-byte key.
; 2. Encrypts the plaintext by applying XOR byte-by-byte,
;    storing the result in a cipher buffer.
; 3. Decrypts the ciphertext with the same key,
;    storing the result in a decrypted buffer.
; 4. Writes the decrypted text to STDOUT (to demonstrate that it
;    matches the original plaintext).
; 5. Exits the program.
;
; Assemble with: nasm -f elf64 xor_cipher.asm && ld -o xor_cipher
↪   xor_cipher.o

        global _start

        section .data
; Define the plaintext message. A newline (0x0A) is appended.
plaintext db    "Hello, XOR Cipher!", 0x0A
; The encryption key (one byte). Modify as desired.
key       db    0x3F
; Calculate the length of the plaintext string.
len       equ   $ - plaintext

        section .bss
; Allocate buffers for the ciphertext and the decrypted message.
cipher    resb  len
decrypted resb  len

        section .text

_start:
        ; -------------------------------
```

218

```
; Encryption Routine:
;   For each byte:
;       c[i] = m[i] XOR key
; -------------------------------
mov     al, [key]          ; Load the key into AL
mov     rsi, plaintext     ; Source pointer (plaintext)
mov     rdi, cipher        ; Destination pointer (cipher text)
mov     rcx, len           ; Set loop counter to the length of
↪   the text

encrypt_loop:
cmp     rcx, 0
je      encrypt_done       ; Exit loop if all bytes processed
mov     bl, [rsi]          ; Load current byte of plaintext
↪   into BL
xor     bl, al             ; c[i] = m[i] XOR key
mov     [rdi], bl          ; Store the result byte in cipher
↪   buffer
inc     rsi                ; Advance plaintext pointer
inc     rdi                ; Advance cipher pointer
dec     rcx                ; Decrement loop counter
jmp     encrypt_loop

encrypt_done:
; -------------------------------
; Decryption Routine:
;   For each byte:
;       m[i] = c[i] XOR key
;   (Exploiting the self-inverting property of XOR)
; -------------------------------
mov     al, [key]          ; Reload the key into AL (for
↪   clarity)
mov     rsi, cipher        ; Source pointer (cipher text)
mov     rdi, decrypted     ; Destination pointer (decrypted
↪   message)
mov     rcx, len           ; Reset loop counter

decrypt_loop:
cmp     rcx, 0
je      decrypt_done       ; Exit loop when done
mov     bl, [rsi]          ; Load current byte of cipher text
↪   into BL
xor     bl, al             ; decrypted byte = cipher byte XOR
↪   key
mov     [rdi], bl          ; Store the result in decrypted
↪   buffer
inc     rsi                ; Advance cipher pointer
inc     rdi                ; Advance decrypted pointer
dec     rcx                ; Decrement loop counter
jmp     decrypt_loop

decrypt_done:
; -------------------------------
```

```
; Output Routine:
; Write the decrypted text to STDOUT to verify the result.
; -------------------------------
mov     rax, 1          ; Syscall number for write
↪  (sys_write)
mov     rdi, 1          ; File descriptor 1 (STDOUT)
mov     rsi, decrypted  ; Pointer to the decrypted text
↪  buffer
mov     rdx, len        ; Number of bytes to write
syscall


; -------------------------------
; Exit Routine:
; Terminate the program cleanly.
; -------------------------------
mov     rax, 60         ; Syscall number for exit (sys_exit)
xor     rdi, rdi        ; Return 0 status
syscall
```

Chapter 42

Checksum Calculation Routine

Fundamental Concepts of Checksum Computation

A checksum represents a compact numerical value derived from a block of data, designed to provide a rudimentary verification of data integrity. The routine under examination computes an aggregate value by processing each data element and subsequently performing arithmetic operations that reduce the result to a predetermined fixed size. In many instances, the checksum is formulated by sequentially adding individual bytes of the data and then applying a modulo reduction, expressed mathematically as

$$\text{checksum} = \left(\sum_{i=0}^{n-1} m_i \right) \bmod M,$$

where m_i represents each data element and M corresponds to the modulus, typically chosen as a power of two (e.g., 256 when the checksum is confined to a single byte). The operational simplicity of this method permits its effective implementation in assembly language, where direct manipulation of registers and memory affords both speed and granular control over the arithmetic process. This conceptual design is pivotal in situations that require rapid verification of data integrity without incurring significant computational overhead.

Mathematical Framework and Error Detection Characteristics

The mathematical underpinnings of the checksum calculation revolve around modular arithmetic. Defining the checksum routine as an additive process, the computed value adheres to the equation

$$S = \left(\sum_{i=0}^{n-1} m_i \right) \mod 2^k,$$

where 2^k represents the range limitation of the chosen accumulator register inherent to the assembly architecture. The modular reduction confines the result within a fixed numerical interval, an attribute that undergirds many error detection schemes. The efficacy of the checksum in detecting anomalies such as single-bit errors or simple burst errors is contingent upon the statistical dispersion of the data and the specific modulus M. Although this mechanism does not offer the cryptographic robustness of more sophisticated error detection codes, its efficiency and ease of computation render it an indispensable tool in various embedded systems and low-level data transfer protocols.

Assembly-Level Considerations in Checksum Computation

The implementation of the checksum algorithm in assembly language necessitates meticulous management of register operations and memory accesses. The routine is typically structured to initialize an accumulator register to zero, thereby establishing a baseline state. Subsequent operations involve iteratively loading data bytes from memory into a temporary register, followed by an additive operation that increments the accumulator. Assembly instructions such as ADD are employed in this context, with the operational semantics ensuring that any overflow is either naturally truncated or explicitly handled using additional instructions if a higher fidelity of modular arithmetic is required. The choice of using a direct accumulation method permits inline optimizations whereby the processor's inherent arithmetic capabilities can be leveraged, thereby minimizing the overall instruction cycle count. Moreover, the absence of conditional branching in the primary arithmetic loop contributes to a streamlined control flow that is compatible with the paradigms of assembly-level data processing.

Implementation Strategy for Data Integrity Verification

A systematic strategy for computing a checksum begins with the allocation of an accumulator that is set to an initial zero value. Data is then accessed sequentially, with each byte undergoing an addition operation to update the accumulator. The algorithm inherently incorporates a modulo reduction, either implicitly through the architecture's fixed register width or explicitly by applying a remainder operation. Following the complete traversal of the data sequence, the resulting checksum is available as a succinct representation of the original data's aggregate properties. This checksum can then be appended to the data sequence or transmitted alongside it to facilitate the subsequent verification of data integrity. The underlying methodology benefits from a deterministic arithmetic process, where the linear summation of data elements ensures that even minor variations in the input sequence will yield a noticeably different checksum. Such sensitivity to data modifications provides a foundational layer of defense against unintentional data corruption, making the checksum calculation routine a critical component in systems where data reliability is paramount.

x64 Assembly Code Snippet

```
; --------------------------------
; x64 Assembly Code: Checksum Calculation Routine
;
; This routine computes a checksum over a block of data by
↪   performing the
; summation of each byte and subsequently applying a modulo
↪   reduction with
; the modulus of 256. The mathematical foundation behind this is:
;     checksum = (m_0 + m_1 + ... + m_(n-1)) mod 256
; where each m_i represents a byte from the data buffer.
;
; The code below is written in NASM syntax for Linux on x64. It
↪   initializes
; an accumulator, iterates over each byte in the data buffer, adds
↪   it to the
```

```
; accumulator while performing an inline modulo reduction (using
↪    bitwise AND
; with 0xFF to keep only the least significant 8 bits), and finally
↪    exits
; returning the checksum as the process exit code.
; -----------------------------

section .data
    ; Data buffer: an example sequence of bytes over which the
    ↪    checksum is computed
    dataBuffer: db 0x12, 0x34, 0x56, 0x78, 0x9A, 0xBC, 0xDE, 0xF0
    dataLength equ $ - dataBuffer    ; Calculate the length of the
    ↪    dataBuffer

section .text
    global _start

_start:
    ; Initialize pointer and counter for the data buffer
    lea rsi, [rel dataBuffer]    ; RSI now points to the start of
    ↪    dataBuffer
    mov rcx, dataLength          ; RCX holds the number of bytes to
    ↪    process

    ; Initialize the accumulator (RBX) to zero; this will hold the
    ↪    checksum
    xor rbx, rbx                 ; RBX = 0

checksum_loop:
    ; Check if all bytes have been processed
    test rcx, rcx                ; Set flags based on RCX
    jz done_checksum             ; If RCX is zero, jump to finalize
    ↪    checksum

    ; Load the next byte from the data buffer into RAX (zero-extend
    ↪    to 64-bit)
    movzx rax, byte [rsi]        ; RAX = next byte from dataBuffer

    ; Accumulate the checksum
    add rbx, rax                 ; RBX = RBX + current byte

    ; Apply modulo reduction (ensuring RBX remains within 8-bit
    ↪    range)
    and rbx, 0xFF                ; RBX = RBX mod 256

    ; Advance the pointer and decrement the counter
    inc rsi                      ; Move to the next byte in dataBuffer
    dec rcx                      ; Decrement the byte counter
    jmp checksum_loop            ; Repeat the loop

done_checksum:
    ; At this point, RBX contains the final computed checksum (0 -
    ↪    255)
```

```asm
; For demonstration purposes, the checksum is returned as the
↪ exit code.
mov rdi, rbx                ; RDI will hold the exit code
↪ (checksum value)
mov rax, 60                 ; syscall number for exit in Linux x64
syscall                     ; Exit the program with the checksum
↪ as the status code
```

Chapter 43

Implementing a Simple Calculator

Mathematical Foundations and Formal Syntax

The calculator operates on arithmetic expressions that are defined within the framework of a formal language. In this setting, expressions are constructed from a finite alphabet of digits, operator symbols (such as $+$, $-$, $\times$, and $\div$), and grouping delimiters such as parentheses. The design follows a context-free grammar, which can be expressed in Backus-Naur Form. For example, one may define the grammar as

$$E \to E + T \mid E - T \mid T,$$

$$T \to T \times F \mid T \div F \mid F,$$

$$F \to (E) \mid N,$$

where E represents a general expression, T denotes terms with higher precedence, F stands for factors, and N corresponds to numeric literals. Such a grammatical foundation ensures that operator precedence and associativity are maintained, allowing for a rigorous evaluation of the expressions.

Lexical Analysis and Tokenization Process

The initial phase in the calculator pipeline involves decomposing the input string into a sequence of tokens. Each token is an elemental unit representing either a number, an operator, or a delimiter. The process of lexical analysis is formally modeled using regular expressions that identify patterns corresponding to valid tokens. For instance, numeric tokens may be characterized by a regular expression such as

$$[0-9]+(\.[0-9]+)?$$

to account for both integer and floating-point representations. Operator tokens, in contrast, are extracted by matching individual characters that denote arithmetic operations. This phase guarantees that the input is transformed into a well-structured sequence of symbols that conform to the predefined syntactic rules of the language.

Syntactical Parsing and Abstract Syntax Tree Construction

Once tokenization is complete, the ensuing step involves syntactical parsing, where the linear sequence of tokens is converted into a hierarchical structure known as an abstract syntax tree (AST). The parser employs techniques such as recursive descent or shift-reduce parsing to analyze the token sequence in accordance with the formal grammar. The resulting AST encapsulates the inherent structure of the arithmetic expression, where each internal node represents an operator and each leaf node represents an operand. The tree structure is vital in preserving the precedence of operations; for example, nodes corresponding to multiplication and division are nested deeper within the AST compared to those representing addition or subtraction. This structural representation is instrumental in ensuring that the subsequent evaluation phase adheres strictly to the intended semantics of the arithmetic operations.

Evaluation Strategies and Computational Semantics

The evaluation of the AST is achieved through a systematic traversal that computes the final numerical result based on the nodes' values and their associated operations. The computation is defined recursively: for a given node, the evaluation function applies the operation indicated by the node to the results obtained from its child nodes. For example, if a node represents the addition operation, its value is computed as

$$f(\text{left}) + f(\text{right}),$$

where f denotes the evaluation function and left and right are the subtrees corresponding to the operands. The semantics of the arithmetic operations are derived directly from conventional mathematical definitions, ensuring that expressions such as $a + b \times c$ are processed by first evaluating the multiplication and then performing the addition, in strict accordance with the prescribed operator hierarchy. This evaluation strategy is both inductive and compositional, rendering the calculator an effective tool for computing aggregated arithmetic results.

Consideration of Operator Precedence and Associativity

A critical dimension in the design of the calculator is the rigorous management of operator precedence and associativity. The formal grammar imposes a hierarchy in which multiplication and division assume higher precedence over addition and subtraction. This hierarchy is reflected in the structure of the AST, with nodes representing higher-precedence operations occupying positions that ensure their evaluation prior to lower-precedence operators. Additionally, the concept of left-associativity is inherently managed within the parsing process; for instance, an expression like

$$a - b - c$$

is parsed in a manner that associates as

$$(a - b) - c,$$

228

thereby preserving the left-to-right evaluation order. Such considerations are essential to maintain the mathematical integrity of complex expressions and are embedded within both the parsing and evaluation stages.

Error Handling and Semantic Validation

The robustness of the calculator is further enhanced through comprehensive error detection and semantic validation mechanisms. During lexical analysis and parsing, the algorithm scrutinizes the sequence of tokens for anomalies such as mismatched delimiters or malformed numeric representations. In the subsequent phase, the AST is examined for structural inconsistencies that could lead to undefined behaviors—for example, the detection of a division operator where the right-hand operand evaluates to zero. Such semantic validations are critical to avoid run-time exceptions and to ensure that the evaluation process is carried out under conditions of mathematical correctness. The integration of these error-handling strategies is predicated on a solid understanding of both formal language theory and the computational semantics of arithmetic expressions, thereby contributing to the overall reliability of the calculator implementation.

x64 Assembly Code Snippet

```
; -------------------------------------
;
; x64 Assembly Code for a Simple Calculator Using Recursive Descent
↪    Parsing
;
; Grammar:
;     E -> T { ('+' | '-') T }
;     T -> F { ('*' | '/') F }
;     F -> '(' E ')' | number
;
; This implementation uses a global pointer "input_ptr" that tracks
↪    the current
; position in the input expression (stored as a null-terminated
↪    string).
;
; The program evaluates an expression like "3+5*2-4" and prints the
↪    result.
;
; Assemble with: nasm -felf64 calculator.asm
```

```
; Link with:      ld -o calculator calculator.o -lc --dynamic-linker
↪ /lib64/ld-linux-x86-64.so.2
;------------------------------------

global main
extern printf, exit

section .data
    expression  db "3+5*2-4", 0            ; Input expression to
    ↪ evaluate
    fmt         db "Result: %d", 10, 0      ; Format string for
    ↪ printf (10 = LF)
    error_msg   db "Error in parsing expression", 10, 0

section .bss
    input_ptr   resq 1                      ; Global pointer to
    ↪ current char in expression

section .text

;------------------------------------
; main: Program entry point.
;------------------------------------
main:
    ; Initialize the input pointer with the address of the
    ↪ expression string.
    mov     rax, expression
    mov     [input_ptr], rax

    ; Parse the expression and compute the result. Result will be in
    ↪ rax.
    call    parse_expr

    ; After parsing, ensure that the entire expression has been
    ↪ consumed.
    mov     rbx, [input_ptr]
    movzx   rcx, byte [rbx]
    cmp     cl, 0
    jne     parse_error

    ; Print the result using printf.
    mov     rsi, rax        ; Argument: evaluated integer result.
    lea     rdi, [rel fmt]  ; Format string.
    xor     rax, rax        ; Clear rax (for variadic functions).
    call    printf

    ; Exit the program with status 0.
    mov     rdi, 0
    call    exit

;------------------------------------
; parse_expr: Parse an expression.
; Implements rule: E -> T { ('+' | '-') T }
```

```
; Returns evaluated result in rax.
;------------------------------------
parse_expr:
    push    rbp
    mov     rbp, rsp
    sub     rsp, 8              ; Allocate 8 bytes for local
    ↪  accumulator.

    ; Parse the first term.
    call    parse_term
    mov     [rbp-8], rax        ; accumulator = first term.

.parse_expr_loop:
    ; Load current character.
    mov     rbx, [input_ptr]
    movzx   rcx, byte [rbx]
    cmp     cl, '+'
    je      .expr_add
    cmp     cl, '-'
    je      .expr_sub
    jmp     .expr_done

.expr_add:
    ; Skip the '+' token.
    inc     rbx
    mov     [input_ptr], rbx
    ; Parse the next term.
    call    parse_term
    ; accumulator = accumulator + parsed term.
    mov     rdx, [rbp-8]
    add     rdx, rax
    mov     [rbp-8], rdx
    jmp     .parse_expr_loop

.expr_sub:
    ; Skip the '-' token.
    inc     rbx
    mov     [input_ptr], rbx
    ; Parse the next term.
    call    parse_term
    ; accumulator = accumulator - parsed term.
    mov     rdx, [rbp-8]
    sub     rdx, rax
    mov     [rbp-8], rdx
    jmp     .parse_expr_loop

.expr_done:
    mov     rax, [rbp-8]
    leave
    ret


;------------------------------------
; parse_term: Parse a term.
```

```
; Implements rule: T -> F { ('*' | '/') F }
; Returns evaluated result in rax.
;-----------------------------------
parse_term:
    push    rbp
    mov     rbp, rsp
    sub     rsp, 8              ; Allocate 8 bytes for local
    ↪  accumulator.

    ; Parse the first factor.
    call    parse_factor
    mov     [rbp-8], rax        ; accumulator = first factor.

.parse_term_loop:
    ; Load current character.
    mov     rbx, [input_ptr]
    movzx   rcx, byte [rbx]
    cmp     cl, '*'
    je      .term_mul
    cmp     cl, '/'
    je      .term_div
    jmp     .term_done

.term_mul:
    ; Skip the '*' token.
    inc     rbx
    mov     [input_ptr], rbx
    ; Parse the next factor.
    call    parse_factor
    ; Multiply: accumulator = accumulator * parsed factor.
    mov     rdx, [rbp-8]
    imul    rdx, rax
    mov     [rbp-8], rdx
    jmp     .parse_term_loop

.term_div:
    ; Skip the '/' token.
    inc     rbx
    mov     [input_ptr], rbx
    ; Parse the next factor.
    call    parse_factor
    ; Divide: accumulator = accumulator / parsed factor.
    ; Save divisor in r8.
    mov     r8, rax
    mov     rax, [rbp-8]        ; Dividend.
    cqo                         ; Sign extend rax into rdx:rax.
    idiv    r8                  ; Quotient in rax.
    mov     [rbp-8], rax
    jmp     .parse_term_loop

.term_done:
    mov     rax, [rbp-8]
    leave
```

```
            ret

;------------------------------------
; parse_factor: Parse a factor.
; Implements rule: F -> '(' E ')' | number
; Returns evaluated result in rax.
;------------------------------------
parse_factor:
        push    rbp
        mov     rbp, rsp
        mov     rbx, [input_ptr]
        movzx   rcx, byte [rbx]
        cmp     cl, '('
        je      .factor_expr

        ; Otherwise, the factor should be a number.
        call    parse_number
        jmp     .factor_done

.factor_expr:
        ; Skip the '(' token.
        inc     rbx
        mov     [input_ptr], rbx
        ; Recursively parse the expression within the parentheses.
        call    parse_expr
        ; After parsing, the current character must be ')'.
        mov     rbx, [input_ptr]
        movzx   rcx, byte [rbx]
        cmp     cl, ')'
        jne     parse_error
        ; Skip the ')' token.
        inc     rbx
        mov     [input_ptr], rbx

.factor_done:
        leave
        ret


;------------------------------------
; parse_number: Convert a sequence of digits into an integer.
; Returns the integer value in rax.
;------------------------------------
parse_number:
        push    rbp
        mov     rbp, rsp
        xor     rax, rax                ; Initialize result = 0.

.parse_number_loop:
        mov     rbx, [input_ptr]
        movzx   rcx, byte [rbx]
        cmp     cl, '0'
        jb      .end_parse_number
        cmp     cl, '9'
```

233

```
        ja      .end_parse_number
        ; Multiply result by 10.
        imul    rax, rax, 10
        ; Convert ASCII digit to numeric value and add it.
        sub     cl, '0'
        add     rax, rcx
        ; Advance the input pointer.
        inc     rbx
        mov     [input_ptr], rbx
        jmp     .parse_number_loop

.end_parse_number:
        leave
        ret


;----------------------------------------
;
; parse_error: Handle parsing errors by printing an error message
↪   and exiting.
;----------------------------------------
parse_error:
        lea     rdi, [rel error_msg]
        xor     rax, rax
        call    printf
        mov     rdi, 1          ; Exit code 1 indicates an error.
        call    exit
```

Chapter 44

Converting Uppercase to Lowercase

ASCII Representation and Character Mapping

The standard ASCII encoding scheme assigns unique numerical values to characters, with uppercase and lowercase letters occupying distinct contiguous ranges. Specifically, uppercase alphabetic characters are encoded with integer values ranging from 65 (corresponding to the character A) to 90 (corresponding to the character Z). In contrast, the lowercase counterparts are represented by the range from 97 (for a) to 122 (for z). A fixed arithmetic offset exists between the corresponding uppercase and lowercase representations. For each uppercase character c in the interval $[65, 90]$, the equivalent lowercase character may be obtained via the transformation

$$f(c) = c + 32.$$

This transformation is a direct consequence of the structured layout of the ASCII table and serves as the foundational principle for the routine under discussion.

Bitwise Transformation Methodology

An alternative perspective on the conversion process involves a bitwise manipulation approach. The binary representation of ASCII values reveals that the difference between an uppercase and its corresponding lowercase letter is isolated to a single bit position. In binary, the value 32 is represented as 0010 0000, wherein the activation of the bit corresponding to 2^5 marks the transition from uppercase to lowercase. Consequently, for any character c satisfying $65 \leq c \leq 90$, the operation

$$f(c) = c \,|\, 32$$

performs a bitwise inclusive OR with the constant 32, effectively setting the required bit. This method dispenses with the need for an arithmetic addition and leverages the efficiency inherent in bitwise operations, underscoring the routine's computational elegance.

Algorithmic Conditions and Correctness Considerations

The conversion routine must ensure that it applies the transformation only to valid uppercase inputs. Formally, if a character c adheres to the constraint

$$65 \leq c \leq 90,$$

then the function $f(c)$ is defined and yields a character within the lowercase range, given either by

$$f(c) = c + 32$$

or equivalently by the bitwise formulation

$$f(c) = c \,|\, 32.$$

A critical aspect of the algorithm is that it performs a conditional check on the input, thereby safeguarding against the inadvertent alteration of characters that do not fall within the designated uppercase interval. This condition contributes to the robustness and correctness of the transformation. In a formal verification setting, proofs of the routine's correctness involve establishing that for every $c \in [65, 90]$, the relation

$$97 \leq f(c) \leq 122$$

holds, while for $c \notin [65, 90]$, the routine is designed either to bypass the transformation or to defer to an alternative handling mechanism. The mathematical rigor embedded in these conditions ensures that the operation not only aligns with the theoretical underpinnings of ASCII encoding but also meets the practical demands of efficiency and correctness in system-level implementations.

x64 Assembly Code Snippet

```
; --------------------------------
; Function: convert_to_lower
; Purpose : Convert an uppercase ASCII character to its lowercase
↪    equivalent.
;           This routine checks if the character (located at the
↪    memory address
;           pointed to by RDI) is in the range 'A' (0x41) to 'Z'
↪    (0x5A).
;           If so, it converts the character using either arithmetic
↪    addition
;           (c + 32) or bitwise OR (c | 32) to set the 2^5 bit,
↪    yielding the
;           lowercase equivalent. If the character does not fall in
↪    the uppercase
;           range, it remains unmodified.
;
; Calling Convention: System V AMD64 calling convention (Linux/Mac).
; Input  : RDI -> pointer to a byte holding the character.
; Output : The converted (or unchanged) character is stored back in
↪    memory
;           and also returned in AL.
; --------------------------------

global convert_to_lower
section .text

convert_to_lower:
    push    rbp                 ; Preserve base pointer
    mov     rbp, rsp            ; Establish stack frame

    ; Load the character from memory (zero-extended into EAX)
    movzx   eax, byte [rdi]

    ; Check if the character is at least 'A' (65 or 0x41)
    cmp     al, 0x41
    jl      .done               ; If less than 'A', do nothing

    ; Check if the character is at most 'Z' (90 or 0x5A)
    cmp     al, 0x5A
```

```
    jg     .done                    ; If greater than 'Z', do
    ↪  nothing

    ; Conversion Method Option:
    ; Method 1 (Arithmetic Addition):
    ;   add    al, 0x20             ; f(c) = c + 32
    ;
    ; Method 2 (Bitwise OR):
         or     al, 0x20            ; f(c) = c | 32

    ; Store the converted character back into memory
    mov    byte [rdi], al

.done:
    pop    rbp                      ; Restore previous base pointer
    ret                             ; Return, with AL holding the
    ↪  result

; --------------------------------
; End of the convert_to_lower routine.
```

Chapter 45

Character Classification Routine

Fundamental Principles of ASCII Encoding

The American Standard Code for Information Interchange (ASCII) represents a fundamental numerical characterization of textual symbols. Each character is assigned a unique integer value, and the structure of the ASCII table is inherently partitioned into contiguous ranges that correspond to distinct character types. For instance, uppercase alphabetic characters are encoded within the interval $[65, 90]$, whereas lowercase letters occupy the interval $[97, 122]$. Digits are situated in the interval $[48, 57]$, and a variety of punctuation marks and control symbols are distributed among other specific ranges. The intrinsic ordering and numerical spacing of these values permit classification routines to exploit simple arithmetic comparisons and mathematical predicates to differentiate between character types based solely on their ordinal values.

Definition and Formalization of Character Classes

Character classification can be formalized by defining a function

$$\chi : \mathbb{Z} \to \mathcal{C},$$

239

where $\mathcal{C}$ is a set of disjoint categories such as *Uppercase, Lowercase, Digit,* and *Other.* For an input character with ASCII code c, the classification function χ is defined by the relations

$$\chi(c) = \begin{cases} \text{Uppercase} & \text{if } 65 \leq c \leq 90, \\ \text{Lowercase} & \text{if } 97 \leq c \leq 122, \\ \text{Digit} & \text{if } 48 \leq c \leq 57, \\ \text{Other} & \text{otherwise.} \end{cases}$$

This precise partition of the domain of standard ASCII values ensures that every valid input is mapped unequivocally to one of the classification subsets. In the above definition, the predicates

$$P_U(c) \equiv (65 \leq c \leq 90), \quad P_L(c) \equiv (97 \leq c \leq 122),$$

$$\text{and} \quad P_D(c) \equiv (48 \leq c \leq 57)$$

serve as the foundational conditions that guarantee the mutual exclusivity and collective exhaustiveness of the categories defined within $\mathcal{C}$.

Logical Decomposition and Predicate Formulation

The task of differentiating between various types of characters can be viewed as decomposing the ASCII set into non-overlapping segments based on numerical intervals. This decomposition is achieved via a series of Boolean predicates. For example, the condition $65 \leq c \leq 90$ is sufficient to assert that the character is an uppercase letter, while an alternative condition, $97 \leq c \leq 122$, establishes the character as lowercase. The predicate for digit recognition, given by $48 \leq c \leq 57$, ensures that numerical characters are segregated from alphabetic symbols. Such predicates form the core of decision procedures within character classification routines. The logical structure underlying these procedures is typically implemented as a cascade of conditional evaluations, where the satisfaction of one predicate precludes the need to assess the subsequent ones. The completeness of this logical framework is underpinned by the comprehensive coverage of the standard ASCII range, thereby allowing the classification function χ to function as an accurate and deterministic mapping from numerical values to character types.

Algorithmic Considerations and Efficiency in Classification

From an algorithmic perspective, the design of a character classification routine must balance logical clarity with operational efficiency. The inherent order of ASCII codes allows for the use of sequential comparison checks that are computationally inexpensive. Given that the cost of a comparison is constant, the determination of the proper character class via conditional evaluation entails a worst-case complexity of only a few comparisons. This efficiency is critical in applications that perform extensive text processing or lexical analysis. Furthermore, the assurance of correctness is bolstered by the formal invariants established by the predicates $P_U(c)$, $P_L(c)$, and $P_D(c)$. The invariants guarantee that for any ASCII code c, the relation

$$c \in [0, 127] \quad \Longrightarrow \quad \exists\, C \in \mathcal{C} \text{ such that } \chi(c) = C,$$

holds true under the standard definition. In situations where c falls outside the canonical ASCII range, extension mechanisms or error-handling procedures may be invoked as dictated by the broader system architecture. The succinct mapping provided by χ not only serves to simplify the classification logic but also facilitates formal verification of the routine's correctness and its adherence to theoretical specifications based on the numerical properties of the ASCII encoding.

x64 Assembly Code Snippet

```
; x64 Assembly Code: Character Classification Routine
; This program classifies an input character (from a predefined
↪   memory location)
; into one of four categories: Uppercase, Lowercase, Digit, or
↪   Other.
; It then prints a corresponding message to stdout using Linux
↪   kernel syscalls.

; Data Section: Define the input character and the message strings.
section .data
    ; Input character for classification (modify as needed).
    input_char    db 'G', 0

    ; Message strings are null-terminated.
```

```asm
        msg_upper      db "Character is Uppercase.", 10, 0      ; 10 =
        ↪ newline
        msg_lower      db "Character is Lowercase.", 10, 0
        msg_digit      db "Character is a Digit.", 10, 0
        msg_other      db "Character is Other.", 10, 0

; BSS Section: For uninitialized data (none needed here).
section .bss

; Text Section: Contains the code.
section .text
global _start

_start:
        ; Load the input character from memory into AL.
        mov al, [input_char]

        ; --------------------------------------------------
        ; Classification Routine: Determine the character class.
        ; --------------------------------------------------
        ; Check if the character is Uppercase (ASCII 65 to 90).
        cmp al, 65
        jl check_lower         ; If less than 'A', not uppercase.
        cmp al, 90
        jg check_lower         ; If greater than 'Z', not uppercase.
        ; Character is uppercase.
        mov rbx, msg_upper     ; Load address of uppercase message.
        jmp prepare_output

check_lower:
        ; Check if the character is Lowercase (ASCII 97 to 122).
        cmp al, 97
        jl check_digit         ; If less than 'a', not lowercase.
        cmp al, 122
        jg check_digit         ; If greater than 'z', not lowercase.
        ; Character is lowercase.
        mov rbx, msg_lower     ; Load address of lowercase message.
        jmp prepare_output

check_digit:
        ; Check if the character is a Digit (ASCII 48 to 57).
        cmp al, 48
        jl check_other         ; If less than '0', not a digit.
        cmp al, 57
        jg check_other         ; If greater than '9', not a digit.
        ; Character is a digit.
        mov rbx, msg_digit     ; Load address of digit message.
        jmp prepare_output

check_other:
        ; Character did not match any of the above categories.
        mov rbx, msg_other     ; Load address of 'Other' message.
```

```asm
; ------------------------------------------------
; Prepare the output: Compute the length of the message string.
; ------------------------------------------------
prepare_output:
    mov rsi, rbx         ; rsi holds the pointer to the chosen
    ↪ message.
    xor rcx, rcx         ; Clear rcx; will use it as a length
    ↪ counter.

compute_length:
    mov al, byte [rsi + rcx] ; Load the next byte of the string.
    cmp al, 0
    je write_output      ; If null terminator found, end loop.
    inc rcx
    jmp compute_length

; ------------------------------------------------
; Write the message to standard output.
; ------------------------------------------------
write_output:
    mov rax, 1           ; Syscall number for sys_write.
    mov rdi, 1           ; File descriptor 1 = stdout.
    mov rsi, rbx         ; Message pointer.
    mov rdx, rcx         ; Message length.
    syscall

    ; ------------------------------------------------
    ; Exit the program.
    ; ------------------------------------------------
    mov rax, 60          ; Syscall number for exit.
    xor rdi, rdi         ; Exit code 0.
    syscall
```

Chapter 46

Implementing a Software Timer Delay

Conceptual Foundations of Delay Loops

Delay loops constitute a software-based mechanism for creating temporal pauses in program execution by repeatedly iterating through a predetermined loop structure. The fundamental premise is that each loop iteration consumes a specific number of processor cycles, and by executing the loop a sufficient number of times, a measurable time delay can be simulated. If the iteration count is denoted by N, the average number of cycles per iteration by C, and the processor clock frequency by f, the induced delay T may be approximated by

$$T \approx \frac{N \cdot C}{f}.$$

This relation encapsulates the core idea that the temporal duration of the delay is directly proportional to the cumulative cycle consumption of the loop. Intrinsic to this approach is the reliance on the processor's deterministic cycle execution characteristics, which allows the delay loop to function as an effective substitute for hardware-based timing solutions in controlled environments.

Analytical Modeling and Cycle Analysis

A rigorous analysis of delay loops necessitates a decomposition of the loop into its constitutive instructions, each contributing a quantifiable delay. The total delay introduced per iteration can be modeled by considering the individual cycle delays, $\tau_1, \tau_2, \ldots, \tau_k$, of the k instructions within the loop. The delay per iteration is then given by

$$\Delta T = \tau_1 + \tau_2 + \cdots + \tau_k,$$

and the overall delay is represented as

$$T = N \cdot \Delta T.$$

Careful cycle analysis must account for factors such as instruction pipelining, execution latency, and inter-instruction dependencies. In advanced microarchitectures, phenomena such as superscalar execution and branch prediction may further influence the aggregate cycle count. The analytical model serves as a theoretical framework that facilitates the prediction of delay durations and enables parameterization of the loop to meet specified timing criteria.

Calibration and Parameter Sensitivity

While the mathematical formulation provides a first-order approximation of the delay, practical implementations require thorough calibration due to variabilities in cycle consumption. Factors such as fluctuations in internal clock rates, microarchitectural behavior, and external system influences can lead to deviations from the idealized model. Accordingly, an empirical calibration process is employed wherein the iteration count N is adjusted to align the theoretical delay with observed real-time performance. This calibration may be represented by the introduction of an empirical factor k_c, such that the effective delay becomes

$$T = k_c \cdot \frac{N \cdot C}{f}.$$

The calibration process involves iterative measurements under controlled conditions and subsequent refinement of the loop parameters to ensure that the intended delay is realized within acceptable tolerance levels. This approach mitigates the impact of system-level discrepancies and ensures that the delay loop remains a viable solution in the absence of dedicated hardware timers.

Microarchitectural and System-Level Considerations

The implementation of a software timer delay must also address the influence of the broader system environment, including microarchitectural features and operating system behavior. Modern processors implement dynamic frequency scaling, speculative execution, and out-of-order processing, all of which can contribute to non-deterministic cycle counts during loop execution. Additionally, asynchronous events such as interrupt handling and context switching may interrupt the execution flow, thereby extending the actual delay beyond the calculated estimate. To address these issues, detailed performance profiling is essential to quantify the impact of such factors. The acquired metrics inform adjustments in the delay loop design, allowing for the integration of compensatory measures that attenuate the variance in timing. This meticulous consideration of microarchitectural and system-level phenomena ensures that the delay loop delivers reliable performance even in the presence of inherent system fluctuations.

x64 Assembly Code Snippet

```
; ----------------------------------------------------------
; x64 Assembly Code: Software Timer Delay with Cycle Count
↪    Measurement
;
; This code implements a software delay loop based on the formula:
;     T  (N * C) / f
; where:
;     - N is the number of iterations (delay_iterations),
;     - C is the number of cycles consumed per iteration (dependent on
↪    the
;       instructions inside the loop),
;     - f is the processor clock frequency.
;
; An empirical calibration factor (k_c) can be applied to adjust for
; microarchitectural variances:
;     T = k_c * (N * C) / f
;
; In this example, we also measure the total number of cycles
↪    consumed by
; the delay loop using the RDTSC instruction. A serialization step
↪    using CPUID
; is employed before and after the RDTSC calls to ensure accurate
↪    readings.
```

```
;
; Assemble with:
;   nasm -f elf64 delay.asm && ld -o delay delay.o
; -------------------------------------------------------

global _start

section .data
    ; The effective iteration count for the delay loop.
    ; Adjust this value as needed to achieve the desired delay.
    delay_iterations: dq 50000000    ; 50,000,000 iterations

section .text
_start:
    ;
    ↪  ------------------------------------------------------------
    ; 1. Measure Start Timestamp using RDTSC
    ;
    ↪  ------------------------------------------------------------
    ; Serialize instruction execution to ensure all previous
    ↪  instructions
    ; have completed. We use CPUID with EAX=0.
    xor     eax, eax        ; Set EAX = 0 to prepare for CPUID
    cpuid                   ; Serialize pipeline

    ; Read the Time Stamp Counter (TSC)
    rdtsc                   ; RDX:EAX ← TSC value
    ; Combine EAX and EDX into a single 64-bit register.
    shl     rdx, 32         ; Shift high-order bits to correct
    ↪  position
    or      rax, rdx        ; RAX now holds full 64-bit TSC value
    mov     r10, rax        ; Save the start timestamp in R10


    ;
    ↪  ------------------------------------------------------------
    ; 2. Execute the Delay Loop
    ;
    ↪  ------------------------------------------------------------
    ; Load the iteration count (N_effective) into RCX.
    mov     rcx, [delay_iterations]

delay_loop:
    ; Dummy operations to simulate cycle consumption per iteration.
    mov     rax, rcx        ; Copy current counter value into RAX
    add     rax, 1          ; Simple arithmetic operation (consumes
    ↪  cycles)
    sub     rax, 1          ; Reverse the operation to preserve
    ↪  value

    ; Decrement the loop counter.
    dec     rcx
    jnz     delay_loop      ; Continue loop until RCX == 0
```

```
;
↪  ----------------------------------------------------------------
; 3. Measure End Timestamp using RDTSC
;
↪  ----------------------------------------------------------------
xor     eax, eax        ; Prepare for CPUID serialization
cpuid                   ; Serialize pipeline again

rdtsc                   ; Read TSC into EDX:EAX
shl     rdx, 32         ; Shift high-order bits
or      rax, rdx        ; Combine into full 64-bit TSC value
mov     r11, rax        ; Save the end timestamp in R11

; Calculate the total cycles consumed by the delay loop.
sub     r11, r10        ; R11 = (end TSC) - (start TSC)
; At this point, R11 holds the total cycle count which can be
↪  used
; for further calibration or analysis in relation to the timing
↪  formula.

;
↪  ----------------------------------------------------------------
; 4. Exit the Program (Linux syscall)
;
↪  ----------------------------------------------------------------
mov     rax, 60         ; system call number for exit (sys_exit)
xor     rdi, rdi        ; status code 0
syscall                 ; invoke operating system to exit
```

Chapter 47

Implementing a Random Number Generator

Theoretical Foundations of Pseudorandom Number Generation

A pseudorandom number generator (PRNG) is an algorithm that produces a deterministic sequence of numbers whose statistical properties emulate those of truly random sequences. In a typical PRNG, an initial seed value, denoted by S_0, is iteratively transformed according to a state update function so that the sequence $\{S_n\}$, where

$$S_{n+1} = f(S_n),$$

exhibits characteristics such as unpredictability and uniform distribution over a specified range. The inherent determinism implies that the generator is entirely defined by its initial condition and its transformation function. A well-designed PRNG ensures that the resulting sequence passes standard randomness tests by diminishing detectable correlations and preserving a long period before the eventual repetition of states.

Arithmetic Transformations in Pseudorandom Generation

Arithmetic operations constitute a core component in the evolution of the internal state of a PRNG. A classical method employs the linear congruential model, which is succinctly expressed as

$$S_{n+1} = (aS_n + c) \mod m,$$

where a, c, and m are carefully chosen constants. In this context, the multiplier a and the increment c are selected based on rigorous number-theoretic principles to yield a maximal period and desirable statistical uniformity. The modulo operation confines the state within a finite range, effectively wrapping around the value space and introducing nonlinearity. Beyond linear congruence, more elaborate arithmetic manipulations may incorporate multiplicative inverses or modular exponentiation, contributing additional complexity to the state update mechanism. These operations enhance the sensitivity of the generator to initial conditions and ensure a thorough dispersion of bits among successive states.

Bitwise Operations in Enhancing Randomness

Bitwise operations furnish the essential non-linear perturbations required to disrupt predictable arithmetic patterns. Operations such as XOR, bit shifts (both left $<<$ and right $>>$), and bitwise negation serve to significantly intermix the bits within the state variable. For example, an exclusive OR (XOR) operation enacts a bitwise comparison that can rapidly diffusely alter the bit pattern of a numerical value when combined with appropriate shifting. Shifting operations reallocate bit significance, consequently breaking up contiguous sequences generated solely through arithmetic manipulation. The swift execution and inherent simplicity of these logical operations, when judiciously combined with arithmetic transformations, contribute to the overall obfuscation of the underlying deterministic process. Their role is central in attaining a statistically robust output that mitigates the risk of discernible patterns in the distribution of pseudorandom values.

Synthesis of Arithmetic and Bitwise Techniques

The integration of arithmetic and bitwise operations yields a composite transformation that capitalizes on the strengths of both approaches. The state update function can be represented as a sequential composition:

$$S_{n+1} = g\Big(h(S_n)\Big),$$

where $h(\cdot)$ denotes a set of arithmetic manipulations and $g(\cdot)$ comprises subsequent bitwise alterations. This synthesis is designed to engender a complex, multi-layered evolution of the state, ensuring that minor variations in the input seed propagate dramatically through subsequent iterations. The arithmetic stage, by introducing multiplicative and additive perturbations, expands the state space and embeds the initial conditions deeply within the computation. The bitwise stage, in turn, scrambles the intermediate results and erases any residual structure that might arise from the arithmetic operations. The order and configuration of these operations are critical; optimal arrangements promote excellent diffusion properties and maximize the period of the generated sequence, even under the constraints of finite state arithmetic.

Statistical Properties and Algorithmic Considerations

The efficacy of a pseudorandom number generator is ultimately judged by the statistical properties of its output. Notably, criteria such as uniformity of distribution, absence of serial correlation, and high entropy are quantitatively assessed using rigorous randomness test suites. The interplay between arithmetic and bitwise operations is engineered to achieve an equilibrium wherein the resulting sequence exhibits an unpredictable and uniform dispersion of values over its operational domain. Algorithmic considerations include the sensitivity to initial conditions and the ability to maintain a large period, ideally approaching the theoretical maximum determined by state size. Moreover, the computational efficiency of the operations is paramount: the low overhead of bitwise operations complements the inherently more resource-intensive arithmetic calculations, ensuring that the generator remains practical for high-performance applications. The design process involves both theoretical analysis, often grounded in number theory and combinatorics, and empirical testing to fine-tune the operational parameters and verify the absence of exploitable patterns within the generated sequence.

x64 Assembly Code Snippet

```
; ----------------------------------------------------------
; x64 Assembly Code for a Pseudorandom Number Generator (PRNG)
;
; This example implements a composite state update:
;    1. Arithmetic Stage (Linear Congruential Generator):
;         S = (S * MULTIPLIER + INCREMENT) mod 2^64
;
;    2. Bitwise Mixing Stage:
;         OUTPUT = S XOR (S >> SHIFT_AMOUNT)
;
; The constants are chosen based on well-established parameters:
;    MULTIPLIER  = 6364136223846793005    ; from Numerical Recipes
;    INCREMENT   = 1442695040888963407    ; odd constant for maximal
; ↪ period
;    SHIFT_AMOUNT= 22                      ; bit mixing shift value
;
; The seed is stored in a global variable "rand_state". In this
; ↪ code,
; the new pseudorandom number is computed by calling the function
; ↪ "next_rand"
; and is then used as the exit status to demonstrate its retrieval.
;
; Assemble with: nasm -f elf64 prng.asm
; Link with: ld -o prng prng.o
; ----------------------------------------------------------

section .data
    ; Global seed for the pseudorandom number generator.
    ; It must be initialized to a nonzero 64-bit value.
    rand_state:    dq 0xDEADBEEFCAFEBABE

    ; Constants for the linear congruential generator.
    multiplier:    dq 6364136223846793005
    increment:     dq 1442695040888963407
    ; SHIFT_AMOUNT is stored as a byte-sized constant.
    shift_amount:  db 22

section .text
    global _start

; ----------------------------------------------------------
```

```asm
; Function: next_rand
; Description:
;   Updates the internal state using a linear congruential formula
↪   and then
;   applies a xorshift mixing step to produce the final pseudorandom
↪   number.
;
;   Calculation:
;       new_state = (old_state * MULTIPLIER + INCREMENT) mod 2^64
;       random    = new_state XOR (new_state >> SHIFT_AMOUNT)
;
; Returns:
;   The pseudorandom number in RAX.
; ---------------------------------------------------------------
next_rand:
    ; Load the current state into RAX.
    mov rax, [rand_state]

    ; Multiply: RAX = old_state * MULTIPLIER.
    mov rbx, [multiplier]
    imul rax, rbx

    ; Add the increment: RAX = RAX + INCREMENT.
    add rax, [increment]

    ; Save the updated state back to memory.
    mov [rand_state], rax

    ; Perform bit mixing: temp = new_state >> SHIFT_AMOUNT.
    ; Copy the new state into RBX.
    mov rbx, rax
    ; Load the shift amount (stored as a byte) into CL.
    mov cl, [shift_amount]
    shr rbx, cl

    ; XOR the new state with its shifted version.
    xor rax, rbx

    ret


; ---------------------------------------------------------------
; Entry Point: _start
; Description:
;   Calls next_rand to generate a pseudorandom number and then exits
;   using that number as the exit status.
; ---------------------------------------------------------------
_start:
    ; Obtain a new pseudorandom number by calling next_rand.
    call next_rand

    ; Use the resulting random number in RAX as the exit code.
    mov rdi, rax
```

253

```
; Invoke the exit system call (sys_exit = 60).
mov rax, 60
syscall
```

Chapter 48

Implementing Modular Arithmetic

Mathematical Foundations of Modular Arithmetic

Modular arithmetic, commonly regarded as arithmetic on residue classes, establishes a framework wherein computations are confined to a finite set of integers defined by a positive modulus, m. The structure is built upon the concept of congruence, where for any two integers a and b, the notation $a \equiv b \pmod{m}$ indicates that m divides the difference $a - b$. This relation partitions the infinite set of integers, $\mathbb{Z}$, into exactly m equivalence classes. Operations such as addition, subtraction, and multiplication are performed with the result reduced modulo m, thereby encapsulating the cyclic nature of the arithmetic. In this system, the existence of a multiplicative inverse for an integer is specifically dependent upon the coprimality of that integer with m. Such properties are not only of intrinsic mathematical interest but are also critical for ensuring robust algorithmic behavior in applications spanning cryptography and cyclic computations.

Algorithmic Approaches to Modular Computations

Algorithmic efficiency in modular arithmetic is paramount due to the frequent necessity to manage large integers and perform repeated reductions. At the core of these computations lies the reduction process: for any integer a, the expression $a \bmod m$ yields the unique remainder in the range 0 to $m-1$. Modular addition and multiplication are defined similarly to their conventional counterparts, yet each operation is followed by a reduction step to maintain the results within the prescribed range. More demanding operations, such as modular exponentiation, require methods like the repeated squaring algorithm, which reduces the computational complexity from linear to logarithmic in the exponent. For situations involving large moduli or the processing of high-precision arithmetic, techniques such as Montgomery reduction are employed to sidestep costly division operations, thus preserving computational resources while upholding mathematical integrity. The design of these algorithms necessitates a careful balance between theoretical correctness and practical efficiency, ensuring that intermediate values are managed appropriately to avoid overflow while sustaining the cyclic characteristics inherent in modular systems.

Integration of Modular Operations in Cryptographic and Cyclic Computations

The application of modular arithmetic in cryptographic schemes and cyclic computations is grounded in its ability to constrain numerical operations within a fixed set of outcomes, thereby introducing a controlled periodicity. Cryptographic algorithms such as RSA and the Diffie-Hellman key exchange exploit the mathematical structure of modular arithmetic to secure communications. In these contexts, operations like modular exponentiation and the computation of modular inverses—often derived via the extended Euclidean algorithm—are indispensable. The cyclical properties of modular systems facilitate the creation of finite groups and rings, whose algebraic characteristics are leveraged to produce pseudorandom sequences and error-detection codes. The inherent non-linearity and periodicity of modular operations contribute to the complexity and unpredictability required in secure communication protocols.

Additionally, cyclic computations based on modular arithmetic are essential in constructing algorithms for cyclic redundancy checks, pseudorandom number generation, and various digital signal processing tasks. The synthesis of these elements underpins a mathematical and algorithmic paradigm where efficient computation and theoretical soundness converge to yield systems capable of withstanding rigorous analysis and practical application alike.

x64 Assembly Code Snippet

```
; x64 Assembly Code for Modular Arithmetic Operations
; This code implements four key routines:
; 1. mod_add:   Compute (a + b) mod m.
; 2. mod_mul:   Compute (a * b) mod m.
; 3. mod_exp:   Compute modular exponentiation a^exp mod m using
↪   repeated squaring.
; 4. mod_inv:   Compute the modular inverse of a mod m via the
↪   Extended Euclidean Algorithm.
;
; Calling Conventions:
;   mod_add: RDI = a, RSI = b, RDX = m -> Returns (a+b) mod m in
↪   RAX.
;   mod_mul: RDI = a, RSI = b, RDX = m -> Returns (a*b) mod m in
↪   RAX.
;   mod_exp: RDI = base, RSI = exponent, RDX = m -> Returns
↪   base^exponent mod m in RAX.
;   mod_inv: RDI = a, RSI = m -> Returns modular inverse of a mod m
↪   in RAX (or 0 if none exists).

global mod_add, mod_mul, mod_exp, mod_inv

section .text

;-----------------------------------------------------------------
; Function: mod_add
; Description: Compute (a + b) mod m.
; Inputs:
;   RDI: a
;   RSI: b
;   RDX: m (modulus)
; Output:
;   RAX: (a + b) mod m
;-----------------------------------------------------------------
mod_add:
    mov rax, rdi        ; rax = a
    add rax, rsi        ; rax = a + b
    mov rcx, rdx        ; rcx = m
    xor rdx, rdx        ; clear rdx prior to division
```

```
    div rcx                ; divide rax by m: quotient in RAX, remainder
    ↪  in RDX
    mov rax, rdx           ; result = remainder
    ret


;-------------------------------------------------------------
; Function: mod_mul
; Description: Compute (a * b) mod m.
; Inputs:
;   RDI: a
;   RSI: b
;   RDX: m (modulus)
; Output:
;   RAX: (a * b) mod m
;-------------------------------------------------------------
mod_mul:
    mov rcx, rdx           ; rcx = m (preserve modulus)
    mov rax, rdi           ; rax = a
    mul rsi                ; unsigned multiply: rax * b -> product in
    ↪  [RDX:RAX]
    div rcx                ; divide [RDX:RAX] by m: quotient in RAX,
    ↪  remainder in RDX
    mov rax, rdx           ; result = remainder
    ret


;-------------------------------------------------------------
; Function: mod_exp
; Description: Compute a^exp mod m using the repeated squaring
; ↪  method.
; Inputs:
;   RDI: base (a)
;   RSI: exponent (exp)
;   RDX: m (modulus)
; Output:
;   RAX: a^exp mod m
;-------------------------------------------------------------
mod_exp:
    push rbx               ; preserve rbx (callee-saved)
    ; Initialize registers:
    ; r8 = base, r9 = exponent, r10 = modulus, rax = result
    mov r8, rdi            ; r8 = base
    mov r9, rsi            ; r9 = exponent
    mov r10, rdx           ; r10 = modulus
    mov rax, 1             ; result = 1

    ; Reduce base modulo m: r8 = r8 mod r10
    mov rcx, r10
    mov rbx, r8            ; copy base to rbx for reduction
    mov rax, rbx
    xor rdx, rdx
    div rcx                ; divide: quotient in RAX, remainder in RDX
    mov r8, rdx            ; new base = remainder
    mov rax, 1             ; reinitialize result to 1
```

258

```
exp_loop:
    test r9, 1          ; check if current exponent bit is 1
    jz skip_mul
    ; Multiply result by current base modulo m:
    ; result = (result * base) mod m
    mov rbx, rax        ; save current result in rbx
    mov rax, rbx
    mul r8              ; multiply: rax * base → [RDX:RAX]
    mov rcx, r10
    div rcx             ; reduce: remainder in RDX
    mov rax, rdx        ; update result with remainder
skip_mul:
    ; Square the base: base = (base * base) mod m
    mov rbx, r8         ; save base in rbx
    mov rax, r8
    mul rbx             ; compute base^2 → [RDX:RAX]
    mov rcx, r10
    div rcx             ; reduction: remainder in RDX
    mov r8, rdx         ; update base with remainder
    ; Shift exponent right by 1 bit for next iteration
    shr r9, 1
    cmp r9, 0
    jne exp_loop
    pop rbx
    ret


;-----------------------------------------------------------------
; Function: mod_inv
; Description: Compute the modular inverse of a mod m using the
;              Extended Euclidean Algorithm. Returns 0 if no inverse
↪ exists.
; Inputs:
;   RDI: a
;   RSI: m (modulus)
; Output:
;   RAX: modular inverse of a mod m (or 0 if none exists)
;-----------------------------------------------------------------
mod_inv:
    push rbx            ; preserve rbx
    ; Initialize:
    ; t = 0          -> r8
    ; newt = 1       -> r9
    ; r = m          -> r10
    ; newr = a       -> r11
    xor r8, r8         ; r8 = 0 (t)
    mov r9, 1          ; r9 = 1 (newt)
    mov r10, rsi       ; r10 = m (r)
    mov r11, rdi       ; r11 = a (newr)

inv_loop:
    cmp r11, 0
    je inv_done_loop   ; exit loop when newr == 0
```

```
    ; Compute quotient = r / newr, where r is in r10 and newr in
    ↪  r11.
    mov rax, r10        ; dividend = r
    xor rdx, rdx
    div r11             ; quotient in RAX, remainder in RDX
    ↪  (discarded)
    mov rbx, rax        ; store quotient in rbx

    ; Update (t, newt): temp = t - quotient * newt
    mov rax, rbx        ; rax = quotient
    imul rax, r9        ; rax = quotient * newt
    mov rdx, r8         ; rdx = t
    sub rdx, rax        ; temp = t - (quotient * newt)
    mov r8, r9          ; t = newt
    mov r9, rdx         ; newt = temp

    ; Update (r, newr): temp = r - quotient * newr
    mov rax, rbx        ; rax = quotient
    imul rax, r11       ; rax = quotient * newr
    mov rdx, r10        ; rdx = r
    sub rdx, rax        ; temp = r - (quotient * newr)
    mov r10, r11        ; r = newr
    mov r11, rdx        ; newr = temp
    jmp inv_loop

inv_done_loop:
    cmp r10, 1
    jne inv_no_inverse   ; if r > 1 then inverse does not exist
    ; If t (r8) is negative then adjust by adding modulus (RSI)
    cmp r8, 0
    jge inv_positive
    add r8, rsi
inv_positive:
    mov rax, r8         ; result (modular inverse) stored in RAX
    pop rbx
    ret

inv_no_inverse:
    mov rax, 0          ; no inverse exists, return 0
    pop rbx
    ret
```

Chapter 49

Exponentiation by Squaring

Overview of the Technique

The exponentiation by squaring algorithm provides an efficient method for computing large integer powers. This approach systematically reduces the number of multiplications by exploiting the algebraic identity expressing a power in terms of the square of a smaller power. In particular, the formulation utilizes the relations

$$a^n = \begin{cases} 1, & \text{if } n = 0, \\ \left(a^{\frac{n}{2}}\right)^2, & \text{if } n \text{ is even}, \\ a \cdot \left(a^{\frac{n-1}{2}}\right)^2, & \text{if } n \text{ is odd}. \end{cases}$$

This recursive decomposition effectively transforms a computation that would otherwise require $O(n)$ multiplications into one that runs in $O(\log n)$ time. The algorithm itself is an exemplar of divide-and-conquer strategies within the field of algorithm design.

Mathematical Foundations

Central to the method is the formal understanding of exponentiation as an operation on the set of real or complex numbers, or more generally on a multiplicative monoid. Let a be an element of such a structure and let n be a nonnegative integer. The defining recursive relations not only ensure that the base case $a^0 = 1$ is satisfied, but they also leverage the parity of the exponent to reduce the problem size efficiently. Given that any positive integer n can be expressed in binary form, the algorithm iterates through the bits of n from least significant to most significant, performing a multiplication only when the current bit is equal to 1. The squaring operation inherently corresponds to the doubling of the exponent, embedding the binary decomposition of the exponent into the computation. This realization is fundamental to appreciating why the algorithm achieves its logarithmic time complexity.

Algorithmic Construction

The construction of the algorithm depends on the iterative or recursive processing of the exponent. In an iterative formulation, a loop is maintained wherein the base is squared at each iteration, and the exponent is right-shifted by one bit. When the least significant bit of the exponent is nonzero, the accumulated result is multiplied by the current value of the base. This process continues until the exponent is reduced to zero. Each iteration effectively halves the magnitude of the remaining exponent, ensuring that the total number of iterations is bounded above by $\lfloor \log_2 n \rfloor + 1$. The method remains robust across diverse applications, whether within numerical computations or within algorithms employed in cryptography, where rapid modular exponentiation is often required.

Complexity Analysis and Performance Characteristics

The efficiency of exponentiation by squaring is best characterized by its asymptotic time complexity. With each iteration of the algorithm performing at most two multiplications and one squaring operation, the total number of multiplicative operations grows logarithmically with respect to the exponent. This yields an overall time complexity of $O(\log n)$, as opposed to the linear $O(n)$ performance of a naive multiplication approach. Additionally, the space complexity is minimal, particularly in iterative implementations, as only a few auxiliary variables are required to maintain the current base, the accumulator for the result, and the residual exponent. This economical use of resources underpins the algorithm's suitability for high-performance applications, especially in environments where large exponents and finite precision arithmetic are commonplace.

x64 Assembly Code Snippet

```
; Exponentiation by Squaring in x64 Assembly (NASM syntax for Linux)
; This program computes a^n using the exponentiation by squaring
↪   algorithm.
; It follows the System V AMD64 calling convention.
;
; The "exp_by_squaring" function:
;    Input:
;      RDI - base (a)
;      RSI - exponent (n)
;    Output:
;      RAX - result (a^n)
;
; The "_start" entry point demonstrates an example computation
↪   (3^5),
; converts the result to a decimal string, outputs it to stdout
↪   using syscalls,
; and then exits the program.
;
; To assemble and link:
;    nasm -f elf64 exp_by_squaring.asm
;    ld -o exp_by_squaring exp_by_squaring.o

global _start
global exp_by_squaring

section .data
    result_msg db "Result: ", 0      ; Message prefix
    msg_len    equ $ - result_msg     ; Length of result_msg
    newline    db 10, 0               ; Newline character

section .bss
    buffer resb 32                    ; Buffer for converting number to
    ↪   string

section .text

;-------------------------------------------------------
; Function: exp_by_squaring
; Computes base^exponent using exponentiation by squaring.
; Input:
;    RDI - base (a)
;    RSI - exponent (n)
; Output:
```

263

```
;    RAX - result (a^n)
;-------------------------------------------------------
exp_by_squaring:
    push rbp
    mov  rbp, rsp
    mov  rax, 1          ; Initialize result = 1
    test rsi, rsi        ; Check if exponent is zero
    jz   .done           ; If exponent == 0, return 1
.loop:
    test rsi, 1
    jz   .skip_multiply  ; If current bit is 0, skip multiplication
    imul rax, rdi        ; result *= base
.skip_multiply:
    imul rdi, rdi        ; Square the base: base = base * base
    shr  rsi, 1          ; exponent = exponent >> 1
    cmp  rsi, 0
    jne  .loop           ; Repeat loop while exponent != 0
.done:
    pop  rbp
    ret


;-------------------------------------------------------
; Entry Point: _start
; Demonstrates usage by computing 3^5, converting the result to a
↪   string,
; and printing it to stdout.
;-------------------------------------------------------
_start:
    ; Set up parameters for exp_by_squaring: base = 3, exponent = 5.
    mov rdi, 3           ; Base = 3
    mov rsi, 5           ; Exponent = 5
    call exp_by_squaring ; Compute 3^5. Result is in RAX (should be
↪   243)

    ; Convert numerical result (in RAX) to an ASCII string.
    mov rbx, rax         ; Preserve the result in RBX
    mov rdi, buffer + 31 ; Initialize pointer to the end of buffer
    mov byte [rdi], 0    ; Null-terminate the string

.convert_loop:
    cmp rbx, 0
    je  .conversion_done
    mov rax, rbx
    xor rdx, rdx         ; Clear RDX for division
    mov rcx, 10
    div rcx              ; Divide RAX by 10; quotient in RAX,
↪   remainder in RDX
    add rdx, '0'         ; Convert remainder into its ASCII digit
    dec rdi
    mov [rdi], dl        ; Store the digit in the buffer (building
↪   the string backwards)
    mov rbx, rax         ; Update RBX with the quotient
    jmp .convert_loop
```

264

```
.conversion_done:
    ; Save pointer to the beginning of the number-string in R8.
    mov r8, rdi         ; R8 now holds the start address of the
    ↳  converted string

    ; Calculate the length of the number string.
    mov rax, buffer + 31
    sub rax, r8         ; rax = length of the number string
    mov r9, rax         ; Save length in R9

    ; Write the result message ("Result: ") to stdout.
    mov rax, 1          ; sys_write system call
    mov rdi, 1          ; File descriptor: stdout
    mov rsi, result_msg
    mov rdx, msg_len
    syscall

    ; Write the converted number string to stdout.
    mov rax, 1          ; sys_write system call
    mov rdi, 1          ; File descriptor: stdout
    mov rsi, r8         ; Pointer to the number string
    mov rdx, r9         ; Length of the number string
    syscall

    ; Write a newline character to stdout.
    mov rax, 1          ; sys_write system call
    mov rdi, 1          ; File descriptor: stdout
    mov rsi, newline
    mov rdx, 1
    syscall

    ; Exit the program.
    mov rax, 60         ; sys_exit system call
    xor rdi, rdi        ; Exit code 0
    syscall
```

Chapter 50

Implementing an RPN Calculator

Theoretical Foundations of Reverse Polish Notation

Reverse Polish Notation (RPN) is a mathematical expression format in which every operator follows all of its operands. In contrast to conventional infix notation, where operators are placed between operands and the order of operations is governed by precedence and associativity rules, RPN eliminates the need for parentheses by design. For example, the infix expression $3 + 4 \times 5$ is represented in RPN as $3\ 4\ 5\ \times\ +$, wherein the multiplication is implicitly performed prior to the addition. This property arises from the postfix placement of operators, ensuring that the sequence of operations is unambiguously determined by the position of the operands relative to their corresponding operators.

Stack-Based Evaluation Mechanism

A central component in the evaluation of RPN expressions is the stack data structure. The stack, which adheres to the last-in-first-out (LIFO) principle, serves as temporary storage for operands and intermediate results during the computational process. When an operand is encountered in the expression sequence, it is placed (pushed) onto the stack. Conversely, when an operator appears, the appropriate number of operands is removed (popped) from the stack, the operator is applied, and the computed result is pushed back onto the stack. This mechanism ensures that operations are performed in the correct order without external bookkeeping. The intrinsic simplicity of this approach also contributes to its efficiency, with the primary operations consisting of constant time push and pop actions.

Tokenization and Symbolic Parsing

The evaluation process begins with the tokenization of the input expression. In this context, the expression is segmented into a sequence of discrete tokens, each of which represents either an operand or an operator. The parsing stage involves examining these tokens to determine their respective roles and ensuring that the classification is consistent with the expected symbol set. Operands are typically numerical values, represented in a format suitable for arithmetic computation, while operators denote the mathematical functions—such as addition, subtraction, multiplication, and division—to be performed. Meticulous attention to this preliminary phase is critical, since subsequent operations rely on the correct identification and ordering of tokens throughout the evaluation process.

Evaluation Algorithm and Control Flow

The core evaluation algorithm for an RPN expression proceeds by processing each token sequentially. Upon encountering an operand, the value is pushed onto the evaluation stack. When an operator is encountered, the algorithm pops the requisite number of operands from the stack; for a binary operator, these operands are typically retrieved in reverse order, yielding a computation of the form b op a. The result of this computation is then pushed back onto the stack. This iterative process continues until all tokens have been examined, leaving a single value on the stack that represents the final result of the expression. The control flow of the algorithm is determined by a loop that iterates over the token list, with conditional branches to handle the distinction between operands and operators. Error conditions, such as unexpected tokens or a stack that is underpopulated when an operator is encountered, are detected through invariant checks performed during each iteration of the loop.

Computational Complexity and Operational Considerations

The efficiency of an RPN calculator is largely attributed to the simplicity of the stack-based evaluation method. The algorithm processes an expression comprising n tokens in a single pass, resulting in a time complexity of $O(n)$. Each token is handled through a constant number of operations involving push or pop actions and, in the case of operators, arithmetic computations that are assumed to execute in constant time with respect to the size of the operands. Memory usage is limited by the maximum depth of the evaluation stack, which in the worst-case scenario correlates directly with the number of operands in the expression. Moreover, the approach inherently accommodates error detection, as any deviation from the expected token arrangement typically manifests as an inconsistency in the stack size. These operational characteristics render the RPN calculator both robust and efficient for a wide range of arithmetic expression evaluations.

x64 Assembly Code Snippet

```
; x64 Assembly Code for an RPN Calculator
; This code implements a simple Reverse Polish Notation (RPN)
↪   calculator.
; It parses a null-terminated RPN expression, tokenizes it, and
↪   evaluates the expression
; using a stack-based mechanism. Supported operators: +, -, *, /.
;
; Assemble with NASM and link with ld on a Linux x64 system.
;
; Example expression: "3 4 5 * +" is equivalent to 3 + (4 * 5) = 23.

section .data
    expr db "3 4 5 * +", 0          ; Null-terminated RPN expression

    err_unknown_token    db "Error: Unknown token", 10, 0
    err_stack_underflow  db "Error: Stack underflow", 10, 0
    err_div_zero         db "Error: Division by zero", 10, 0

section .bss
```

268

```
    stack resq 64                    ; Stack storage for 64 quadwords
    ↪ (8 bytes each)
    sp    resq 1                     ; Stack pointer (stores the number
    ↪ of elements pushed)

section .text
    global _start

_start:
    ; Initialize the stack pointer to 0
    mov qword [sp], 0

    ; Set RSI to point to the start of the expression string
    mov rsi, expr

parse_loop:
    ; Load the current character into AL
    mov al, byte [rsi]
    ; If the null terminator is reached, finish evaluation
    cmp al, 0
    je evaluate_done
    ; Skip spaces between tokens
    cmp al, ' '
    je skip_space

    ; Check if the token is a digit (i.e. '0' to '9')
    cmp al, '0'
    jb check_operator
    cmp al, '9'
    ja check_operator

    ; Convert the ASCII digit to its numeric value by subtracting
    ↪ '0'
    sub al, '0'
    movzx rax, al              ; rax now holds the numeric value
    ; Push the value onto the stack
    mov rcx, [sp]
    lea rdx, [stack + rcx*8]   ; each element is 8 bytes
    mov [rdx], rax
    inc rcx
    mov [sp], rcx
    jmp next_token

check_operator:
    ; Token is not a digit; check for supported operators: +, -, *,
    ↪ /
    cmp al, '+'
    je op_add
    cmp al, '-'
    je op_sub
    cmp al, '*'
    je op_mul
    cmp al, '/'
```

```
        je op_div

        ; If token does not match any known operator, signal an error.
        mov rdi, err_unknown_token
        call print_error_and_exit

op_add:
        ; Addition: Pop two values, compute (second + first), and push
        ↪ result.
        call pop_value          ; Operand a is now in RAX
        mov rbx, rax            ; Save a in RBX
        call pop_value          ; Operand b is now in RAX
        add rax, rbx            ; b + a
        call push_value
        jmp next_token

op_sub:
        ; Subtraction: Compute (second - first)
        call pop_value          ; Operand a in RAX
        mov rbx, rax
        call pop_value          ; Operand b in RAX
        sub rax, rbx            ; b - a
        call push_value
        jmp next_token

op_mul:
        ; Multiplication: Compute (second * first)
        call pop_value          ; Operand a in RAX
        mov rbx, rax
        call pop_value          ; Operand b in RAX
        imul rax, rbx           ; b * a
        call push_value
        jmp next_token

op_div:
        ; Division: Compute (second / first)
        call pop_value          ; Operand a (divisor) in RAX
        mov rbx, rax
        cmp rbx, 0
        je error_div_zero       ; Prevent division by zero
        call pop_value          ; Operand b (dividend) in RAX
        xor rdx, rdx            ; Clear RDX before division
        div rbx                 ; Divide RAX by RBX; quotient in RAX
        call push_value
        jmp next_token

skip_space:
        ; Skip over the space character.
        inc rsi
        jmp parse_loop

next_token:
        ; Advance the pointer to the next character in the expression.
```

270

```asm
        inc rsi
        jmp parse_loop

evaluate_done:
        ; After processing all tokens, the final result is at the top of
        ↪   the stack.
        call pop_value
        ; Exit with the result as the exit status.
        mov rdi, rax
        call exit_with_code

; Subroutine: pop_value
; Pops the top value from the stack.
; The value is returned in RAX.
pop_value:
        mov rcx, [sp]           ; Load current number of elements
        cmp rcx, 0
        je error_stack_underflow
        dec rcx
        mov [sp], rcx
        lea rdx, [stack + rcx*8]
        mov rax, [rdx]
        ret

; Subroutine: push_value
; Pushes the value in RAX onto the stack.
push_value:
        mov rcx, [sp]
        lea rdx, [stack + rcx*8]
        mov [rdx], rax
        inc rcx
        mov [sp], rcx
        ret

; Subroutine: print_error_and_exit
; Prints the error message (pointed to by RDI) and exits with error
↪   code 1.
print_error_and_exit:
        ; Preserve the error message pointer in RSI for writing.
        mov rsi, rdi
        call strlen             ; Determine string length; result in RDX
        mov rax, 1              ; sys_write system call number
        mov rdi, 2             ; File descriptor 2 (stderr)
        syscall
        ; Exit with an error code.
        mov rax, 60            ; sys_exit system call number
        mov rdi, 1
        syscall

error_stack_underflow:
        mov rdi, err_stack_underflow
        call print_error_and_exit
        jmp finish
```

271

```
error_div_zero:
    mov rdi, err_div_zero
    call print_error_and_exit
    jmp finish

; Subroutine: exit_with_code
; Exits the program with the status code provided in RDI.
exit_with_code:
    mov rax, 60              ; sys_exit system call number
    syscall

; Subroutine: strlen
; Computes the length of the null-terminated string pointed to by
↪  RSI.
; Returns the length in RDX.
strlen:
    xor rdx, rdx
.strlen_loop:
    cmp byte [rsi + rdx], 0
    je .strlen_done
    inc rdx
    jmp .strlen_loop
.strlen_done:
    ret

finish:
    ; End of program (should not reach this point)
    hlt
```

Chapter 51

Matrix Addition and Subtraction

Representation of Two-Dimensional Arrays

A two-dimensional array, often conceptualized as a matrix, is an ordered set of data elements organized in rows and columns. In mathematical terms, a matrix is denoted by A, where each element is referenced as A_{ij} with indices i and j indicating the row and column positions, respectively. The organization of these arrays in computer memory typically adheres to a row-major or column-major ordering, which determines the mapping from the two-dimensional index space to a one-dimensional memory address sequence. This mapping is essential for the efficient traversal and processing of matrix elements. The physical layout of the matrix in memory impacts cache utilization and the performance of the subsequent arithmetic routines.

Element-wise Operations in Matrices

Matrix arithmetic in the context of addition and subtraction is performed on an element-by-element basis, meaning that the computation for each position in the resultant matrix is entirely independent of computations for other positions. Such operations are mathematically defined and implemented by iterating over all corresponding indices of the operand matrices.

1 Matrix Addition

Consider two matrices, A and B, each of dimension $n \times m$, where n and m represent the number of rows and columns respectively. The process of matrix addition yields a new matrix C of the same dimensions such that each element is computed according to the relation

$$C_{ij} = A_{ij} + B_{ij} \quad \text{for all} \quad 1 \leq i \leq n,\ 1 \leq j \leq m.$$

The addition operation is performed by systematically accessing each element A_{ij} and B_{ij}, applying the summation, and storing the result in the corresponding position in C. This element-wise property ensures that the operation is both conceptually straightforward and amenable to parallelization. The independence of the computations provides opportunities for improving performance on architectures that support concurrency.

2 Matrix Subtraction

Analogous to the addition of matrices, matrix subtraction is also executed on an element-wise basis. For two matrices, A and B, of identical dimensions $n \times m$, the subtraction producing matrix C is given by

$$C_{ij} = A_{ij} - B_{ij} \quad \text{for all} \quad 1 \leq i \leq n,\ 1 \leq j \leq m.$$

Each individual operation subtracts the element from B from the corresponding element in A and assigns the result to C_{ij}. The universality of the index range across the matrices dictates that the routine must verify the conformity of their dimensions prior to executing the subtraction. This conditional check is crucial not only from a correctness standpoint but also in preventing runtime errors associated with dimension mismatches.

Algorithmic Considerations

The implementation of routines for processing two-dimensional arrays via element-wise matrix addition and subtraction requires careful attention to algorithmic efficiency and memory access patterns. The computational complexity of these operations is directly proportional to the number of elements, yielding a time complexity of $O(n \times m)$ for an $n \times m$ matrix.

The algorithms must be designed to iterate over the entire set of elements without incurring redundant computations. Moreover, optimal performance is achieved when the memory layout is taken into account; contiguous and predictable memory accesses facilitate better cache performance. In implementing these routines, it is imperative that checks for the consistency of matrix dimensions are performed prior to the element-wise operations. Such validation ensures that every corresponding pair of elements, A_{ij} and B_{ij}, is well-defined, thus safeguarding the algorithm against errors that could arise from incompatible input dimensions.

The analysis of these algorithms further underscores their inherent suitability for parallel execution. With each operation on an element being independent of others, the addition and subtraction routines represent excellent candidates for vectorized implementations or execution on parallel computing architectures. The abstraction provided by the matrix model, combined with the rigorous adherence to element-wise arithmetic operations, forms a robust framework for advanced computational tasks in scientific and engineering domains.

x64 Assembly Code Snippet

```
; ----------------------------------------------------------
; x64 Assembly Code for Matrix Addition and Subtraction
; NASM syntax for Linux (System V AMD64 calling convention)
; This complete snippet demonstrates element-wise matrix addition
; and subtraction on two-dimensional arrays (matrices).
; ----------------------------------------------------------

SECTION .data
        ; Define two 3x3 matrices (9 integers each)
        matrixA     dd 1,   2,   3,  \
                    4,   5,   6,  \
                    7,   8,   9

        matrixB     dd 9,   8,   7,  \
                    6,   5,   4,  \
                    3,   2,   1

        ; Matrix dimensions (3 rows x 3 columns)
        row_count   dd 3
        col_count   dd 3
```

```
SECTION .bss
    ; Reserve space for the result matrices (each 3x3)
    matrixAddRes resd 9
    matrixSubRes resd 9

SECTION .text
    global main

;-------------------------------------------------------------
; Function: matrix_add
; Description: Performs element-wise addition of two matrices.
; Parameters:
;    rdi - pointer to first matrix (A)
;    rsi - pointer to second matrix (B)
;    rdx - pointer to result matrix (C)
;    rcx - number of rows
;    r8  - number of columns
;-------------------------------------------------------------
matrix_add:
    push rbp
    mov rbp, rsp

    ; Compute total number of elements: total = rows * cols
    mov rax, rcx
    imul rax, r8
    test rax, rax
    je .matrix_add_done

.loop_add:
    ; Load element from matrix A and matrix B, then add them
    mov eax, dword [rdi]
    add eax, dword [rsi]
    ; Store the result in matrix C
    mov dword [rdx], eax

    ; Advance pointers (each integer is 4 bytes)
    add rdi, 4
    add rsi, 4
    add rdx, 4

    dec rax
    jnz .loop_add

.matrix_add_done:
    pop rbp
    ret

;-------------------------------------------------------------
; Function: matrix_sub
; Description: Performs element-wise subtraction of two matrices.
; Parameters:
;    rdi - pointer to first matrix (A)
;    rsi - pointer to second matrix (B)
```

```
;    rdx - pointer to result matrix (C)
;    rcx - number of rows
;    r8  - number of columns
;-------------------------------------------------------------
matrix_sub:
    push rbp
    mov rbp, rsp

    ; Compute total number of elements: total = rows * cols
    mov rax, rcx
    imul rax, r8
    test rax, rax
    je .matrix_sub_done

.loop_sub:
    ; Load element from matrix A and matrix B, then subtract B from
    ↪  A
    mov eax, dword [rdi]
    sub eax, dword [rsi]
    ; Store the result in matrix C
    mov dword [rdx], eax

    ; Advance pointers for next element
    add rdi, 4
    add rsi, 4
    add rdx, 4

    dec rax
    jnz .loop_sub

.matrix_sub_done:
    pop rbp
    ret


;-------------------------------------------------------------
; Main Entry Point
; Demonstrates the usage of matrix_add and matrix_sub routines.
;-------------------------------------------------------------
main:
    ; Set up stack frame
    push rbp
    mov rbp, rsp

    ; Load matrix dimensions from the data segment
    mov ecx, [row_count]     ; Number of rows (3)
    mov r8d, [col_count]     ; Number of columns (3)

    ;-------------------------------------------------------------
    ; Perform Matrix Addition
    ; Compute: matrixAddRes = matrixA + matrixB
    ;-------------------------------------------------------------
    mov rdi, matrixA         ; Pointer to matrix A
    mov rsi, matrixB         ; Pointer to matrix B
```

277

```asm
    mov rdx, matrixAddRes    ; Pointer to result matrix for addition
    call matrix_add

;---------------------------------------------------------
; Perform Matrix Subtraction
; Compute: matrixSubRes = matrixA - matrixB
;---------------------------------------------------------
    mov rdi, matrixA         ; Pointer to matrix A
    mov rsi, matrixB         ; Pointer to matrix B
    mov rdx, matrixSubRes    ; Pointer to result matrix for
    ↳ subtraction
    call matrix_sub

    ; Exit the program (using Linux syscall)
    mov rax, 60              ; Syscall number for exit
    xor rdi, rdi             ; Exit status 0
    syscall

; End of x64 Assembly Code
```

Chapter 52

Data Serialization Routine

Overview of Data Serialization

Data serialization is the process of converting complex internal binary data structures into a linear, sequential byte stream. This transformation is essential for enabling persistent storage and facilitating data transmission over communication channels. In the context of computer systems, internal data structures are often represented in memory in a non-contiguous or platform-specific manner. The serialization process imposes an explicit ordering on these data structures, thereby eliminating ambiguities arising from memory layout variations. The serialized output is constructed as a contiguous sequence of bytes, each of which occupies a well-defined position in the overall data stream. This method ensures that a faithful representation of the internal state can be reconstructed when the byte stream is parsed by a corresponding deserialization routine.

Internal Binary Data Structures

Internal binary data structures are designed to optimize in-memory efficiency and processor cache utilization. These data structures, which may include arrays, records, trees, and graphs, are typically tailored to the architecture-specific memory alignment and padding conventions. For instance, a data structure that encapsulates multiple fields of differing sizes may include compiler-inserted padding bytes to satisfy native alignment requirements. Let S denote the binary representation of a data structure in memory and $|S|$ represent its size in bytes. The intrinsic organization of S is based on the order and types of individual fields, with each field possibly subject to architecture-dependent ordering. Serialization requires a meticulous extraction of each constituent field of S in a predetermined order, ensuring that the transformation from the in-memory format to the serialized sequence is both reversible and independent of the system's endianness and alignment particulars.

Methodology for Sequential Conversion

The conversion of internal binary data structures into a sequential byte stream encompasses several methodical stages. Initially, the serialization routine identifies the boundaries of each data field within the structure. Let $F_1, F_2, \ldots, F_k$ denote the constituent fields of a structure such that the original binary layout can be expressed as

$$S = F_1 \parallel F_2 \parallel \cdots \parallel F_k,$$

where the symbol $\parallel$ signifies the concatenation of field representations. The serialization mechanism proceeds by extracting each field F_i in sequence and appending its byte representation to the output stream. This process is typically implemented recursively for fields that themselves possess internal structures. For structures containing dynamically allocated components or self-referential links, additional metadata—such as size descriptors or identifier tags—may be incorporated to facilitate accurate deserialization. The systematic conversion of each F_i into a corresponding segment of the byte stream ensures that the complete internal state is replicated in a format that is inherently sequential and suitable for storage or transmission.

Byte Ordering and Alignment Considerations

A critical consideration in the serialization process is the treatment of byte ordering and data alignment. Different hardware architectures may employ varying endianness conventions, with some representing multi-byte data in little-endian order and others in big-endian order. Without appropriate handling, a byte stream generated on one platform may be misinterpreted when deserialized on a platform with an alternative byte ordering. To achieve cross-platform compatibility, serialization routines must either standardize on a canonical byte order or embed sufficient metadata within the serialized stream to indicate the byte order used. Moreover, alignment requirements intrinsic to the data types must be addressed. Internal representations often include implicit padding to meet alignment criteria; such padding bytes may need to be explicitly managed, either by omitting them from the serialized stream or by including well-defined placeholders to preserve field boundaries. Let B denote the canonical byte stream, which is produced by reordering the bytes of each multi-byte field as necessary:

$$B = \text{Serialize}(F_1, F_2, \ldots, F_k).$$

Ensuring that B conforms to a predetermined ordering and alignment specification is indispensable for the reliable reconstruction of original data structures.

Data Integrity and Verification Mechanisms

Guaranteeing data integrity during serialization is paramount, particularly when the byte stream is destined for storage or long-distance transmission. Mechanisms for verifying the completeness and correctness of the serialized output are typically integrated into the serialization routine. Such mechanisms may include the insertion of header information delineating the total byte stream length, field-specific size markers, and checksums or cyclic redundancy checks (CRC). The inclusion of a checksum computed over the serialized data, denoted by χ, can serve as an error-detection measure:

$$\chi = \text{Checksum}(B),$$

where B is the finalized byte stream. This checksum is appended to the stream and subsequently used during deserialization to validate the integrity of the transferred data. Additionally, explicit markers or type identifiers embedded within the byte stream facilitate the detection of inconsistencies between the expected and actual data layouts. The rigorous application of such verification mechanisms ensures that any anomalies introduced during serialization, transmission, or storage are reliably identified, thereby maintaining the robustness of the data communication system.

x64 Assembly Code Snippet

```
; Data Serialization Routine in x64 Assembly
; --------------------------------------------------
; This routine demonstrates the serialization of an example
↪   structure S
; into a contiguous byte stream B, based on the equation:
;
;    B = Serialize(F1 || F2 || F3)
;
; It also calculates a simple checksum  over B, defined as:
;
;    = Checksum(B)
;
; Structure S Layout (total 14 bytes):
;    Offset 0: Field1 (F1) - a 4-byte integer
;    Offset 4: Field2 (F2) - an 8-byte integer
;    Offset 12: Field3 (F3) - a 2-byte integer
;
; The routine performs the following operations:
;    1. Extracts each field from S in memory.
;    2. Converts multi-byte fields to a canonical big-endian byte
↪   order
;       using the BSWAP (or manual rotation) instruction.
;    3. Serializes F1, F2, and F3 into a contiguous output buffer.
;    4. Computes a simple additive checksum over the 14 bytes of
↪   serialized data.
;    5. Appends the 4-byte checksum to the output stream.
;
; Input:
;    rdi: pointer to structure S (in-memory layout as described)
;    rsi: pointer to output buffer where the serialized byte stream
↪   will be stored
;
; Output:
;    The output buffer will contain 18 bytes:
;       - The first 14 bytes: serialized fields F1, F2, and F3
;       - The following 4 bytes: the checksum value computed over the
↪   14 bytes
;
; Assemble with an x64 assembler that supports Intel syntax.
;
; Global Entry Point for this routine
global SerializeData

SerializeData:
```

```asm
; --- Serialize Field1 (4 bytes) ---
; Load Field1 from S, located at offset 0
mov eax, dword [rdi]        ; eax = Field1
; Convert Field1 to canonical big-endian byte order
bswap eax                   ; Swap byte order of 32-bit value
; Store serialized Field1 into output buffer at offset 0
mov dword [rsi], eax


; --- Serialize Field2 (8 bytes) ---
; Load Field2 from S, located at offset 4
mov rax, qword [rdi + 4]    ; rax = Field2
; Convert Field2 to canonical big-endian byte order
bswap rax                   ; Swap byte order of 64-bit value
; Store serialized Field2 into output buffer at offset 4
mov qword [rsi + 4], rax


; --- Serialize Field3 (2 bytes) ---
; Load Field3 from S, located at offset 12
movzx ecx, word [rdi + 12]  ; ecx = Field3 (zero-extended)
; For a 16-bit value, manually swap the two bytes:
rol cx, 8                   ; Rotate left 8 bits to swap the byte
↪   order
; Store serialized Field3 into output buffer at offset 12
mov word [rsi + 12], cx


; At this point, 14 bytes (F1 || F2 || F3) have been stored in
↪   the buffer.
; ----------------------------------------------------
; Compute the checksum over these 14 bytes.
; Here, we compute a simple additive checksum:
;   For each byte in the 14-byte sequence, add its value to the
↪   accumulator.

mov rcx, 14                 ; rcx = number of bytes to process
mov rdx, rsi                ; rdx points to the beginning of the
↪   serialized data
xor eax, eax                ; Clear eax, will be used as checksum
↪   accumulator

checksum_loop:
cmp rcx, 0                  ; Have we processed all 14 bytes?
je checksum_done
movzx ebx, byte [rdx]       ; Load the next byte (zero-extend to
↪   32 bits)
add eax, ebx                ; Accumulate the checksum
inc rdx                     ; Move pointer to the next byte
dec rcx                     ; Decrement the byte counter
jmp checksum_loop

checksum_done:
; --- Append the Checksum ---
; The computed checksum in eax is appended immediately after the
↪   14 bytes,
```

```asm
; at offset 14 in the output buffer.
mov dword [rsi + 14], eax

; Total size of the output buffer now is 14 bytes (data) + 4
↪ bytes (checksum) = 18 bytes.
ret
```

Chapter 53

Implementing Base64 Encoding

Fundamentals of Base64 Encoding

The Base64 encoding scheme is an established method for converting binary data into a textual representation that is both compact and compatible with transmission protocols designed for text. In this transformation, the binary input is interpreted as a stream of bits that is segmented into groups of 24 bits. Each 24-bit block is subsequently divided into four groups of 6 bits, where each 6-bit group represents a number in the range of 0 to 63. This numerical value is then mapped, via a predetermined lookup table, to a corresponding character in the Base64 alphabet. The process ensures that every group of 6 bits is uniquely translated into a textual symbol, thereby permitting a deterministic and reversible conversion between binary and text.

Mapping Strategy for the Base64 Alphabet

The mapping from a 6-bit binary value to its associated character is governed by a canonical Base64 alphabet consisting of 64 distinct symbols. This alphabet is designed such that each value, denoted by an integer i where $0 \le i \le 63$, is assigned to a specific character.

Mathematically, the conversion can be expressed as

$$c = \text{Alphabet}[i],$$

where c is the resulting character and Alphabet represents the lookup table for Base64 encoding. The selection of the alphabet ensures compatibility with various text-based transmission standards, as it is composed exclusively of alphanumeric characters and a small subset of punctuation symbols that are universally recognizable in text processing environments.

Segmentation and Bit-level Processing

The conversion algorithm operates by first treating the input binary data as a continuous sequence of bits. This sequence is partitioned into blocks of 24 bits each. Given an input stream with length not necessarily a multiple of 24 bits, the final block may contain fewer than 24 bits. In such cases, the missing bits are assumed to be zero, which ensures that the block is correctly padded to reach the required 24-bit length before processing. Following segmentation, each 24-bit block is subdivided into four segments, each consisting of 6 bits. The bit-level manipulation involved in this process guarantees that each subset is accurately isolated and prepared for mapping by means of bit-wise shifting and masking operations. This methodical extraction of 6-bit groups is fundamental to preserving the integrity of the original binary data during the transformation.

Padding and Alignment Considerations

When the length of the binary data is not an exact multiple of 3 bytes (or 24 bits), the encoding process must incorporate a mechanism to signal the absence of data in the final block. If the number of remaining bytes is either 1 or 2, then an appropriate number of padding characters is added to the resulting encoded string. Specifically, if only 1 byte remains, then two padding characters are appended; if 2 bytes remain, a single padding character is added. Symbolically, the padding operation can be understood by considering the length L of the binary input and computing $n = L \bmod 3$. The final output is augmented with $3 - n$ instances of the padding character, conventionally denoted by the symbol "=".

This approach ensures that the length of the Base64 encoded output is a multiple of 4, a property that is essential for the accurate reversal of the encoding process.

Implications for Text-based Data Transmission

The transformation of binary data into a Base64 encoded string supports reliable text-based transmission across systems that may impose restrictions on permissible characters. By encapsulating raw binary information within a framework of printable characters, the encoding process mitigates issues related to data corruption and misinterpretation. The resulting textual representation is particularly valuable in environments where the transport medium is optimized for character data, ensuring that the original binary content can be faithfully reconstructed by an appropriate decoding mechanism. The design choices inherent in the Base64 encoding scheme address both the needs of data integrity and the constraints imposed by heterogeneous communication protocols, thereby establishing it as a versatile solution for modern data transmission challenges.

x64 Assembly Code Snippet

```
global base64_encode

section .data
base64_table: db
  ↪ "ABCDEFGHIJKLMNOPQRSTUVWXYZabcdefghijklmnopqrstuvwxyz0123456789+/"
padding_char: db '='

section .text
;--------------------------------
; Function: base64_encode
; Description:
;   Encodes binary data into its Base64 text representation.
;
; Inputs:
;   RDI - pointer to the input data buffer
;   RSI - length of the input data in bytes
;   RDX - pointer to the output buffer (must be large enough to hold
  ↪   the result)
;
```

```
; Registers used (volatile): RAX, RBX, RCX, RDX, RDI, R8, R9, R10,
↪ R11, R12, R13, R14
; Calling Convention: System V AMD64
;-------------------------------
base64_encode:
    push rbp
    mov rbp, rsp

    ; r8 will hold the number of remaining input bytes.
    mov r8, rsi

;---------------------------
; Process full 3-byte groups
;---------------------------
.full_loop:
    cmp r8, 3
    jl .remaining

    ; Load 3 bytes from the input and combine them into a 24-bit
    ↪ triple:
    ;    triple = (byte0 << 16) | (byte1 << 8) | byte2
    movzx eax, byte [rdi]         ; Load first byte into EAX.
    movzx ecx, byte [rdi+1]       ; Load second byte into ECX.
    movzx edx, byte [rdi+2]       ; Load third byte into EDX.
    shl eax, 16                   ; Shift first byte to bits 16-23.
    movzx ebx, cl                 ; Move second byte into EBX.
    shl ebx, 8                    ; Shift second byte to bits 8-15.
    or eax, ebx                   ; Combine first and second bytes.
    movzx ebx, dl                 ; Load third byte into EBX.
    or eax, ebx                   ; Triple now stored in EAX.

    ; Break the 24-bit triple into four 6-bit groups.
    ; Group 0: bits 23-18, Group 1: bits 17-12,
    ; Group 2: bits 11-6, Group 3: bits 5-0.
    mov r11d, eax                 ; Copy triple to r11d.
    shr r11d, 18                  ; Group0 = triple >> 18.
    and r11d, 0x3F                ; Mask lower 6 bits.

    mov r12d, eax
    shr r12d, 12                  ; Group1 = triple >> 12.
    and r12d, 0x3F

    mov r13d, eax
    shr r13d, 6                   ; Group2 = triple >> 6.
    and r13d, 0x3F

    mov r14d, eax
    and r14d, 0x3F                ; Group3 = triple & 0x3F.

    ; Lookup the corresponding Base64 characters using the table.
    lea r10, [rel base64_table]

    mov al, byte [r10 + r11d]
```

```
    mov [rdx], al
    inc rdx

    mov al, byte [r10 + r12d]
    mov [rdx], al
    inc rdx

    mov al, byte [r10 + r13d]
    mov [rdx], al
    inc rdx

    mov al, byte [r10 + r14d]
    mov [rdx], al
    inc rdx

    ; Move to the next 3-byte block.
    add rdi, 3
    sub r8, 3
    jmp .full_loop

;---------------------------
; Process remaining 1 or 2 bytes
;---------------------------
.remaining:
    cmp r8, 0
    je .done

    ; Clear EAX to build the final triple.
    xor eax, eax

    ; For remaining bytes we need to fill the missing bits with
    ↪ zeros.
    cmp r8, 2
    jb .process_one_byte

    ; --- Case: 2 remaining bytes ---
    ; Build triple = (byte0 << 16) | (byte1 << 8)
    movzx eax, byte [rdi]          ; Load the first remaining byte.
    shl eax, 16                    ; Shift it to bits 16-23.
    movzx ebx, byte [rdi+1]        ; Load the second remaining byte.
    shl ebx, 8                     ; Shift it to bits 8-15.
    or eax, ebx                    ; Combine to form the 24-bit triple.

    ; Extract three 6-bit groups (fourth group will be padded).
    mov r11d, eax
    shr r11d, 18                   ; Group0.
    and r11d, 0x3F

    mov r12d, eax
    shr r12d, 12                   ; Group1.
    and r12d, 0x3F

    mov r13d, eax
```

289

```asm
        shr r13d, 6                     ; Group2.
        and r13d, 0x3F

        lea r10, [rel base64_table]
        mov al, byte [r10 + r11d]
        mov [rdx], al
        inc rdx

        mov al, byte [r10 + r12d]
        mov [rdx], al
        inc rdx

        mov al, byte [r10 + r13d]
        mov [rdx], al
        inc rdx

        ; Add one padding character '=' for the missing fourth output.
        mov al, byte [rel padding_char]
        mov [rdx], al
        inc rdx
        jmp .done

.process_one_byte:
        ; --- Case: 1 remaining byte ---
        ; Build triple = (byte0 << 16)
        movzx eax, byte [rdi]
        shl eax, 16

        mov r11d, eax
        shr r11d, 18                    ; Group0.
        and r11d, 0x3F

        mov r12d, eax
        shr r12d, 12                    ; Group1.
        and r12d, 0x3F

        lea r10, [rel base64_table]
        mov al, byte [r10 + r11d]
        mov [rdx], al
        inc rdx

        mov al, byte [r10 + r12d]
        mov [rdx], al
        inc rdx

        ; Add two padding characters '=' for the missing outputs.
        mov al, byte [rel padding_char]
        mov [rdx], al
        inc rdx

        mov al, byte [rel padding_char]
        mov [rdx], al
        inc rdx
```

```
.done:
    pop rbp
    ret
```

Chapter 54

Implementing Base64 Decoding

Foundations and Rationale of Decoding

The process of Base64 decoding is defined as the precise inversion of the Base64 encoding mechanism. In this transformation, an input sequence consisting solely of printable characters is mapped back to its original binary form. The decoding process exploits the deterministic nature of the encoding scheme by interpreting each character as a 6-bit numerical value. This reconstruction proceeds by aggregating groups of four such characters into a composite 24-bit block that is subsequently partitioned into three original bytes. The inherent reversibility of this transformation is predicated on the establishment and preservation of a canonical mapping between each character in the Base64 alphabet and its corresponding integer value in the range 0 to 63.

Character-to-Index Mapping

A critical element of the decoding procedure is the conversion of each encoded character to its corresponding integer value. Let each character, denoted as c, in the Base64 alphabet be associated with an index i, where this index satisfies $0 \leq i \leq 63$. This mapping is formally expressed by the relation

$$i = \text{Index}(c),$$

which instantiates a bijective link between the character set and the set of 6-bit numerical values. The integrity of the overall decoding process is maintained by ensuring that every character is unequivocally mapped back to its original numerical representation.

Reconstitution of Binary Data from Bit Groups

Once the individual 6-bit values have been obtained, the subsequent step involves the assembly of these bits into a coherent binary sequence. The decoding algorithm processes the input in clusters of four characters, each cluster yielding four numerical values B_0, B_1, B_2, and B_3. These values are combined to form a 24-bit composite number, T, via the operation

$$T = (B_0 \ll 18) \vee (B_1 \ll 12) \vee (B_2 \ll 6) \vee B_3,$$

where $\ll$ denotes the left-shift operator and $\vee$ represents the bitwise OR operation. This 24-bit number is then segmented into three individual 8-bit bytes, corresponding to the original data, by employing both right-shift and bit masking operations. The extraction process ensures that the positional significance of each byte is correctly restored.

Processing of Padding Characters

Due to the nature of Base64 encoding, it is common for the final block of the encoded data to be padded with one or more instances of the padding character, conventionally represented by the symbol =. The use of padding arises when the total number of binary input bytes is not an integer multiple of three, resulting in a final encoded block comprising fewer than four meaningful characters. In the reconstruction phase, the presence of one or two padding characters indicates that the final 24-bit block does not contain a complete set of bits derived from the original data. The padding characters signal the decoder to disregard the extraneous zero bits that were introduced during the encoding process. Consequently, in scenarios where padding is detected, only the appropriate subset of the 24-bit block is converted back to produce the original one or two bytes of data, ensuring that no superfluous bits are incorporated.

Detailed Bit-Level Reconstruction

The meticulous reassembly of binary data from the Base64 encoded representation is underpinned by precise bit-level operations. Consider a quartet of Base64 symbols, each converted to its corresponding 6-bit integer. The concatenation of these values into a singular 24-bit word is performed by strategically positioning each 6-bit block at designated bit offsets. Explicitly, the most significant 6 bits, extracted from the first character, are shifted left by 18 positions; this is followed by the next block shifted left by 12, then the subsequent block shifted left by 6, and finally, the least significant block is retained without shift. The composite 24-bit integer, T, embodies the entirety of the four segments. Subsequent utilization of bitwise masking operations with the mask $0xFF$ enables the extraction of each of the three original bytes. This analytical procedure emphasizes the importance of bit alignment and arithmetic in achieving an exact reversal of the encoding process, thereby restoring the original binary sequence with high fidelity.

x64 Assembly Code Snippet

```
; x64 Assembly Code for Base64 Decoding of a 4-Character Block
; This routine decodes four Base64 characters into a 24-bit
↪   composite (up to 3 bytes)
; and handles padding characters ('=') according to the Base64
↪   standard.
;
; Input:
;   RDI - pointer to a 4-byte encoded Base64 block
;   RSI - pointer to output buffer (must have space for 3 bytes)
;
; Output:
;   The decoded bytes are stored at the memory location pointed by
↪   RSI.
;   RAX returns the number of decoded bytes (3 bytes with no
↪   padding, 2 if one '=' and 1 if "==").
;
; Registers used: RAX, RBX, RCX, RDX, R8, R9, R10, R11, R12.
; R12 is used to count padding characters.
;
; The algorithm follows these steps:
; 1. Load the 4 input characters.
; 2. Convert each character into its corresponding 6-bit value
;    using a mapping routine that distinguishes between 'A'-'Z',
↪   'a'-'z',
;      '0'-'9', '+', '/', and '=' (padding).
```

```
;   3. Combine the four 6-bit values into a 24-bit integer according
↪   to:
;           T = (B0 << 18) | (B1 << 12) | (B2 << 6) | B3
;   4. Extract three output bytes from T.
;   5. Adjust the output length based on the number of padding
↪   characters.
;
; Assemble with your favorite x64 assembler (NASM/YASM).
;

section .text
    global base64_decode_block

;---------------------------------------------------------------------
; Function: base64_decode_block
; Description:
;   Decodes a block of 4 Base64 characters pointed to by RDI and
↪   stores
;   the resulting bytes (1 to 3 bytes) at the location pointed to by
↪   RSI.
;   Returns the count of decoded bytes in RAX.
;---------------------------------------------------------------------
base64_decode_block:
    push    r12             ; Save r12 (used for padding count)
    push    rbx             ; Save rbx (used as temporary storage)
    xor     r12, r12        ; Initialize pad_count (r12) to 0

    ;--- Load 4 Base64 characters from the input block ---
    movzx   eax, byte [rdi]         ; Load first character into EAX
    movzx   ebx, byte [rdi + 1]     ; Load second character into EBX
    movzx   ecx, byte [rdi + 2]     ; Load third character into ECX
    movzx   edx, byte [rdi + 3]     ; Load fourth character into EDX

    ;--- Convert each character to its corresponding 6-bit value ---
    ; Process first character: result will be in r8b
    mov     r8d, eax                ; Copy char0 into R8D
    call    base64_char_to_val      ; R8b = mapped 6-bit value (or 0
↪   if '=')

    ; Process second character: result in r9b
    mov     r9d, ebx                ; Copy char1 into R9D
    call    base64_char_to_val

    ; Process third character: result in r10b
    mov     r10d, ecx               ; Copy char2 into R10D
    call    base64_char_to_val

    ; Process fourth character: result in r11b
    mov     r11d, edx               ; Copy char3 into R11D
    call    base64_char_to_val

    ;--- Compute the 24-bit composite value T ---
    ; T = (B0 << 18) | (B1 << 12) | (B2 << 6) | B3
    movzx   rax, r8b                ; RAX = B0
```

295

```
shl     rax, 18              ; B0 shifted left by 18
movzx   rbx, r9b             ; RBX = B1
shl     rbx, 12              ; B1 shifted left by 12
or      rax, rbx             ; Combine into RAX

movzx   rcx, r10b            ; RCX = B2
shl     rcx, 6               ; B2 shifted left by 6
or      rax, rcx             ; Combine into RAX

movzx   rbx, r11b            ; RBX = B3 (no shift)
or      rax, rbx             ; Final composite 24-bit value in
↪    RAX

; Save composite value for output extraction
mov     rbx, rax

;--- Extract output bytes from the 24-bit composite ---
; Note: The extraction uses bit shifts and implicit 0xFF
↪    masking.
; First output byte: bits [23:16]
mov     byte [rsi], byte (rbx >> 16)
; Second output byte: bits [15:8]
mov     byte [rsi + 1], byte (rbx >> 8)
; Third output byte: bits [7:0]
mov     byte [rsi + 2], byte rbx

;--- Determine actual number of bytes to output based on padding
↪    ---
; No padding (r12==0): output 3 bytes.
; One '=' (r12==1): output 2 bytes.
; Two '=' (r12==2): output 1 byte.
cmp     r12, 0
je      .store3
cmp     r12, 1
je      .store2
cmp     r12, 2
je      .store1

.store3:
mov     rax, 3
jmp     .decode_done
.store2:
mov     rax, 2
jmp     .decode_done
.store1:
mov     rax, 1
jmp     .decode_done

.decode_done:
pop     rbx
pop     r12
ret
```

```asm
;----------------------------------------------------------------------
; Subroutine: base64_char_to_val
; Description:
;   Maps a Base64 character (in the low 8 bits of the appropriate
; ↪  register)
;   to its corresponding 6-bit value. The conversion covers:
;       'A'-'Z'  => values 0 to 25
;       'a'-'z'  => values 26 to 51
;       '0'-'9'  => values 52 to 61
;       '+'      => value 62
;       '/'      => value 63
;   If the character is '=' (padding), it returns 0 and increments
; ↪  r12.
;
; The calling convention assumes that the input character is in AL
; ↪  of the
; register used by the caller (for instance, R8b, R9b, etc.) and
; ↪  that
; the result is returned in that same 8-bit portion.
;----------------------------------------------------------------------
base64_char_to_val:
    ; Check if character equals '=' (padding)
    cmp     al, '='
    je      .handle_pad

    ; Check for uppercase letters: 'A' to 'Z'
    cmp     al, 'A'
    jl      .check_lower
    cmp     al, 'Z'
    jg      .check_lower
    sub     al, 'A'
    ret

.check_lower:
    ; Check for lowercase letters: 'a' to 'z'
    cmp     al, 'a'
    jl      .check_digit
    cmp     al, 'z'
    jg      .check_digit
    sub     al, 'a'
    add     al, 26
    ret

.check_digit:
    ; Check for digits: '0' to '9'
    cmp     al, '0'
    jl      .check_special
    cmp     al, '9'
    jg      .check_special
    sub     al, '0'
    add     al, 52
    ret
```

```
.check_special:
    ; Check for the special character '+'
    cmp     al, '+'
    je      .plus_case
    ; Check for the special character '/'
    cmp     al, '/'
    je      .slash_case
    ; For any non-valid character, set result to 0.
    mov     al, 0
    ret

.plus_case:
    mov     al, 62
    ret

.slash_case:
    mov     al, 63
    ret

.handle_pad:
    ; For padding character '=', return 0 and increment the padding
    ↪ counter in R12.
    mov     al, 0
    inc     r12
    ret
```

Chapter 55

Performing Bit Masking for Flag Checks

Conceptual Underpinnings of Bit Masks in Register Operations

A bit mask is a binary pattern specifically designed to isolate or manipulate selected bits within a register. In an n-bit register, a bit mask can be mathematically represented by

$$M = \sum_{i=0}^{n-1} m_i 2^i,$$

where each coefficient m_i takes a value from the set $\{0, 1\}$, and the index i identifies the bit position. This formulation facilitates the extraction or modification of individual bits by applying logical operations directly on the binary representation of the register. The geometric arrangement of set and cleared bits in M ensures that specific flag positions are targeted in subsequent operations.

Formulation of Bit Masks for Flag Manipulation

In the context of managing conditional flags, the construction of a bit mask is predicated on the precise localization of the flag within the register. When a flag is located at the kth bit position, where $0 \leq k < n$, an elementary mask is constructed as

$$M_k = 2^k.$$

This simple mask consists of a single bit set to 1 at the designated position and zero elsewhere, thereby allowing unambiguous identification of that flag. More elaborate masks may be defined to simultaneously target multiple flags by computing the bitwise OR of individual masks, resulting in a composite mask

$$M = \sum_{j \in S} 2^j,$$

where S is the set of bit positions corresponding to the flags of interest. The systematic construction of these masks underpins the deterministic manipulation of register values through bitwise operations.

Bitwise Operations for Setting, Clearing, and Testing Flags

Three fundamental bitwise operations are used in conjunction with masks to perform flag manipulations: bitwise OR, bitwise AND, and bitwise NOT. To activate a specific flag in a register R, the mask M_k is applied via the bitwise OR operation,

$$R \leftarrow R \vee M_k.$$

This operation guarantees that the designated flag bit is set to 1, regardless of its previous state. Conversely, to clear a flag, the inverse of the mask, denoted by $\neg M_k$, is used in a bitwise AND operation,

$$R \leftarrow R \wedge \neg M_k,$$

which ensures that the targeted bit is reset to 0 while leaving the remaining bits unaltered. Testing whether a flag is active is accomplished through the expression

$$(R \wedge M_k) \neq 0.$$

A nonzero result indicates that the flag is set, thereby enabling conditions to be inferred from the current register state through subsequent conditional logic in processing.

Integration of Bit Masks into Conditional Processing

The precise manipulation of bit-level flags via masking is integral to conditional processing in systems programming and computer architecture. By altering register values in a controlled fashion, the state of various system or application-specific flags is maintained in a manner that is both efficient and reliable. Logical operations performed on bit masks adhere to the laws of Boolean algebra, which ensure that the transformations are both predictable and reversible. The composite procedures for setting, clearing, and testing flags underpin a range of conditional constructs, where the output of a bitwise operation directly influences branching decisions in the instruction flow. Such robust manipulation of flags contributes to the efficiency of low-level control mechanisms, thereby optimizing performance in computational routines.

x64 Assembly Code Snippet

```
; This comprehensive x64 Assembly snippet demonstrates the use of
↪    bit masks
; for flag checks, in accordance with the formulas and algorithms
↪    discussed
; in the chapter:
;
;    1. Constructing a bit mask for a single flag:
;          M_k = 2^k
;
;    2. Setting a flag:
;          R <- R OR M_k
;
;    3. Clearing a flag:
;          R <- R AND (NOT M_k)
;
;    4. Testing if a flag is set:
;          (R AND M_k) != 0
;
;    5. Constructing and processing a composite mask for multiple
↪    flags:
;          M = 2^(k1) OR 2^(k2) OR ...
```

```
;
; Assemble this code with NASM and link it on a Linux x64 system:
;    nasm -f elf64 bitmask.asm && ld -o bitmask bitmask.o

global _start

section .text
_start:

    ↪   ;-------------------------------------------------------------------
    ; Example 1: Single Flag Manipulation

    ↪   ;-------------------------------------------------------------------
    ; Use RAX as register R. Begin with RAX = 0.
    mov rax, 0              ; RAX = 0

    ; We want to manipulate the flag at bit position k = 3.
    ; Compute the mask M_k = 2^3.
    mov rcx, 3             ; k = 3
    mov rbx, 1             ; Start with 1
    shl rbx, cl           ; rbx = 1 << 3, so rbx = 8 (mask for bit 3)

    ; Set the flag in RAX using a bitwise OR:
    ; RAX <- RAX OR M_k.
    or rax, rbx            ; Now RAX has bit 3 set (RAX becomes 8).

    ; Test if the flag is set by computing (RAX AND M_k).
    mov rdx, rax           ; Copy RAX into RDX for testing
    and rdx, rbx           ; rdx = RAX AND mask; expected nonzero if
    ↪   flag is set.
    cmp rdx, 0
    jne flag_set           ; If nonzero, the flag is set.

    ; (This branch is not taken in this demo since the flag was just
    ↪   set.)
    jmp continue_single

flag_set:
    ; Since the flag is set, demonstrate clearing the flag:
    ; Clear the flag using RAX <- RAX AND (NOT M_k).
    mov rdx, rbx           ; Copy the mask M_k to RDX
    not rdx                ; rdx now holds NOT M_k
    and rax, rdx           ; Clear bit 3 in RAX

continue_single:
    ; At this point, the flag at bit position 3 in RAX is cleared.


    ↪   ;-------------------------------------------------------------------
    ; Example 2: Composite Flag Manipulation

    ↪   ;-------------------------------------------------------------------
```

```asm
    ; Construct a composite mask for two flags at bit positions k1 =
↪     2 and k2 = 5.
    ; Compute M1 = 2^2 and M2 = 2^5, then combine:
    ;     M = M1 OR M2 = (1 << 2) OR (1 << 5) = 4 OR 32 = 36.
    mov rcx, 2          ; k1 = 2
    mov rdx, 1
    shl rdx, cl         ; rdx = 1 << 2, rdx = 4 (mask for bit 2)

    mov rcx, 5          ; k2 = 5
    mov rsi, 1
    shl rsi, cl         ; rsi = 1 << 5, rsi = 32 (mask for bit 5)

    ; Combine the individual masks to form the composite mask.
    mov r8, rdx         ; r8 = M1
    or r8, rsi          ; r8 = M1 OR M2 = 4 OR 32 = 36

    ; Set the composite flags in RAX.
    or rax, r8          ; RAX <- RAX OR composite mask

    ; Test if both composite flags are set:
    mov r9, rax
    and r9, r8          ; r9 = RAX AND composite mask
    cmp r9, r8
    jne composite_not_set   ; If r9 != composite mask, at least one
↪     flag is not set.

    ; If the composite flags are set, clear them:
    mov r9, r8
    not r9              ; Compute NOT composite mask
    and rax, r9         ; Clear the composite flags in RAX

composite_not_set:

↪   ;-----------------------------------------------------------------
    ; End of Demonstration: Exit Program

↪   ;-----------------------------------------------------------------
    ; Use the Linux exit system call.
    mov rax, 60         ; syscall number for exit
    xor rdi, rdi        ; exit status 0
    syscall
```

303

Chapter 56

CSV String Tokenization

Formal Definition and Structural Properties of CSV Data

A CSV string is defined as a sequence of characters drawn from a finite set Σ, structured such that individual data fields are separated by a designated delimiter, most commonly the comma character. Formally, a CSV string S may be represented as

$$S = f_1, f_2, \ldots, f_n,$$

where each f_i represents a field token. In many implementations, fields that contain embedded delimiters, newline characters, or leading and trailing whitespace are encapsulated in quotation marks, so that a field may alternatively assume the form

$$f_i = {}^{"}\alpha{}^{"},$$

with $\alpha \in \Sigma^*$ representing an arbitrary string of characters. This formal structure encapsulates both the simplicity and the potential complexity inherent in data represented in CSV format.

Theoretical Foundations for Data Tokenization

Tokenization of a CSV string is conceptually modeled by methods from formal language theory. The process can be analyzed using both deterministic finite automata (DFA) and context-free grammar specifications. Given the input string S, the tokenization routine sequentially processes each character by transitioning between states that represent different parsing contexts. For example, the automaton includes states corresponding to unquoted and quoted fields. In the unquoted state, a delimiter character, such as the comma, is interpreted as a token separator, while in the quoted state the same character is treated as part of the field content. The design of the automaton ensures that each field is accurately recognized according to the rules of the CSV formalism.

Algorithmic Strategies for Token Extraction

The extraction of tokens from a CSV string relies on a systematic scanning procedure that differentiates field content from structural delimiters. During a left-to-right traversal of the input, the algorithm maintains a working buffer in which characters of the current token are accumulated. When a delimiter is encountered in the appropriate state, the algorithm finalizes the current token and commences accumulation for the next. Mathematically, if the CSV string is represented as

$$S = c_1 c_2 \ldots c_k,$$

then the tokenization function $\tau : \Sigma^* \to T$, where $T = [t_1, t_2, \ldots, t_m]$, is defined by the sequential partitioning of S into substrings t_i based on the occurrence of delimiter symbols. The procedure is efficient, owing to its single-pass approach and minimal auxiliary storage, and its correctness is predicated upon the strict enforcement of delimiter and encapsulation semantics.

Management of Quoted Fields and Embedded Delimiters

A significant aspect of CSV tokenization involves the treatment of fields enclosed in quotation marks. Quoted fields are designed to permit the inclusion of characters that would otherwise be interpreted as field separators. When an opening quotation mark is encountered, the parser transitions into a quoted state, wherein all subsequent characters are treated as literal components of the field until a corresponding closing quotation mark is identified. Particular attention must be given to sequences of quotation marks within a quoted field; for instance, a pair of successive quotation marks is conventionally interpreted as an encoded quotation mark within the field content. This is mathematically captured by the transformation rule

$$\texttt{""} \rightarrow \texttt{"},$$

which ensures that embedded quotation marks are duly represented as a single character within the final token. Such rigor in handling quoted fields precludes premature token termination due to the inadvertent detection of delimiters and maintains the semantic integrity of the extracted tokens.

Implications for Subsequent Data Processing

Once a CSV string has been partitioned, the resulting sequence of tokens

$$T = [t_1, t_2, \ldots, t_m]$$

constitutes a structured representation of the original data. The exact preservation of field boundaries and the appropriate interpretation of encapsulated content underpin the dependability of subsequent computational processes, such as data validation, transformation, and persistence. The comprehensive tokenization of the CSV string ensures that inherent ambiguities arising from nonstandard formatting or escape sequences are resolved in a consistent manner. This rigorous preprocessing step serves as the foundation for any further analysis that seeks to leverage the structured nature of CSV data.

x64 Assembly Code Snippet

```
; Comprehensive CSV Tokenization Example in x64 Assembly (NASM)
; This program tokenizes a CSV string with support for quoted
↪   fields,
; embedded delimiters, and escaped quotation marks. Each extracted
↪   token
; is printed to the console using the C library function printf.

global main
extern printf

section .data
    ; Sample CSV input string with various cases:
    ; - Unquoted field: "field1"
    ; - Quoted field with an embedded comma: "field,2"
    ; - Quoted field with escaped quotes: "field with ""escaped
    ↪   quotes"""
    ; - Unquoted field: "field4"
    csv_input    db "field1,"field,2","field with ""escaped
    ↪   quotes""",field4", 0
    ; Format string for printing tokens using printf.
    token_format db "Token: %s", 10, 0

section .bss
    ; Buffer to accumulate characters for the current token.
    tokenBuffer resb 256

section .text

main:
    ; Initialize pointer to CSV input in RSI.
    mov rsi, csv_input

process_next_token:
    ; Check for end of CSV string (null terminator).
    mov al, byte [rsi]
    cmp al, 0
    je done_processing

    ; Set RDI to the beginning of the token buffer for accumulation.
    mov rdi, tokenBuffer

    ; If the current character is a double quote, process as a
    ↪   quoted field.
    cmp al, '"'
    je process_quoted_field

    ; Otherwise, process as an unquoted field.
    jmp process_unquoted_field

;-------------------------------------------------------------
```

```
; Process a field that starts with a quotation mark.
; Handles escaped quotes by converting double double-quotes
; into a single quote character.
;-----------------------------------------------------------
process_quoted_field:
    ; Skip the opening quotation mark.
    inc rsi

quote_loop:
    mov al, byte [rsi]
    cmp al, 0
    je finish_token   ; End-of-string reached unexpectedly; finish
    ↪   token.
    ; Check if current character is a quotation mark.
    cmp al, '"'
    jne copy_quoted_char

    ; At a quote, check for an escaped quote by examining the next
    ↪   character.
    mov bl, byte [rsi+1]
    cmp bl, '"'
    je  escaped_quote

    ; If not an escaped quote, this is the closing quote.
    inc rsi        ; Skip the closing quote.
    jmp finish_token_field

escaped_quote:
    ; An escaped quote: output a single quote into tokenBuffer.
    mov al, '"'
    stosb          ; Store AL at [RDI] and increment RDI.
    add rsi, 2     ; Skip both quote characters.
    jmp quote_loop

copy_quoted_char:
    ; Copy the current character from the CSV input to tokenBuffer.
    stosb          ; Stores AL (already in register from mov) and
    ↪   increments RDI.
    inc rsi
    jmp quote_loop

finish_token_field:
    ; After a closing quote, skip optional whitespace or a
    ↪   delimiter.
    mov al, byte [rsi]
    cmp al, ','
    je skip_delimiter
    ; Skip any trailing spaces following the quoted field.
skip_spaces_after_quote:
    cmp al, ' '
    jne finish_token
    inc rsi
    mov al, byte [rsi]
```

```nasm
    jmp skip_spaces_after_quote

skip_delimiter:
    inc rsi      ; Skip the comma delimiter.
    jmp finish_token


;------------------------------------------------------------
; Process an unquoted field.
; Characters are copied until a comma delimiter or null terminator
↪  is reached.
;------------------------------------------------------------
process_unquoted_field:
unquoted_loop:
    mov al, byte [rsi]
    cmp al, 0
    je finish_token
    cmp al, ','
    je finish_token_delim
    ; Copy the character to tokenBuffer.
    mov al, byte [rsi]
    mov byte [rdi], al
    inc rsi
    inc rdi
    jmp unquoted_loop

finish_token_delim:
    ; Skip the comma delimiter in the input.
    inc rsi


;------------------------------------------------------------
; Finalize the token by null-terminating the tokenBuffer,
; then print the token using the printf function.
;------------------------------------------------------------
finish_token:
    ; Null-terminate the current token.
    mov byte [rdi], 0

    ; Prepare parameters for printf:
    ; RDI = pointer to the format string, RSI = pointer to the
    ↪  token.
    lea rdi, [token_format]
    lea rsi, [tokenBuffer]
    xor rax, rax     ; Clear RAX as required for variadic function
    ↪  calls.
    call printf

    ; Process next token.
    jmp process_next_token

done_processing:
    ; Exit the program gracefully (return 0 to the caller).
    mov rax, 0
```

ret

Chapter 57

Computing Basic Statistics on Data

Mathematical Framework and Notation

Let $A = \{a_1, a_2, \ldots, a_n\}$ denote an ordered finite set of numerical values with each $a_i \in \mathbb{R}$ and $n \in \mathbb{N}$ representing the number of elements in A. The elements are indexed in a natural order, thereby preserving the inherent sequence of data. Such a representation facilitates the definition and computation of fundamental statistical measures. The structure of the data set is preserved throughout subsequent operations by rigorously defining arithmetic operations over the elements of A, thereby creating a foundation for quantitative analysis.

Sum and Arithmetic Mean Computation

The first statistical measure is the sum, denoted by S, which is computed as

$$S = \sum_{i=1}^{n} a_i.$$

This computation involves a sequential accumulation of the elements of A, providing an aggregate quantity that reflects the total magnitude of the data set.

The arithmetic mean, symbolized by μ, offers a measure of central tendency and is derived from the calculated sum. The arithmetic mean is defined by the relation

$$\mu = \frac{1}{n} \sum_{i=1}^{n} a_i,$$

which may alternately be expressed as

$$\mu = \frac{S}{n}.$$

The mean encapsulates the balancing point of the distribution of values in A, serving as an essential reference for further statistical computations. The derivation underscores the inherent linearity of the summation process, aligning the index-based accumulation with a multiplicative normalizing factor.

Variance Computation

Variance, denoted by σ^2, is a statistical parameter that quantifies the dispersion of the elements of A relative to their arithmetic mean. Formally, the variance is defined as the average of the squared differences between each element and the mean:

$$\sigma^2 = \frac{1}{n} \sum_{i=1}^{n} (a_i - \mu)^2.$$

The process begins with the computation of the arithmetic mean μ. Subsequently, for each element a_i, the deviation $(a_i - \mu)$ is determined, squared, and then the aggregates of these squared deviations are summed. Dividing the total by the number of elements n yields the variance. This measure provides a rigorous quantification of the spread inherent in the data set, with higher variance denoting a wider distribution of values from the central tendency. The squaring of the deviations ensures that all contributions are non-negative and that extreme deviations exert a proportionally greater influence on the overall metric.

x64 Assembly Code Snippet

```
; x64 Assembly program to compute the sum, arithmetic mean, and
↪    variance
; of an array of double precision numbers.
```

312

```nasm
; Assemble with: nasm -felf64 stats.asm && ld -o stats stats.o

section .data
    ; Data array A with 5 double precision values (example values)
    arr:        dq 4.0, 7.0, 1.5, 3.0, 9.0

    ; Floating point representation of n (number of elements = 5)
    n_float:  dq 5.0

    ; Memory locations to hold computed results
    sum:        dq 0.0        ; Sum S = a1 + a2 + ... + an
    mean:       dq 0.0        ; Arithmetic mean μ = S/n
    variance: dq 0.0          ; Variance ² = (1/n) * (a_i - μ)²

    ; Temporary storage for variance accumulation and intermediate
    ↪ results
    var_sum:  dq 0.0          ; Accumulator for the sum of squared
    ↪ differences
    tmp:        dq 0.0        ; Temporary storage for a squared
    ↪ difference

%define n 5                   ; Define constant n = 5

section .text
    global _start

_start:
    ; Initialize the FPU
    finit

    ;-------------------------------
    ; Compute the Sum S = (a_i)
    ;-------------------------------
    fldz                      ; ST(0) = 0.0, initialize sum
    ↪ accumulator
    mov rsi, arr              ; rsi points to the first element of arr
    mov rcx, n                ; Set loop counter to n (5)

sum_loop:
    cmp rcx, 0
    je done_sum
    fld qword [rsi]           ; Load current element a_i into ST(0)
    faddp st1, st0            ; Add a_i to the accumulator (ST(1) =
    ↪ ST(1) + ST(0)), then pop
    add rsi, 8                ; Move pointer to next double (8 bytes)
    dec rcx
    jmp sum_loop

done_sum:
    fstp qword [sum]          ; Store the computed sum S into memory
    ↪ and clear FPU stack

    ;-------------------------------------------------
```

313

```
; Compute the Arithmetic Mean μ = S / n
;--------------------------------------------------
fld qword [sum]          ; Load sum S into ST(0)
fdiv qword [n_float]     ; Divide by n (as a double), now ST(0) =
↪ μ
fstp qword [mean]        ; Store the mean μ in memory


↪ ;-----------------------------------------------------------------
; Compute the Variance ² = (1/n) * (a_i - μ)²

↪ ;-----------------------------------------------------------------
; Initialize the variance accumulator var_sum to 0.0
fldz
fstp qword [var_sum]

mov rsi, arr             ; Reset pointer to the beginning of arr
mov rcx, n               ; Reset loop counter to n (5)
variance_loop:
    cmp rcx, 0
    je done_variance_loop

    ; Compute difference: (a_i - μ)
    fld qword [rsi]          ; Load a_i into ST(0)
    fsub qword [mean]        ; Subtract μ: now ST(0) = (a_i - μ)

    ; Square the difference: (a_i - μ)²
    fld st0                  ; Duplicate (a_i - μ); ST(0) and ST(1)
↪ both hold (a_i - μ)
    fmulp st1, st0           ; Multiply: ST(0) = (a_i - μ)² (pops one
↪ duplicate)

    ; Store the squared result temporarily in tmp
    fstp qword [tmp]

    ; Add the squared difference to the cumulative variance
↪ accumulator (var_sum)
    fld qword [var_sum]      ; Load current var_sum into ST(0)
    fld qword [tmp]          ; Load squared difference into ST(0)
    faddp st1, st0           ; Add: ST(1) + ST(0) -> ST(0) and pop;
↪ now ST(0) = new var_sum
    fstp qword [var_sum]     ; Store the updated accumulator back to
↪ var_sum

    add rsi, 8               ; Move to the next element of arr
    dec rcx
    jmp variance_loop

done_variance_loop:
    ; Finalize variance: ² = var_sum / n
    fld qword [var_sum]      ; Load the total sum of squared
↪ differences into ST(0)
```

```
fdiv qword [n_float]      ; Divide by n to obtain variance ²
fstp qword [variance]     ; Store the computed variance in memory

;--------------------------
; Exit the Program (Linux)
;--------------------------
mov rax, 60               ; Syscall number for exit
xor rdi, rdi              ; Exit code 0
syscall
```

Chapter 58

Implementing Naive String Pattern Matching

Problem Formulation and Theoretical Underpinnings

Let T denote a finite character array representing the text in which the search is performed, and let P denote another finite character array representing the pattern to be located within T. Denote the length of T by n and the length of P by m, where $n, m \in \mathbb{N}$ and $m \leq n$. The objective is to determine all positions i, with $0 \leq i \leq n - m$, such that the subarray of T beginning at position i matches P exactly. This matching condition is expressed as

$$T[i + j] = P[j] \quad \text{for all} \quad 0 \leq j < m.$$

The method described here follows a naive approach where every candidate position in T is exhaustively examined. The simplicity of this formulation allows the algorithm to be implemented with a straightforward loop structure that sequentially compares segments of T against the pattern P.

Algorithmic Strategy Using Step-by-Step Comparisons

The algorithm employs a dual-loop mechanism. The outer loop iterates over every possible starting index i within the range $0 \leq i \leq n-m$, establishing a tentative alignment between T and P. For each such index, an inner loop is activated to verify if the segment of T starting at i corresponds elementwise to P. During the inner iteration, the comparison

$$T[i+j] \stackrel{?}{=} P[j]$$

is conducted for every j in the interval $0 \leq j < m$. If a mismatch is encountered at any point in the inner loop, the algorithm terminates that particular inner iteration and increments the candidate index in the outer loop. Conversely, if all corresponding characters are equal, the current index i is recognized as a valid starting position of a match.

The time complexity of this approach in the worst-case scenario becomes $\mathcal{O}(n \cdot m)$, as every character in P may be compared against every potential substring position in T. Despite its theoretical inefficiency in worst-case conditions, the algorithm is appreciated for its clarity and ease of implementation, especially in low-level programming contexts where control over loop mechanics and memory access is paramount.

Mapping the Algorithm to Assembly Loop Constructs

The implementation in an assembly environment requires careful mapping of the abstract algorithm to concrete processor instructions. Central to this mapping is the organization of memory accesses and the explicit management of loop counters and pointer arithmetic. The text array T and the pattern array P are stored in contiguous memory locations, and pointer registers are employed to traverse these arrays sequentially.

The outer loop is implemented using a dedicated register to track the current index i in T. At each iteration of this loop, the pointer corresponding to T is set to the ith element, and another pointer is initialized to the starting address of P. The inner loop then iterates over the pattern by incrementing both pointers in lockstep, comparing the byte or word values at each respective location. Conditional branch instructions are used to assess whether a mismatch occurs. If a non-matching pair is detected, control is transferred to the routine responsible for adjusting the outer loop pointer to the next candidate position.

Moreover, the assembly implementation must ensure that registers used during the inner loop do not inadvertently affect those managed by the outer loop. This necessitates a clear convention for register usage and an efficient strategy for saving and restoring register states. The explicit loop constructs in assembly, such as jump instructions and decrements of loop counters, provide the granular control needed to implement the naive string pattern matching algorithm with precision.

In this context, the step-by-step comparison mechanism is realized by iterating over each potential alignment and executing a series of load, compare, and branch instructions. The reliance on direct memory manipulation and condition checks enables a faithful representation of the naive approach, whereby each character comparison is explicitly executed, thereby mirroring the theoretical underpinnings of the algorithm within the constraints and capabilities of the assembly language environment.

x64 Assembly Code Snippet

```
; Naive String Pattern Matching in x64 Assembly (NASM Syntax)
; This program searches for a given pattern within a text using a
; brute-force (naive) approach. For each possible starting index in
; the text, it compares byte-for-byte against the pattern. When all
; characters in the pattern match, a counter is incremented to
↪   record
; that a match was found.

global _start

section .data
    ; Define the text to be searched.
    ; A null byte is appended but not used by the algorithm.
    text    db "THIS IS A SIMPLE TEXT FOR NAIVE STRING MATCHING", 0
    ; Calculate text length excluding the trailing null.
    text_len   equ $ - text - 1

    ; Define the pattern to search for.
    pattern db "SIMPLE"
    ; Calculate pattern length (number of characters).
    pat_len equ $ - pattern
```

```
section .bss
    ; (Optional) Space to store match indices can be reserved here
    ↪  if needed.
    ; For this snippet, we simply count the number of matches found
    ↪  in r11.

section .text
_start:
    ; Set up base pointers:
    ; rsi will point to the beginning of the text.
    ; rdi will point to the beginning of the pattern.
    mov rsi, text
    mov rdi, pattern

    ; Initialize match counter (r11) to 0.
    xor r11, r11

    ; Outer loop index (candidate starting index within text) stored
    ↪  in r8.
    xor r8, r8

    ; Compute the maximum valid starting index:
    ; Last index = text_len - pat_len. Store this in r10.
    mov r10, text_len
    sub r10, pat_len
    ; Now, valid starting positions are 0 <= r8 <= r10.

outer_loop:
    ; If r8 > r10, then all candidate positions have been examined.
    cmp r8, r10
    ja exit_program

    ; Initialize inner loop index (offset within the pattern) in r9.
    xor r9, r9

inner_loop:
    ; Check whether we have compared all characters of the pattern.
    cmp r9, pat_len
    je record_match

    ; Compute effective offset in text: r8 (candidate index) + r9
    ↪  (current offset).
    mov rax, r8
    add rax, r9

    ; Load byte from text at address (rsi + (r8 + r9)).
    mov bl, byte [rsi + rax]
    ; Load corresponding byte from pattern at address (rdi + r9).
    mov cl, byte [rdi + r9]

    ; Compare the two bytes.
    cmp bl, cl
```

319

```
        ; If the characters do not match, abandon this candidate.
        jne no_match

        ; Characters match; increment the inner loop index and check the
        ↪  next one.
        inc r9
        jmp inner_loop

record_match:
        ; Full match found: the pattern matches text at index in r8.
        ; Increment the match counter (r11). (Optional: The index can be
        ↪  stored if needed.)
        inc r11

no_match:
        ; Proceed to the next candidate starting position by
        ↪  incrementing r8.
        inc r8
        jmp outer_loop

exit_program:
        ; Exit the program. The number of matches is left in r11.
        mov rax, 60       ; syscall: exit
        xor rdi, rdi      ; exit status 0
        syscall
```

Chapter 59

Implementing a Reverse String Function

Problem Formulation

Consider a string S represented as a contiguous sequence of characters, that is,

$$S = \{s_0, s_1, \ldots, s_{n-1}\},$$

where n denotes the length of S. The task is to construct a function that produces the reversed string, denoted by

$$S^R = \{s_{n-1}, s_{n-2}, \ldots, s_0\}.$$

This reversal operation is fundamental when performing tasks such as palindromic checks, where the equality $S = S^R$ determines palindromic properties. The operation must be executed with precise memory manipulations, ensuring that each element s_i is correctly relocated to the complementary index $n - 1 - i$.

Algorithmic Methodology

The reversal function is efficiently implemented using a two-pointer technique. Designate two indices, l and r, initially assigned to 0 and $n - 1$, respectively. The algorithm repeatedly exchanges the elements s_l and s_r, updating the pointers according to

$$l \leftarrow l + 1 \quad \text{and} \quad r \leftarrow r - 1,$$

until the condition $l \geq r$ is met. Each exchange operation ensures that the character originally positioned at index l is relocated to index r in the reversed string, and vice versa. This process is performed in situ, thereby achieving an optimal space complexity of $O(1)$ while maintaining a linear time complexity of $O(n)$, where the number of operations scales directly with the length of the string.

Memory Layout and Pointer Arithmetic

Within the assembly language implementation, the string S is stored in a contiguous block of memory. Two pointer registers reference the base address of the string and facilitate access to individual characters at offsets corresponding to indices l and r. The memory addressing is formalized by computing the effective addresses as:

$$\text{Address}(s_l) = \text{Base} + l, \quad \text{Address}(s_r) = \text{Base} + r.$$

During each swap, a temporary register is employed to hold one character value while transferring the value from one memory location to another. The meticulous management of register states ensures that the base pointer remains unaltered throughout the operation, thereby preserving the integrity of the string's memory layout. Additionally, precise pointer arithmetic guarantees that no inadvertent memory access occurs beyond the defined bounds of the string.

Considerations for Assembly Implementation

The assembly implementation of the reverse string function demands a rigorous control flow that leverages conditional branching and explicit loop constructs. Each iteration of the loop comprises a sequence of load and store operations to execute the swap operation between s_l and s_r. The algorithmic structure minimizes the

number of instructions executed per iteration while ensuring that
the temporary storage and register usage do not compromise the
persistence of critical data. Particular care is given to adherence to
the architectural constraints, such as alignment requirements and
the preservation of register states. The in situ reversal strategy,
combined with efficient pointer arithmetic, culminates in a robust
implementation that faithfully reverses the string as defined by the
transformation $S \to S^R$.

x64 Assembly Code Snippet

```
; Reverse String Function using two-pointer technique in x64
↪    Assembly.
;
; Problem Formulation:
;    Given a string S = { s0, s1, ..., s(n-1) } stored in consecutive
↪    memory locations,
;    the goal is to compute S^R = { s(n-1), s(n-2), ..., s0 } by
↪    swapping the elements.
;
; Algorithm Overview:
;    1. Initialize two pointers:
;         left pointer  (r8) = Base address of S.
;         right pointer (r9) = Base + (n - 1).
;
;    2. Loop while (left pointer < right pointer):
;         a. Load the character at left pointer into a temporary
↪    register.
;         b. Swap the characters: store character from right pointer
↪    into left pointer.
;         c. Store the temporary value into the right pointer.
;         d. Increment left pointer and decrement right pointer.
;
;    3. Terminate when left pointer is no longer less than right
↪    pointer.
;
; Memory Layout & Pointer Arithmetic:
;    - Address(s_l) = Base + l.
;    - Address(s_r) = Base + r.
;
; Calling Convention:
;    - Input:
;         RDI: Pointer to the beginning of the string S.
;         RSI: Length (n) of the string S.
;    - Output:
;         The string S is reversed in place.
;
; This routine fully adheres to the in situ reversal, ensuring O(1)
↪    space and O(n) time.
```

```asm
global reverse_string      ; Export the function for the linker

section .text

reverse_string:
    ; Check if string length is 0 or 1; nothing to do in that case.
    cmp rsi, 1
    jle .done

    ; Initialize pointers:
    ; r8 will serve as the left pointer: Base address of S.
    ; r9 will serve as the right pointer: Base + (n - 1).
    mov r8, rdi                ; r8 = Base address of S (left
    ↪   pointer)
    lea r9, [rdi + rsi - 1]    ; r9 = Base + (n - 1) (right pointer)

.reverse_loop:
    ; Check loop condition: continue while left pointer < right
    ↪   pointer.
    cmp r8, r9
    jge .done                  ; Exit loop when r8 >= r9

    ; Swap the bytes at addresses r8 and r9.
    mov al, byte [r8]          ; Load byte from left pointer (s[l])
    ↪   into AL.
    mov bl, byte [r9]          ; Load byte from right pointer (s[r])
    ↪   into BL.
    mov byte [r8], bl          ; Store the byte from BL (s[r]) into
    ↪   left position.
    mov byte [r9], al          ; Store the byte from AL (s[l]) into
    ↪   right position.

    ; Update the pointers:
    inc r8                     ; Move left pointer to the next
    ↪   element (l = l + 1).
    dec r9                     ; Move right pointer to the previous
    ↪   element (r = r - 1).
    jmp .reverse_loop          ; Repeat the swapping loop.

.done:
    ret                        ; Return from the function.
```

Chapter 60

Implementing Circular Buffer Operations

Circular Buffer Architecture and Invariants

A circular buffer, often denominated as a ring buffer, is a fixed-size data structure that relies on contiguous memory allocation and cyclic index manipulation. The underlying construct comprises an array of elements of predetermined capacity N, along with a pair of index pointers, typically referred to as the head and tail pointers. The head pointer, denoted by H, identifies the position of the oldest element in the buffer, while the tail pointer, denoted by T, indicates the position where the subsequent element shall be inserted. The invariant conditions governing the buffer ensure that consistency is maintained throughout its operational cycles. For instance, when H equals T, the buffer is in an empty state, whereas a full state is customarily characterized by the condition $(T + 1) \mod N = H$. Such invariants are imperative for avoiding ambiguity between full and empty conditions in a system that leverages modulo arithmetic to facilitate wrapping.

Insertion Operation Techniques

The insertion routine is tasked with introducing a new element into the circular buffer at the position indicated by the tail pointer T.

Upon insertion, the value is stored in the underlying array at index T, after which the tail pointer is advanced according to the update rule $T \leftarrow (T + 1) \mod N$. This modulo operation guarantees that the pointer seamlessly cycles back to the beginning of the array when the maximum index is surpassed, thereby establishing the wrap-around behavior inherent in circular buffers. It is crucial that the routine verifies the buffer's state prior to insertion to preclude the possibility of overwriting valid data. In designs where buffer capacity is rigidly enforced, the insertion operation must incorporate a check for the full condition, namely $(T + 1) \mod N = H$, and respond appropriately by aborting the operation or by employing a predetermined overwrite strategy. The efficient management of pointer arithmetic and the adherence to invariant conditions ensure that the insertion routine operates in constant time, $O(1)$, with minimal overhead.

Deletion Operation Mechanisms

The deletion operation in a circular buffer is defined by the systematic removal of the element residing at the head pointer H. This process involves the extraction of the element located at the corresponding index within the array, followed by the advancement of the head pointer via the update rule $H \leftarrow (H + 1) \mod N$. Analogous to the insertion process, this modulo-based update is critical in preserving the circular nature of the buffer, as it seamlessly translates the pointer position from the terminal index back to the initial index upon reaching the boundary. Prior to the execution of a deletion operation, the routine must ascertain that the circular buffer is non-empty; this is typically validated by confirming that $H \neq T$. The deletion mechanism, therefore, not only retrieves and subsequently invalidates the element from its original location, but also reinstates the buffer's invariant properties. The elimination of an element is accomplished in $O(1)$ time, thereby ensuring that the deletion process remains both efficient and scalable.

Wrap-around Handling Strategies

Wrap-around handling constitutes a core element in the management of circular buffers, whereby the logical continuity of the buffer is maintained even as the tail or head pointer reaches the extreme ends of the underlying array. The mechanism is implemented through modulo arithmetic, wherein both pointers are updated using the expressions $H \leftarrow (H+1) \mod N$ and $T \leftarrow (T+1) \mod N$. This arithmetic ensures that when a pointer value attains the upper bound $N - 1$, the subsequent incrementation wraps around to index 0, thereby recycling the memory space in a continuous loop. Such wrap-around behavior necessitates rigorous consistency checks within insertion and deletion routines to prevent pointer misalignment that could violate the buffer's invariant conditions. In scenarios where pointer wrapping is not meticulously managed, there exists a heightened potential for off-by-one errors, leading to either inadvertent data loss or erroneous overwriting of active data. Thus, the explicit incorporation of modulo operations in pointer updates is indispensable for ensuring the robust operation of circular buffer manipulation routines under all conditions of buffer utilization.

x64 Assembly Code Snippet

```
;-----------------------------------------------------
; Circular Buffer Implementation in x64 Assembly (NASM Syntax)
; This complete code snippet demonstrates:
;    - Initialization of a fixed-size circular (ring) buffer.
;    - Insertion of elements with full-buffer checking.
;        (Full condition: (tail + 1) mod N equals head)
;    - Deletion of elements with empty-buffer checking.
;        (Empty condition: head equals tail)
;    - Wrap-around of head and tail pointers using modulo arithmetic.
;
; Buffer capacity is defined by N. In this example, N is set to 8.
;
; To assemble and link on Linux:
;    nasm -felf64 circular_buffer.asm -o circular_buffer.o
;    ld circular_buffer.o -o circular_buffer
;-----------------------------------------------------

section .data
    N            equ 8                    ; Circular buffer
    ↪  capacity
    ; The buffer is an array of 8 32-bit integers initialized to 0.
    buffer       dd 0, 0, 0, 0, 0, 0, 0, 0
    ; Head and tail indices (both 32-bit).
    head         dd 0                     ; Head pointer: index of
    ↪  oldest element
    tail         dd 0                     ; Tail pointer: index where
    ↪  next element will be inserted

section .text
```

```
        global _start

;-------------------------------------------------------------------
; _start: Program entry point for demonstration.
; It performs a few insertions into the buffer followed by a
↳   deletion,
; then exits the program via a Linux exit system call.
;-------------------------------------------------------------------
_start:
        ; --- Insert three elements into the circular buffer ---
        mov edi, 10            ; First element: 10
        call cb_insert         ; Call insertion routine

        mov edi, 20            ; Second element: 20
        call cb_insert         ; Call insertion routine

        mov edi, 30            ; Third element: 30
        call cb_insert         ; Call insertion routine

        ; --- Delete one element from the circular buffer ---
        call cb_delete         ; Call deletion routine; deleted element
        ↳   returned in eax
        ; (For this demonstration, the deleted value is not further
        ↳   used.)

        ; --- Exit the program with exit code 0 ---
        mov edi, 0             ; Exit code 0
        call sys_exit


;-------------------------------------------------------------------
; cb_insert: Inserts an element into the circular buffer.
; Input:  edi = element to be inserted (32-bit integer)
; Output: Buffer updated; if buffer is full, insertion is skipped.
;         (Full condition: (tail + 1) mod N == head)
;-------------------------------------------------------------------
cb_insert:
        ; Load current tail index from memory.
        mov eax, [tail]
        ; Compute (tail + 1) mod N.
        add eax, 1
        mov ecx, N
        xor edx, edx
        div ecx               ; eax = quotient, edx = remainder =
        ↳   (tail+1) mod N.
        mov r8d, edx          ; r8d holds next index (next_tail).

        ; Check if the buffer is full:
        ; If next_tail equals head, then the buffer is full.
        cmp r8d, [head]
        je cb_insert_full

        ; Compute the address of buffer element at index = current tail.
        mov eax, [tail]       ; Reload current tail index.
```

328

```
        shl eax, 2              ; Multiply index by 4 (size of a dword).
        lea r9, [buffer]        ; Load base address of the buffer.
        add r9, rax             ; r9 points to buffer[tail].
        mov [r9], edi           ; Store the element from edi into the
        ↪ buffer.

        ; Update tail pointer to next_tail.
        mov [tail], r8d
        ret

cb_insert_full:
        ; Buffer full condition encountered.
        ; In this demonstration, we simply do not insert the element.
        ret


;--------------------------------------------------------------------
; cb_delete: Deletes an element from the circular buffer.
; Output: eax = deleted element (32-bit integer).
;         If the buffer is empty (head == tail), eax is set to -1.
;--------------------------------------------------------------------
cb_delete:
        ; Check if the buffer is empty.
        mov eax, [head]
        cmp eax, [tail]
        je cb_delete_empty

        ; Calculate address of element to delete: buffer + (head * 4)
        mov ecx, eax
        shl ecx, 2              ; Multiply head index by 4.
        lea r8, [buffer]
        add r8, rcx
        mov eax, [r8]           ; Retrieve the element from the buffer.

        ; Update head pointer: head = (head + 1) mod N.
        mov eax, [head]
        add eax, 1
        mov ecx, N
        xor edx, edx
        div ecx                 ; After division, edx = (head+1) mod N.
        mov [head], edx
        ret

cb_delete_empty:
        ; Buffer is empty; return -1 to indicate the error.
        mov eax, -1
        ret


;--------------------------------------------------------------------
; sys_exit: Exits the program using the Linux exit system call.
; Input: edi = exit status code.
;--------------------------------------------------------------------
sys_exit:
```

```
mov eax, 60           ; System call number for exit (Linux
 ↪   x86-64).
syscall
```

Chapter 61

Run-Length Encoding Compression

Overview of the Methodology

Run-length encoding exploits the occurrence of consecutive, identical data elements within a fixed sequence. The essence of the method is the replacement of a sequential block of repeated symbols with a compact representation, typically expressed as an ordered pair containing the repeated symbol and an integer count. Formally, given an input sequence $S = s_1 s_2 \ldots s_n$, where each s_i belongs to an alphabet Σ, a contiguous segment of k identical symbols (with $k \geq 1$) is transformed into (d, k), where d denotes the repeated symbol. This transformation reduces data redundancy when sequences of repeating elements are present, condensing the overall representation while preserving the capacity for lossless decompression.

Algorithmic Foundation

The run-length encoding process is underpinned by the rigorous application of invariant conditions and iterative scanning techniques. As the algorithm processes the input sequence, it maintains a counter that reflects the run-length of the current symbol. Upon encountering a symbol distinct from the active run, the algorithm emits a corresponding pair (d, k) and resets the counter for the new run. The formal invariant maintained during processing is that for each emitted pair the condition $k \geq 1$ holds, and the sum of all individual run-lengths satisfies $\sum_i k_i = n$, where n is the total number of symbols in the original sequence. Such a formulation ensures that the encoding is both complete and reversible.

Mechanics of the Encoding Process

The procedure commences with an initial assignment of the first symbol of the sequence to a temporary register and sets the run-length counter to 1. The algorithm then sequentially examines each subsequent symbol. If the examined symbol matches the one currently in the temporary register, the counter is incremented. In the event of a mismatch—or at the terminal element of the sequence—the algorithm registers the run by outputting the pair, and updates the temporary register with the new symbol while resetting the counter to 1. This process guarantees a linear traversal over the dataset, and the use of modulo arithmetic is not mandatory here, as the update operation simply requires comparison and reassignment. The mechanics are designed such that each step adheres strictly to the invariant that no run-length counter is ever zero, thereby ensuring fidelity during the compression and eventual decompression phases.

Invariant Conditions and Handling of Edge Cases

Crucial to the efficacy of run-length encoding is the adherence to robust invariant conditions throughout the compression routine. The condition $k \geq 1$ for any run, where k denotes the count of a repeated symbol, is essential to avoid spurious encoding of non-existent data. Furthermore, in scenarios where the numerical representation of a run-length is constrained by system-specific limitations (for example, fixed-width fields), the algorithm must accommodate runs that exceed such bounds by partitioning them into a series of valid, consecutive pairs. Maintaining the precise relation $\sum_i k_i = n$ is vital to ensure that the decompression process can reconstruct the original sequence exactly. Edge cases, such as sequences that either contain no repetition or are entirely composed of a single repeated element, are addressed within this framework by ensuring that the compression and subsequent decompression processes adhere to the defined invariant constraints.

Efficiency Considerations and Compression Efficacy

The computational complexity of run-length encoding is $\mathcal{O}(n)$, as it inspects each element of the sequence exactly once. This linear complexity ensures that the algorithm scales appropriately with the size of the input. The efficacy of the compression, however, is heavily dependent on the statistical characteristics of the input data. Sequences with extensive, long runs of identical symbols yield highly favorable compression ratios, whereas data with minimal repetition may result in an output representation that is equivalent to or even larger than the original input. Such variability accentuates the importance of contextual data analysis for optimal utilization of run-length encoding techniques. The method's simplicity, coupled with its low computational overhead, positions it as a fundamental algorithm in scenarios where repetitive data patterns are predominant.

x64 Assembly Code Snippet

```
; x64 Assembly Code for Run-Length Encoding Compression
; This example is written in NASM syntax for a Linux x64
↪   environment.
; It implements the RLE algorithm by processing an input string and
; outputting pairs of [symbol, count]. Each run of consecutive
↪   characters
; results in one such pair. The invariant maintained is that every
↪   run has
; a count of at least 1 and the sum of all run lengths equals the
↪   length
; of the original input string.

section .data
    ; Define the input string (null-terminated)
    input_string db "AAABBBCCDAA", 0
    ; Allocate an output buffer sufficiently large to hold the
    ↪   encoded data.
    ; Each run is stored as two bytes: one for the symbol and one
    ↪   for the count.
    output_buffer times 256 db 0

section .text
```

```
        global _start

_start:
    ; Initialize pointers:
    ;    RSI will point to the input string.
    ;    RDI will point to the output buffer.
    mov rsi, input_string
    mov rdi, output_buffer

    ; Load the first byte from the input.
    mov al, byte [rsi]
    cmp al, 0
    je  exit_program          ; Exit if the input string is empty.

    ; Set up the initial run:
    ;    Store the current symbol in BL.
    ;    Initialize the run-length counter in r8b to 1.
    mov bl, al                ; BL holds the current symbol.
    mov r8b, 1                ; r8b holds the run-length count (must
    ↳  be 1).
    inc rsi                   ; Advance the input pointer to the next
    ↳  character.

encode_loop:
    ; Read the next character from the input.
    mov al, byte [rsi]
    cmp al, 0
    je  output_run            ; If the null terminator is reached,
    ↳  output the current run.

    ; Compare the read character with the current symbol in BL.
    cmp al, bl
    je  same_char             ; If they match, continue the current
    ↳  run.

    ; If a different character is encountered, output the current
    ↳  run.
    jmp output_run

same_char:
    ; Increment the run-length counter since the current symbol
    ↳  repeats.
    inc r8b
    inc rsi                   ; Move to the next input character.
    jmp encode_loop

output_run:
    ; Store the encoded pair [symbol, count] into the output buffer.
    mov byte [rdi], bl        ; Write the symbol.
    mov byte [rdi+1], r8b     ; Write the run-length count.
    add rdi, 2                ; Advance the output pointer by 2 bytes.

    ; Check if we have reached the end of the input.
```

```
        cmp al, 0
        je  finish_encoding

        ; Prepare for the next run:
        ;    Update the current symbol to the new character.
        ;    Reset the run-length counter to 1.
        mov bl, al              ; Set the new current symbol.
        mov r8b, 1              ; Reset counter for the new run.
        inc rsi                 ; Advance the input pointer.
        jmp encode_loop

finish_encoding:
        ; (Optional) Append a null terminator to the output buffer for
        ↪  safety.
        mov byte [rdi], 0

exit_program:
        ; Exit the program using the Linux syscall (exit code 0).
        mov rax, 60             ; Syscall for exit.
        xor rdi, rdi            ; Set exit status to 0.
        syscall
```

Chapter 62

Run-Length Decoding

Fundamentals of Decoding

Decoding in the context of run-length compression entails reconstituting the original data sequence from an encoded representation consisting of ordered pairs. Each pair, designated as (d, k), comprises a data symbol d and a positive integer count k that indicates the number of consecutive occurrences of d in the original sequence. Formally, given an encoded sequence

$$E = \{(d_1, k_1), (d_2, k_2), \ldots, (d_m, k_m)\},$$

the decoding process reconstructs the original sequence S as

$$S = \underbrace{d_1 \, d_1 \, \cdots \, d_1}_{k_1 \text{ times}} \underbrace{d_2 \, d_2 \, \cdots \, d_2}_{k_2 \text{ times}} \cdots \underbrace{d_m \, d_m \, \cdots \, d_m}_{k_m \text{ times}},$$

with the invariant

$$\sum_{i=1}^{m} k_i = n,$$

where n denotes the length of S. This formulation ensures that the reversal process is both complete and lossless.

Algorithmic Construction

The reconstruction of the original data sequence from the encoded pairs is achieved by an iterative procedure that processes each pair in turn. For every pair (d, k), the algorithm generates a subsequence consisting of k successive instances of the symbol d. The replication mechanism implicitly relies on a controlled iteration that guarantees the exact reproduction of the symbol-run prescribed by the count k. Conceptually, the operation can be viewed as a mapping from the compressed representation back to a string concatenation operation, where the function

$$f : (d, k) \mapsto \underbrace{d\, d \cdots d}_{k \text{ times}}$$

is applied sequentially over the set of encoded pairs. This systematic generation of repeated symbols constitutes the core mechanism by which the original sequence is fully restored.

Invariant Conditions and Correctness Assurance

The integrity of the decoding process rests upon the maintenance of precise invariant conditions. First, for each pair (d, k), the invariant $k \geq 1$ must consistently hold to ensure that only valid symbol runs contribute to the reconstruction process. Second, as each encoded pair is processed, the aggregate count of symbols produced must accumulate to match the length of the original sequence, as characterized by

$$n = \sum_{i=1}^{m} k_i.$$

Furthermore, at any point during the iterative expansion, the partially decoded sequence must accurately reflect the prefix of the original data, thereby reinforcing the correctness of the intermediate states. The adherence to these invariants can be rigorously proven via mathematical induction, thereby establishing a sound foundation for the lossless reconstruction guarantees offered by the decoding algorithm.

Performance and Resource Considerations

The computational complexity associated with the decoding process is linear, denoted as $\mathcal{O}(n)$ with respect to the uncompressed sequence length n. This linear complexity arises from the necessity to output each of the n symbols, regardless of the compressed form's brevity. Additionally, the space complexity is directly proportional to n, as memory allocation must accommodate the entire reconstructed sequence. Such predictable resource utilization renders the algorithm particularly efficient, especially in applications where the overhead of decompression is a critical factor.

Edge Case Considerations

Robust implementations of run-length decoding require careful handling of edge cases to ensure unerring reconstruction. In instances where the encoded data comprises a single pair, or when multiple pairs representing a logical continuous run are segmented due to constraints in the encoding process, the decoding algorithm must meticulously replicate the appropriate number of symbols without introducing anomalies. Moreover, validation of input integrity plays an essential role in precluding cases where an encoded pair might inadvertently violate the invariant condition $k \geq 1$. Under the assumption of well-formed encoded data, however, the systematic expansion of symbol counts guarantees that the decoded output precisely mirrors the original sequence, thereby fulfilling the objective of lossless recovery.

x64 Assembly Code Snippet

```
; Run-Length Decoding x64 Assembly Implementation
; This program decodes an encoded sequence of (symbol, count) pairs
↪   into its original form.
; Each encoded pair is structured as follows:
;    - 1 byte  : symbol (the character to be repeated)
;    - 7 bytes : padding for alignment
;    - 8 bytes : count (the number of repetitions, with invariant
↪   count >= 1)
;
; The algorithm iterates through the encoded pairs, replicates the
↪   symbol
; by its count, and writes the resulting decoded sequence into an
↪   output buffer.
; Finally, the decoded result is written to stdout using Linux
↪   system calls.
;
; To assemble and link (using NASM and ld on Linux):
;    nasm -f elf64 run_length_decode.asm -o run_length_decode.o
```

```
;    ld run_length_decode.o -o run_length_decode

global _start

section .data
    ; Encoded data: three pairs representing the strings "AAAAA",
    ↪   "BBB", and "CCCC"
    encoded_data:
        db 'A'                  ; symbol 'A'
        db 0,0,0,0,0,0,0        ; padding to align the count
        dq 5                    ; count = 5

        db 'B'                  ; symbol 'B'
        db 0,0,0,0,0,0,0
        dq 3                    ; count = 3

        db 'C'                  ; symbol 'C'
        db 0,0,0,0,0,0,0
        dq 4                    ; count = 4

    num_pairs     dq 3    ; Total number of encoded pairs
    total_length  dq 12   ; Total decoded length: 5 + 3 + 4 = 12

section .bss
    ; Output buffer for storing the decoded sequence (allocate
    ↪   sufficient space)
    output_buffer: resb 64

section .text

_start:
    ; Initialize pointers:
    ; rsi -> pointer to the start of encoded_data.
    ; rdi -> pointer to the start of output_buffer.
    mov     rsi, encoded_data
    mov     rdi, output_buffer
    mov     rcx, [num_pairs]        ; outer loop counter for encoded
    ↪   pairs

decode_pairs:
    ; Check if all pairs have been processed
    test    rcx, rcx
    jz      write_output

    ; Load the symbol from the current encoded pair (at offset 0)
    mov     al, byte [rsi]
    ; Load the replication count from offset 8 (64-bit value)
    mov     r8, [rsi + 8]

decode_symbol:
    ; If count (r8) becomes zero, break out of the inner loop
    test    r8, r8
    jz      next_pair
```

```
        ; Store the symbol into the output buffer
        mov     byte [rdi], al
        inc     rdi             ; advance the output buffer pointer
        dec     r8              ; decrement the remaining count
        jmp     decode_symbol

next_pair:
        ; Move to the next encoded pair; each pair occupies 16 bytes
        add     rsi, 16
        dec     rcx             ; processed one pair
        jmp     decode_pairs

write_output:
        ; Prepare for the write syscall to output the decoded result
        mov     rdx, [total_length] ; total number of decoded bytes to
    ↪ write
        mov     rax, 1          ; syscall number for write
    ↪ (sys_write)
        mov     rdi, 1          ; file descriptor for stdout
        mov     rsi, output_buffer  ; pointer to the decoded output
    ↪ buffer
        syscall

        ; Exit the program cleanly using the exit syscall
        mov     rax, 60         ; syscall number for exit (sys_exit)
        xor     rdi, rdi        ; exit status 0
        syscall
```

Chapter 63

Memory Alignment Utility

Conceptual Framework of Memory Alignment

Memory alignment is defined by the placement of data in memory at addresses that adhere to specified boundary conditions, typically determined by powers of two. This alignment is integral to the efficient operation of contemporary computer architectures. When data elements are aligned to boundaries such as 2^n, the processor can access memory in fixed-size chunks, thereby optimizing the usage of cache lines and reducing the likelihood of performance penalties associated with misaligned accesses. The adherence to these fixed boundaries ensures that memory retrieval operations are streamlined, thus bolstering data throughput and overall computational efficiency.

Mathematical Underpinnings and Theoretical Formulation

Consider an arbitrary memory address A and an alignment boundary B, where B is usually a power of two. The condition for A to be considered properly aligned is given by

$$A \bmod B = 0.$$

When this condition is not met, the address is regarded as misaligned. In order to compute the next aligned address A', one must first determine the remainder r where

$$r = A \bmod B.$$

If $r \neq 0$, then the adjusted address is obtained by the equation

$$A' = A + (B - r),$$

thereby guaranteeing that

$$A' \bmod B = 0.$$

This mathematical foundation provides a robust framework for designing routines that adjust memory pointers to meet alignment constraints, ensuring that subsequent memory accesses are performed under optimal conditions.

Adjustment Routines for Memory Alignment

Routines for adjusting memory addresses to meet alignment requirements can be constructed on the basis of the aforementioned mathematical formulation. A typical alignment routine examines an initial pointer value A and computes the alignment offset using the modulo operation with respect to the boundary B. If A is found to be misaligned, the minimal offset required to reach the next address that satisfies the alignment condition is determined by $B - (A \bmod B)$. The resultant address

$$A' = A + (B - (A \bmod B))$$

is then used for all subsequent memory operations. Such routines are indispensable in ensuring that data structures and buffers in memory conform to the stringent requirements of hardware memory controllers, thereby minimizing latency and maximizing the efficiency of memory transfers.

System-Level Implications and Computational Efficiency

The strategic adjustment of memory addresses to align with fixed boundaries has significant implications at the system architecture level. Aligned memory accesses facilitate more predictable cache behavior and leverage hardware-level optimizations such as burst transfers and prefetching mechanisms. The imposition of proper alignment reduces the likelihood of processor stalls resulting from cache-line splits, and it enhances the throughput of vectorized operations often employed in high-performance computing environments. Additionally, this approach helps in maintaining the structural integrity of memory access patterns, thereby reducing the overhead associated with misaligned data retrieval. The implementation of precise alignment routines is therefore fundamental to both the stability and performance augmentation of systems that rely on rigorous memory management paradigms.

x64 Assembly Code Snippet

```
; --------------------------------
; x64 Assembly Routine for Memory Alignment Utility
;
; This complete code snippet demonstrates an alignment routine which
; calculates the next memory address A' that is aligned to a given
; boundary B (typically a power-of-two). The algorithm uses the
↪   equation:
;
;    If A mod B = 0, then A' = A
;    Else, A' = A + (B - (A mod B))
;
; For power-of-two alignments, the modulo operation is optimized
↪   using a
; bit mask: remainder = A & (B - 1)
;
; This program includes:
;    - A function "align_memory" which accepts:
;         RDI = Original memory address (A)
;         RSI = Alignment boundary (B)
;      and returns the aligned address in RAX.
;
;    - A simple "main" routine which demonstrates the usage of
↪   align_memory.
;      It aligns a sample misaligned address (e.g., 0x1003 to an
↪   8-byte boundary)
;      and then prints the resulting aligned address using the C
↪   library
;      routine printf.
; --------------------------------

section .data
    fmt db "Aligned address: 0x%016lx", 10, 0    ; Format string for
    ↪   output
```

```
        section .text
            global main, align_memory
            extern printf

        ; ------------------------------
        ; align_memory:
        ;
        ; Input:
        ;   RDI - Original memory address (A)
        ;   RSI - Alignment boundary (B) [Assumed to be a power-of-two]
        ;
        ; Output:
        ;   RAX - Aligned memory address (A')
        ;
        ; Algorithm:
        ;   1. Compute the remainder using: remainder = A & (B - 1)
        ;   2. If remainder is 0, the address is already aligned.
        ;   3. Otherwise, compute the offset: offset = B - remainder and add
        ;↪  it to A.
        ; ------------------------------
        align_memory:
            mov rax, rdi        ; rax = A (store original address)
            mov rcx, rsi        ; rcx = B (alignment boundary)
            dec rcx             ; rcx = B - 1, which will act as a mask
            mov rdx, rdi        ; rdx = A (duplicate A for remainder
            ↪  calculation)
            and rdx, rcx        ; rdx = remainder = A & (B - 1)
            test rdx, rdx       ; Check if remainder is zero (A is aligned)
            jz .aligned         ; If zero, jump to return A unchanged
            mov rcx, rsi        ; Reload B into rcx (for offset calculation)
            sub rcx, rdx        ; rcx = B - remainder, this is the needed
            ↪  offset
            add rax, rcx        ; rax = A + (B - remainder), thus the
            ↪  aligned address
        .aligned:
            ret                 ; Return aligned address in RAX


        ; ------------------------------
        ; main:
        ;
        ; Demonstrates the memory alignment of a sample address. In this
        ↪  example,
        ; a misaligned address (0x1003) is aligned to an 8-byte boundary.
        ;
        ; The aligned address is then printed using printf.
        ; ------------------------------
        main:
            ; Set up a sample misaligned address and alignment boundary.
            mov rdi, 0x1003     ; Original memory address A = 0x1003
            ↪  (misaligned)
            mov rsi, 8          ; Alignment boundary B = 8 bytes
            ↪  (power-of-two)
```

344

```
    call align_memory    ; Call the alignment routine, result in RAX

    ; Prepare parameters to call printf:
    ;   First argument (format string) in RDI,
    ;   Second argument (aligned address) in RSI.
    lea rdi, [rel fmt]   ; Load address of the format string into RDI
    mov rsi, rax          ; Move the aligned address result into RSI
    xor rax, rax          ; Clear RAX as required for variadic
    ↪  functions (SysV ABI)
    call printf           ; Call printf to print the aligned address

    ; Exit the program with return code 0.
    mov rax, 0
    ret
```

Chapter 64

Circular Shift on Arrays

Problem Formulation

A circular shift of an array is defined as the operation that repositions each element of a data sequence by a fixed number of positions
in a designated direction, such that elements exiting one boundary
reappear at the opposite boundary. Consider an array represented
as $A = \{a_0, a_1, \ldots, a_{n-1}\}$; a circular shift by k positions to the
right is formally described by the mapping

$$a_i \mapsto a_{(i+k) \bmod n},$$

where $i \in \{0, 1, \ldots, n-1\}$ and the modulo operation ensures the
wrap-around effect inherent to the cyclic structure. Analogously,
a shift to the left can be characterized by an adjusted index transformation. This operation preserves the cyclic ordering of the elements while effecting a systematic reordering of the array.

Mathematical Framework and Formal Definitions

The circular shift operation can be rigorously modeled within the
context of modular arithmetic. Let the transformation $T : \mathbb{Z}_n \to
\mathbb{Z}_n$ be defined by

$$T(i) = (i + k) \mod n,$$

where n denotes the length of the array and k is the shift constant. The transformation T is bijective, ensuring that each array element occupies a unique position in the rotated configuration. The inverse operation is realized by a complementary shift of $n - k$ positions (or an appropriate negative value of k), thereby reestablishing the original ordering. Furthermore, analysis shows that the cyclic structure of the operation is intimately connected with the greatest common divisor, $\gcd(n, k)$, which determines the number of disjoint cycles present in the permutation induced by T.

Algorithmic Design Considerations

The design of an algorithm to perform a circular shift necessitates careful consideration of several factors, including the direction of the shift and the handling of boundary conditions. One may employ a direct cyclic permutation mechanism wherein each element is relocated to its destination position according to the transformation index. This approach requires that the cyclic dependencies be resolved without overwriting unprocessed values, a factor that is critically influenced by the value of $\gcd(n, k)$. Alternatively, methods based on sequential reversals offer an elegant solution by partitioning the array into segments and applying a series of inplace reversals. Both strategies must address the special cases in which $k = 0$ or when k is an integral multiple of n, wherein the array remains invariant under the shift operation. The algorithm must ensure that the data integrity is preserved throughout the element rearrangement, maintaining a coherent mapping between the initial and the final states.

Analysis of Computational Complexity and Data Movement

The efficiency of a circular shift algorithm is predominantly measured by its computational complexity and the associated data movement. In typical implementations, each element is visited a constant number of times, yielding an overall time complexity of $O(n)$. In the context of in-place operations, the algorithm minimizes additional memory overhead by performing the reordering within the original array. The cycle-based approach requires careful management of element swaps, particularly when multiple cycles are present, while reversal-based techniques entail a fixed number of passes over the array. The analysis of the movement cycles, especially with respect to the factor $\gcd(n, k)$, provides valuable insight into the number of independent cycles that must be resolved to complete the transformation. Such detailed scrutiny of the data movement patterns is essential for assessing the performance implications in scenarios where large arrays and high throughput are of concern.

Memory Layout and Hardware Considerations

The success of an in-place circular shift algorithm is closely related to the physical layout of memory and the characteristics of the underlying hardware architectures. Since the elements of the array are stored contiguously, the reordering process benefits from spatial locality and cache-friendly access patterns. However, non-sequential memory accesses, which may occur during the shift operation, can introduce cache inefficiencies and impose penalties due to cache-line splits. The algorithm must therefore be designed to align with the memory hierarchy, ensuring that the movement of elements does not adversely impact the cache performance. Careful analysis of the memory access patterns, combined with an understanding of hardware prefetching and burst transfer mechanisms, is imperative for optimizing the data throughput. Furthermore, in large-scale applications, the potential parallelization of the circular shift operation across multiple processing units offers additional avenues for performance enhancements, provided that the synchronization and coherence among concurrent operations are meticulously managed.

x64 Assembly Code Snippet

```
; This complete x64 Assembly snippet demonstrates an in-place
↪   circular shift to the right
; on an array of 32-bit integers using the reversal algorithm. It
↪   implements the key
; steps discussed in the chapter: applying modular arithmetic to
↪   compute an effective
; shift, reversing the entire array, and then reversing sub-segments
↪   to restore cyclic order.
```

```
; The code is written in NASM syntax and follows the System V AMD64
↪   calling convention.
; It defines two subroutines:
;   1. reverse_array: reverses a sub-array (from index RSI to index
↪   RDX) in place.
;   2. circular_shift_right: performs a right circular shift on an
↪   entire array.
; Finally, the main function demonstrates the operation on a sample
↪   array.

global main
extern printf

section .data
    fmt      db "Array after circular shift right: ", 0xa, 0
    numFmt   db "%d ", 0
    newLine  db 0xa, 0
    ; Sample array of 8 integers
    arr      dd 1, 2, 3, 4, 5, 6, 7, 8
    arr_len  equ 8

section .text

;
↪   -----------------------------------------------------------------------
; reverse_array:
;   Reverses the elements in the sub-array defined by indices in RSI
↪   (start)
;   and RDX (end) within the array pointed to by RDI.
;   Each element is 4 bytes (32-bit integer).
;
;   Input:
;       RDI - pointer to the base of the array
;       RSI - start index of the sub-array to reverse
;       RDX - end index of the sub-array to reverse
;
;   The subroutine swaps elements [RDI + RSI*4] and [RDI + RDX*4]
↪   continuously
;   until the entire segment is reversed.
;
↪   -----------------------------------------------------------------------
reverse_array:
    cmp rsi, rdx
    jge .reverse_done
.reverse_loop:
    cmp rsi, rdx
    jge .reverse_done
    ; Load elements from the two ends of the sub-array
    mov eax, [rdi + rsi*4]
    mov ebx, [rdi + rdx*4]
    ; Swap the two elements
    mov [rdi + rsi*4], ebx
    mov [rdi + rdx*4], eax
```

349

```
    ; Move inward
    inc rsi
    dec rdx
    jmp .reverse_loop
.reverse_done:
    ret


;
↪   -------------------------------------------------------------------
; circular_shift_right:
;   Performs an in-place circular shift to the right on the array
↪   pointed by RDI.
;   It rotates the array by k positions as specified in RDX.
;
;   Input:
;       RDI - pointer to the array
;       RSI - number of elements in the array (n)
;       RDX - shift amount (k)
;
;   The effective shift is computed as k mod n. The reversal
↪   algorithm is then applied:
;       1. Reverse the entire array.
;       2. Reverse the first k elements.
;       3. Reverse the remaining n-k elements.
;
↪   -------------------------------------------------------------------
circular_shift_right:
    ; Return immediately if the array is empty.
    test rsi, rsi
    jz .shift_done
    ; Compute effective shift: k = k mod n.
    mov rax, rdx      ; RAX = k
    xor rdx, rdx      ; Clear RDX for division
    mov rcx, rsi      ; RCX = n
    div rcx           ; After division: RAX = quotient, RDX =
    ↪   remainder (effective k)
    cmp rdx, 0
    je .shift_done    ; No rotation needed if effective k is 0
    mov r8, rdx       ; Save effective shift in R8
    mov r9, rsi       ; Save n (number of elements) in R9
    ;
    ; Step 1: Reverse the entire array (indices 0 to n-1)
    mov rsi, 0
    mov rdx, r9
    dec rdx           ; Set RDX = n - 1
    call reverse_array
    ;
    ; Step 2: Reverse the first k elements (indices 0 to k-1)
    mov rsi, 0
    mov rdx, r8
    dec rdx           ; Set RDX = k - 1
    call reverse_array
    ;
```

```
    ; Step 3: Reverse the remaining elements (indices k to n-1)
    mov rsi, r8          ; Start index = k
    mov rdx, r9
    dec rdx              ; End index = n - 1
    call reverse_array
.shift_done:
    ret


;
↪   ------------------------------------------------------------------------
; main:
;   Demonstrates the circular shift right algorithm on an example
↪   array.
;   It calls circular_shift_right to rotate the array by 3
↪   positions.
;   Then it prints the modified array using the C library printf
↪   function.
;
↪   ------------------------------------------------------------------------
main:
    ; Parameters for circular_shift_right(arr, arr_len, 3):
    mov rdi, arr         ; Pointer to the array
    mov rsi, arr_len     ; Number of elements in the array
    mov rdx, 3           ; Shift amount (k)
    call circular_shift_right
    ;
    ; Print the header string.
    lea rdi, [rel fmt]
    xor rax, rax
    call printf
    ;
    ; Loop to print each element of the shifted array.
    mov rcx, arr_len     ; Loop counter
    xor rbx, rbx         ; Index = 0
.print_loop:
    cmp rbx, rcx
    jge .print_done
    lea rdi, [rel numFmt]      ; Load format string for an integer
    mov eax, [arr + rbx*4]     ; Load the array element at index RBX
    mov esi, eax               ; Move element into ESI as argument
    xor rax, rax
    call printf
    inc rbx
    jmp .print_loop
.print_done:
    ; Print a newline.
    lea rdi, [rel newLine]
    xor rax, rax
    call printf
    ;
    ; Exit the program using the Linux syscall.
    mov rax, 60          ; Syscall number for exit
    xor rdi, rdi         ; Exit code 0
```

syscall

Chapter 65

Binary Tree Insertion Routine

Binary Search Tree Fundamentals

A binary search tree (BST) is a structured data organization in which each node contains a key and pointers to at most two child nodes, conventionally referred to as the left and right children. The BST property mandates that for any given node with key k, every key in the left subtree is strictly less than k, while every key in the right subtree is strictly greater than k. This invariant is fundamental to the proper operation of search, insertion, and deletion routines, and forms the basis of the efficiency of these operations. The structure is typically defined recursively, thereby permitting both recursive and iterative strategies for traversing and manipulating the tree. In the context of an insertion routine, the maintenance of the BST property is paramount, as any violation may impair subsequent operations that rely on the ordering of keys.

The Insertion Process

The insertion routine is designed to integrate a new node into an already established BST while preserving the inherent order of its elements. The process commences from the root of the tree and involves successive comparisons between the key of the node to be inserted and the key contained in the current node. If the key under consideration is less than that of the current node, the routine proceeds to the left subtree; conversely, if the key is greater, it advances towards the right subtree. This iterative or recursive descent continues until a $NULL$ pointer is encountered, indicating the appropriate position where no further child node exists. At this vacancy, the new node is allocated and inserted as either the left or right child of the terminal node encountered during the descent. Such a process ensures that the ordering property is maintained, and that the tree's structure is adjusted dynamically through a series of pointer assignments.

Pointer Manipulation and Node Linkage

The precision of pointer manipulation is of crucial importance in the physical implementation of the insertion routine. As the algorithm traverses the BST, each comparison yields a decision that results in the assignment or reassignment of pointer values to correctly link nodes. When the new node is generated, its pointer fields are initialized to denote the absence of children, typically by setting its left and right pointers to $NULL$. Subsequently, the pointer of the parent node—corresponding to the vacant left or right position—is updated to reference the newly allocated node. This procedure necessitates a careful handling of memory addresses and register values to avoid common pitfalls such as dereferencing invalid pointers or inadvertently overwriting existing links. The manipulation of pointers must also account for special conditions, including the scenario where the BST is initially empty; in such a case, the root pointer itself is set to reference the new node, thereby establishing the tree's initial state.

Algorithmic and Complexity Considerations

The operational complexity of the insertion routine is intrinsically linked to the height, h, of the BST. In a balanced tree, the height is $O(\log n)$, where n is the number of nodes, ensuring an insertion complexity of $O(\log n)$. However, in the worst case of a degenerate or unbalanced tree, the complexity degrades to $O(n)$, as the routine may need to traverse each node along a single branch. In addition to the complexity analysis, the routine must rigorously manage the structural adjustments that accompany each pointer change. A precise accounting of the number of pointer updates and the conditional checks employed in the traversal is essential for a comprehensive understanding of the routine's performance characteristics. The detailed scrutiny of these operations provides insight into the efficiency trade-offs inherent in pointer-based manipulations and the maintenance of dynamic data structures such as binary search trees.

x64 Assembly Code Snippet

```
; x64 Assembly code for Binary Tree Insertion Routine
; Function: bst_insert
; Description:
;    This routine inserts a new node into a Binary Search Tree (BST)
↪   while
;    preserving the BST property. It assumes that the node structure
↪   is defined as:
;       Offset 0x00: Key (8 bytes)
;       Offset 0x08: Pointer to left child (8 bytes)
;       Offset 0x10: Pointer to right child (8 bytes)
;
; Input:
;    rdi: Address of the root pointer (Node**)
;    rsi: Pointer to the new node to be inserted (Node*)
; Output:
;    The BST is updated with the new node inserted at the correct
↪   position.
;
global bst_insert
bst_insert:
    ; Check if the tree is empty.
    mov     rax, [rdi]          ; Load the root pointer (*root) into
    ↪   rax.
    cmp     rax, 0
    jne     .not_empty
    ; If the tree is empty, set the new node as the root.
    mov     [rdi], rsi
    ret

.not_empty:
    ; Begin traversal from the root.
.L_loop:
    ; Load current node's key.
    mov     rdx, [rax]          ; rdx = current->key
    ; Load new node's key.
    mov     rcx, [rsi]          ; rcx = new_node->key
    cmp     rcx, rdx
```

```
jl      .go_left            ; If new key is less, go to left
↪    subtree.
jg      .go_right           ; If new key is greater, go to right
↪    subtree.
; For equal keys, decide to insert in the right subtree.
jmp     .go_right

.go_left:
    ; Process left child.
    mov     rdx, [rax + 8]      ; rdx = current->left pointer
    cmp     rdx, 0
    je      .insert_left        ; If left child is NULL, insert new
↪    node here.
    ; Otherwise, move to the left child.
    mov     rax, rdx
    jmp     .L_loop

.insert_left:
    mov     [rax + 8], rsi      ; Set current->left = new_node
↪    pointer
    ret

.go_right:
    ; Process right child.
    mov     rdx, [rax + 16]     ; rdx = current->right pointer
    cmp     rdx, 0
    je      .insert_right       ; If right child is NULL, insert new
↪    node here.
    ; Otherwise, move to the right child.
    mov     rax, rdx
    jmp     .L_loop

.insert_right:
    mov     [rax + 16], rsi     ; Set current->right = new_node
↪    pointer
    ret
```

Chapter 66

Set Operations on Bit Masks

Foundations and Definitions

In the framework of set representation, a finite set S is considered as a subset of a universal set U with cardinality n. Each element of U is assigned a unique index, and the membership of an element in S is indicated by a corresponding bit in a binary vector belonging to $\{0,1\}^n$. Formally, the indicator function $\chi_S : U \to \{0,1\}$ is defined by

$$\chi_S(x) = \begin{cases} 1, & \text{if } x \in S, \\ 0, & \text{if } x \notin S. \end{cases}$$

This binary representation permits the encoding of the set S in the compact form of a bit mask, where the ith bit is set to 1 if and only if the ith element of U is a member of S. The inherent structure of these bit masks renders them particularly amenable to elementary bitwise operations.

Representation of Data Sets via Bit Masks

A data set can be efficiently represented by a bit mask, in which each bit serves as a flag denoting the presence or absence of a particular element. Given a universal set U of fixed size, a set

$A \subseteq U$ is encoded by a bit mask $a \in \{0,1\}^n$, where the relation

$$a_i = \begin{cases} 1, & \text{if the } i^{\text{th}} \text{ element of } U \text{ is in } A, \\ 0, & \text{otherwise,} \end{cases}$$

holds for each index i in the range $1 \le i \le n$. This representation not only minimizes memory overhead but also facilitates the execution of set operations in a manner that exploits parallelism available in modern processor architectures. In hardware, a series of bitwise operations can manipulate such bit masks rapidly, often in constant time when the size of the set is bounded by the word length of the underlying machine.

Set Union Operation

The union of two sets, when expressed in terms of their corresponding bit masks, is achieved through the bitwise OR operation. Let A and B be two subsets of U, represented by bit masks a and b respectively. The union $A \cup B$ is then encoded by a bit mask c, defined by

$$c = a \vee b,$$

where the operation is performed elementwise; that is, for every index i,

$$c_i = a_i \vee b_i.$$

The bit c_i is set to 1 if either $a_i = 1$ or $b_i = 1$. This operation consolidates the membership information from both sets, ensuring that an element appears in the union if it is present in at least one of the original sets. The union operation, by its definition, satisfies commutativity and associativity, aligning perfectly with the corresponding algebraic properties in classical set theory.

Set Intersection Operation

The intersection of two sets is determined by the bitwise AND operation applied to their respective bit masks. For subsets A and B of U, represented by bit masks a and b, the intersection $A \cap B$ is represented by a bit mask c, which is computed as

$$c = a \wedge b.$$

This operation is conducted in an elementwise fashion such that for all indices i,

$$c_i = a_i \wedge b_i.$$

A bit c_i is set to 1 if and only if both $a_i = 1$ and $b_i = 1$, thereby capturing only those elements that are common to both sets A and B. The intersection operation is inherently commutative and associative, mirroring the foundational properties of intersection in set theory. Its efficient computation using bitwise hardware instructions underlines its suitability for high-performance applications where rapid, repeated evaluation of common set membership is required.

Algebraic Properties of Bit Mask Operations

The union and intersection operations, as executed through bit masks, adhere to the axioms of a Boolean lattice. The bitwise OR operation used for set union is idempotent, meaning that

$$a \vee a = a,$$

and exhibits both commutativity,

$$a \vee b = b \vee a,$$

and associativity,

$$(a \vee b) \vee c = a \vee (b \vee c).$$

Similarly, the bitwise AND operation defining set intersection is idempotent,

$$a \wedge a = a,$$

commutative,

$$a \wedge b = b \wedge a,$$

and associative,

$$(a \wedge b) \wedge c = a \wedge (b \wedge c).$$

Furthermore, these operations satisfy the distributive laws, such that

$$a \wedge (b \vee c) = (a \wedge b) \vee (a \wedge c),$$

and

$$a \vee (b \wedge c) = (a \vee b) \wedge (a \vee c).$$

The comprehensive conjunction of these properties establishes that the manipulation of data sets via bit masks is not only computationally efficient but also theoretically robust. The alignment of these operations with Boolean algebra provides a rigorous foundation for analyzing and optimizing algorithms that perform set operations at the bit level.

x64 Assembly Code Snippet

```
; x64 Assembly Code for Set Operations on Bit Masks
; This complete code demonstrates how to perform:
;    - Set Union using the bitwise OR operation (c = a OR b)
;    - Set Intersection using the bitwise AND operation (c = a AND b)
; It also includes a helper routine to convert a 64-bit value to its
; hexadecimal string representation.
;
; Assemble with NASM and link on a Linux system.
; Example (using NASM and ld):
;    nasm -felf64 set_operations.asm -o set_operations.o
;    ld set_operations.o -o set_operations

global _start

section .data
    ; Example 64-bit bit masks (each bit represents an element's
    ↪ membership)
    maskA:     dq 0x0F0F0F0F0F0F0F0F      ; Bit mask for Set A
    maskB:     dq 0x3333333333333333      ; Bit mask for Set B

    unionMsg:  db "Union: 0x", 0          ; Message for union
    ↪ result
    interMsg:  db "Intersection: 0x", 0   ; Message for
    ↪ intersection result
    newline:   db 10, 0                   ; Newline character

section .bss
    ; Buffer to store the hexadecimal string (16 characters + null
    ↪ terminator)
    buffer:    resb 17

section .text

;-----------------------------------------------------------------------
; Function: set_union
; Description:
;    Compute the union of two bit masks using the bitwise OR
↪ operation.
```

360

```asm
; Inputs:
;   rdi - first bit mask (maskA)
;   rsi - second bit mask (maskB)
; Output:
;   rax - result of (maskA OR maskB)
;-------------------------------------------------------------------------
set_union:
    mov rax, rdi            ; Load first mask into rax
    or rax, rsi             ; OR with second mask => union of masks
    ret


;-------------------------------------------------------------------------
; Function: set_intersection
; Description:
;   Compute the intersection of two bit masks using the bitwise AND
;   ↪  operation.
; Inputs:
;   rdi - first bit mask (maskA)
;   rsi - second bit mask (maskB)
; Output:
;   rax - result of (maskA AND maskB)
;-------------------------------------------------------------------------
set_intersection:
    mov rax, rdi            ; Load first mask into rax
    and rax, rsi            ; AND with second mask => intersection of
    ↪  masks
    ret


;-------------------------------------------------------------------------
; Function: convert_to_hex
; Description:
;   Converts a 64-bit value in rax into a hexadecimal string.
;   The resulting null-terminated string is stored in the global
;   ↪  buffer.
;   The conversion writes 16 hex digits.
; Clobbers: rax, rcx, rdx, rbx.
;-------------------------------------------------------------------------
convert_to_hex:
    mov rcx, 16             ; Process 16 hex digits
    lea rbx, [buffer+16]    ; Point rbx to the end of the buffer
    mov byte [rbx], 0       ; Null-terminate the string
.convert_loop:
    dec rbx                 ; Move pointer backwards
    ; Get the lowest nibble from rax
    mov rdx, rax
    and rdx, 0xF
    cmp rdx, 9
    jbe .digit
    ; For values 10-15 add 55 to convert into ASCII letters A-F
    add rdx, 55
    jmp .store_digit
.digit:
```

```
        add rdx, 48                 ; For numeric digits convert to ASCII
        ↳   ('0' = 48)
.store_digit:
        mov [rbx], dl               ; Store converted character into buffer
        shr rax, 4                  ; Shift rax right by 4 bits (one hex
        ↳   digit)
        loop .convert_loop
        ret


;--------------------------------------------------------------------------
; Entry point _start
; Description:
;     Demonstrates the set union and intersection operations on bit
↳   masks.
;     It then converts the results to hexadecimal strings and writes
↳   them
;     to stdout using Linux sys_write syscall.
;--------------------------------------------------------------------------
_start:
        ;----------------------------------------------------
        ; Calculate Union: union_result = maskA OR maskB
        ;----------------------------------------------------
        mov rdi, [maskA]        ; Load maskA into rdi
        mov rsi, [maskB]        ; Load maskB into rsi
        call set_union          ; rax now holds (maskA OR maskB)
        ; Save union result for conversion
        push rax                ; Preserve union result on the stack

        ; Convert union result to a hexadecimal string
        call convert_to_hex     ; The result string is stored in 'buffer'
        ; Write union result message
        mov rax, 1              ; sys_write syscall number
        mov rdi, 1              ; stdout (file descriptor 1)
        mov rsi, unionMsg      ; Address of unionMsg string
        mov rdx, 10            ; Length of unionMsg (approx.)
        syscall

        ; Write the converted union result string
        mov rax, 1
        mov rdi, 1
        lea rsi, [buffer]
        mov rdx, 16            ; 16 hex digits
        syscall

        ; Write newline
        mov rax, 1
        mov rdi, 1
        mov rsi, newline
        mov rdx, 1
        syscall

        ;----------------------------------------------------
        ; Calculate Intersection: intersection_result = maskA AND maskB
```

```asm
;----------------------------------------------------
mov rdi, [maskA]        ; Load maskA into rdi again
mov rsi, [maskB]        ; Load maskB into rsi
call set_intersection   ; rax now holds (maskA AND maskB)
; Convert intersection result to hexadecimal string
call convert_to_hex

; Write intersection result message
mov rax, 1              ; sys_write syscall number
mov rdi, 1              ; stdout file descriptor
mov rsi, interMsg       ; Address of interMsg string
mov rdx, 18             ; Length of interMsg (approx.)
syscall

; Write the converted intersection result string
mov rax, 1
mov rdi, 1
lea rsi, [buffer]
mov rdx, 16             ; 16 hex digits
syscall

; Write newline
mov rax, 1
mov rdi, 1
mov rsi, newline
mov rdx, 1
syscall


;----------------------------------------------------
; Exit program
;----------------------------------------------------
mov rax, 60             ; sys_exit syscall number
xor rdi, rdi            ; Exit status 0
syscall
```

www.ingramcontent.com/pod-product-compliance
Lightning Source LLC
LaVergne TN
LVHW051428050326
832903LV00030BD/2965